BATTLE FOR THE SOUL

(MAN'S QUEST FOR GODHOOD)

By
Rayola Kelley

Hidden Manna Publications

BATTLE FOR THE SOUL
Copyright © 2002 & 2022 by Rayola Kelley

ISBN: 978-1-7347503-1-7

Cover Design: Pamela Wester

Except where otherwise indicated, all Scripture quotations in this book are taken from the King James Version of the Bible.

Printed in the United States of America

All rights reserved. No portion of this book may be reproduced in any form without the written permission of the publisher.

Hidden Manna Publications
PO Box 3572
Oldtown, ID 83822

Facebook:
https://www.facebook.com/HiddenMannaPublications/

DEDICATION:

I want to dedicate this book to all the sheep that desire to hear and follow their precious Shepherd.

SPECIAL ACKNOWLEDGMENT:

I want to acknowledge the editing
work of Crystal Garvin,
as well as Jeannette Haley
for proof-reading this book.

Contents

- Important Information 7
- Introduction 11
1. Just Where Is the Battle? 13
2. Reality vs. Truth 21
3. Delusion or Truth 32
4. A Sad Commentary 42
5. Out of Balance 51
6. Testing the Spirits 63
7. Frame of Reference 77
8. Patterns! 87
9. Worldview 97
10. The Bottom Line 107
11. The Powerless Church 114
12. Oppression or Possession? 124
13. Unbelief and Idolatry 142
14. Witchcraft, Heresy, and Rebellion 154
15. Self-centeredness 164
16. In Pursuit of Nirvana 175
17. The Sins of the Tongue 188
18. Soul Ties 198
19. Curses 202
20. Self-serving Prayer 214
21. Wrong Laying on of Hands 222
22. The Great Physician 227
23. The Glorious Light 234
24. Whole Heart 241
25. The Key to Freedom 250
26. Sight At Last 262
27. A Large Place 270
- Bibliography 277

IMPORTANT INFORMATION:

This would normally be the foreword, but I am aware that some people skip the forward and move into the main text of the book. Before a person begins to read this book, I would like to lay a simple foundation.

Of all the different books I have written, this one has been the most intense. People encouraged me to write this book because I could not clone myself or individually impart to others all of my understanding about deliverance. This project initially brought the realization that I had only understood in part, and as the information developed about such subjects as frame of reference, depression, worldview, street mentality, soul ties, curses, psychic prayer, and wrong laying on of hands, I became more aware of how little I understood.

I realize that what I possess is not simply insightful knowledge of deliverance but a gift that God used in spite of me. God gave me this gift after I had watched many people go up to altars in different churches seeking deliverance from some unseen bondage. They walked away from these altars with tearful hope in their eyes. Subsequently, as I watched these people in action, I realized they were still very much captive. I reminded the Lord what He said in *Luke 4:18*,

> *The Spirit of the Lord is upon me, because he hath anointed me to preach the gospel to the poor; he hath sent me to heal the brokenhearted, to preach deliverance to the captives, and recovering of sight to the blind, to set at liberty them that are bruised.*

Since He came to set all captives free, why were these people still in bondage? After all, they appeared to come to the altars in sincerity. I never realized this simple question would launch me on an incredible journey in which the Lord would answer the question. He gave me gifts in which to take this journey. The first was child-like faith to trust Him in every facet of this exploration, and the second was wisdom to discern and understand.

God showed me the first steps of child-like faith were to ask to understand His will and mind, to seek out the truth in every situation, and to knock over every obstacle that I encountered. Eventually He revealed which questions to ask, the unchanging truth that must not only be sought after but also embraced, and the endless doors to go through that required me to persevere in faith.

In His faithfulness, the Lord showed me, it was within His heart to bring wholeness to wounded, lost souls but such deliverance remains far from some people because of the various avenues of bondage that subtly entangle them.

He allowed me to walk through many areas of bondage with people while keeping me safe from its tentacles. He protected me when ministering to people with murder in their heart, surrounded me when I encountered the pigpens of pornography, and allowed me to observe Him as He healed the brokenhearted, brought truth to the captives, gave sight to the blind, and healed those wounded and bruised by life in general and sin in particular.

I realized early on that He was the deliverer from all bondages and I was the vessel. He was allowing me to co-labor with Him in the lives of others, but He was the One doing the majority of the work. I was the student who often sat in awe of His love, power, and desire to set captives free.

He also allowed me to see the dangers surrounding the area of deliverance. Deliverance in these times is often nothing more than a glorified scam whereby people make money off of the helplessness of others. Certain "deliverance ministries" claim to have special insight into the kingdom of darkness (or human nature) that gives them the ability to deliver souls. But what is often missing in these different types of "deliverance ministries" is the Deliverer Himself. Only Jesus can deliver.

I also learned that at the core of every bondage are the same lie, same sin, and same solution. In fact, the lie is constantly brought to the light, and both the sin and the solution comprise the largest sections of this book.

The course people must travel is the same as well. You will consistently encounter this route of deliverance throughout this book. It will be presented from different perspectives, but it brings you back to the same scriptural responsibility.

I realize that some people want to understand this information because they have watched it set people free and establish them on the right path to healing and reconciliation. On the other hand, I am aware that others want to get their hands on this information to be a "somebody" in Christendom or to start their own ministry. The latter can be a dangerous scenario that leaves victims behind. However, as I began to write this book, it became clear that God is not making it easy for just anyone to become the latest expert in deliverance or to refine some kind of procedure with which to start his or her own deliverance ministry. As the steps to deliverance progressed with each chapter, I was struck by the reality of how much work God does in delivering a person.

As a co-laborer with Him, my work involves that which is visible while God works on that which is unseen. God's workings to set people free are limitless, but my ways and knowledge are limited. As the book project neared completion, I rejoiced to see how a person who might approach this book to become the next "expert in deliverance" would only be overwhelmed by every angle that must be considered. It also struck me that if such an individual were honest, he or she would have to concede only God knows how deep He will have to go and how far He has to reach to unlock the many prisons that enslave people. As a result, God will get the glory He alone deserves.

It is humbling to know that this book is not written to the wannabe "experts" but to individuals who truly want to be set free. This book is a discovery that allows a person to see various areas of bondage that can enslave him or her, and then it allows the individual to seek the real Deliverer for deliverance.

This book is for those truly seeking deliverance. My prayer is that your journey through it will not only be life-changing, but I hope that you

Battle For the Soul

will come out knowing the Deliverer in ways that will produce awe, invoke worship, and cause your heart to rejoice in His beauty, power, and faithfulness as well.

INTRODUCTION

Why do so many people in the Christian realm insist on losing? This is one of the most haunting questions I have striven to answer as a minister of the Gospel. When I talk about losing, I am talking about people who are offered the solution for their problems and yet reject it and walk away. For example, to me one of the biggest losers in the Bible was the rich young ruler in *Matthew 19:16-22*. He was offered eternal life, and he actually walked away from it.

Although I am aware that Scripture repeatedly states only a few people (or a remnant) will gain eternal life, I still struggle with how people seem to prefer darkness over light. Many of these people start out right, but something in their makeup causes them to change directions. I shake my head in disbelief as people chose deception over truth. My heart breaks as I watch people on the right path take a detour down the road of seduction and delusion.

The reality of how only a few will make it concerns me even more as I have watched well-known spiritual leaders fall into sin and deception. Each of these failures has made me realize no one is exempt from spiritual destruction and that maturity, position, and respect hold no protection or guarantee from the evil tentacles that have the ability to ensnare even "the best."

My need to understand has escalated with each soul that is caught up in these tentacles. This search has allowed me to rediscover basic truths of the Word of God that have been lost in the rise of modern-day Christianity and drowned out by the worldly gospel that is being presented.

As I consider the times in which we live, I feel an urgency for the church to rediscover its real roots in order to stop this onslaught of the destruction of souls. Some will probably say it is too late for the church to get a reality check. I will not accept such a conclusion because I know there are sheep out there who want to rediscover the truths that turned the world upside down centuries ago.

The pilgrimage we are about to take in this book is not for the faint-hearted. In fact, it is only for those who recognize there is a real battle raging for the souls of men and that their souls could be in danger as well. In essence, this book is for those who, like the Apostle Paul, are serious about fighting a good fight, finishing the course, and keeping the faith *(2 Timothy 4:7)*.

My prayer for this book is that the Holy Spirit may use it to encourage those who desire to win, help others make some realistic conclusions about the battle that is raging, and even pull some out of the fires of delusion and destruction.

Therefore, may God prepare each reader to understand the battle and open his or her heart and mind to embrace the solution.

Chapter One

JUST WHERE IS THE BATTLE?

I am sure you have seen war films in which young, zealous men become caught up with the idea of fighting for their country. You can tell that their enthusiasm is not necessarily a product of patriotism but of immaturity and fantasy. They are excited about the idea of something that is often glamorized through various means of propaganda prepared either to stir up heroic nobility or to create guilt. This excitement remains until these young people come face to face with the ugly realities of war.

These young war enthusiasts do not understand the dynamics of war. They fail to recognize that war is often not about protecting one's country but about promoting an unseen ideology that is usually upheld by a few. It is not about patriotism but about sinister agendas and pursuits for ultimate power and control by unseen groups and forces.

Many of these soldiers had no idea where the war was taking place, but they were quick to volunteer and follow others into battle. Many of these noble enthusiasts who were considered the brightest and the best faced the harsh realities of war as they spilled their blood and sacrificed their lives on the soil of foreign lands. Sadly, many paid a high price without really understanding what they were fighting for.

Today there is a great battle going on in the spiritual realm. This is not a new war. It has been raging before Adam was ever formed in the Garden of Eden. The Word of God speaks consistently about this battle. In fact, Christians are called to be soldiers and are provided with armor that allows them to survive any attack from the enemy.[1]

Today the church is busy trying to raise up a new army that will outdo the old army by actually winning the war that started before time

---
[1] 2 Timothy 2:3; Ephesians 6:10-18

began in the Garden of Eden. This new breed of soldier marches to war songs in rallies called worship services that threaten and taunt the enemy. Their boot camp consists of clever indoctrination that is turning the brightest and best into hardhearted militants who will have no problem destroying those who are regarded as enemies.

Rather than commissioning leaders, the elite of this army imparts the rank of apostle, prophet, pastor, etc. on those who agree with their agenda. This army wears an imaginary uniform while claiming to have more effective, powerful weapons than the sword that the old army carried.

Like many soldiers of the past, members of this new army are ready to go into battle to secure the kingdom of heaven without realizing they are not fighting for the cause of Christ but for a sinister ideology that in the end will sacrifice them. Like Saul of Tarsus who persecuted Christians prior to his conversion in *Acts 9,* they believe they are on the right path, marching forward to promote a new movement. And like Saul, this new army will end up fighting against God by trying to eliminate those who truly belong to His kingdom simply on the basis that these renegades will not go along with the leaders' agenda and beliefs.

As you can see, the new army that is being recruited in the Christian realm is dangerous, but not to the real enemy.

Biblically speaking there are many problems with this new army. But since this army subtly discards, ignores, or twists the sword (the Word of God) to suit its own agendas, it has no sound boundaries or criteria in which to properly discern its activities or beliefs.

The first indication that this army does not represent God or His kingdom is that it is aggressive and quick to fight. *Ephesians 6:11, 13-14a* states,

> *Put on the whole armour of God, that ye may be able to <u>stand</u> against the wiles of the devil. . . . Wherefore take unto you the whole armour of God, that ye may be able to <u>withstand</u> in the evil day, and having done all, to <u>stand</u>. <u>Stand</u> therefore. . . .* (emphasis added).

As you can see, the army of God is not called to fight against the wiles of the devil but to stand against his advances. According to *Strong's Concordance*, "stand" in this text means to abide, appoint, bring, continue, covenant, establish, hold up, lay, present, set (up), and stanch.

The reason we are to stand against the wiles of the devil is because this is his world and he has the right to do as he desires. It was Adam who turned the world over to this enemy of God in the Garden of Eden. From that moment, Satan became the god of this world or age and the prince of the power of the air.[2]

Even when Jesus came the first time, He did not take Satan's domain away from him; He only secured the keys to death and hell by dying on the cross. Between His death, burial, and resurrection, He opened some of the graves of the saints of old and preached to the spirits in prison (or hell), proving He held the keys to the grave but not to Satan's world. It is upon His second advent that Jesus will come as King and personally take Satan's domain away from him.[3]

Here is another reality check about Satan's domain. If the Christian church were meant to bring down Satan from his domain, the likes of the first apostles, Peter, John, and Paul, would have done it in their generation. They were men of great authority and power. They knew their God and understood their enemy, and yet it was Peter who said we must be sober and vigilant because the devil is seeking people to devour. The Apostle John talked about young men who had overcome the devil on a personal level, and it was Paul who said we must stand.[4]

Story after story reminds us that God often delivers His people out of the jaws of the enemy, but He never totally destroys the enemy. We must not forget that the people of Israel stood at the Red Sea as God delivered them from Egypt and that King David believed God, who brought down the Philistine giant, Goliath, in utter defeat, but both the

---

[2] 2 Corinthians 4:4; Ephesians 2:2; John 16:11
[3] Revelation 1:18; Matthew 27:52-53; 1 Peter 3:19-20; Revelation 19:11-16
[4] 1 Peter 5:2; 1 John 2:12-20; Ephesians 6:11

Egyptians and the Philistines continued to be snares to Israel throughout its history.[5]

Up until Jesus comes as ruling Lord and King, Christian soldiers are to stand against Satan's attacks. "To stand" means you are not taking ground, but holding your ground. We see this even in the case of Michael the archangel in *Jude 9, "Yet Michael that archangel, when contending with the devil he disputed about the body of Moses, durst not bring against him a railing accusation, but said, The Lord rebuke thee."* Obviously, Michael was not trying to take any territory, but he maintained that which already belonged to God.

In the case of Peter, Jesus told him that Satan had desired to sift him but that He had prayed for him. This shows us that Jesus recognized Satan's rights to sift and test Peter. He did not fight to keep Peter from being sifted, but He stood in prayer on Peter's behalf to ensure his deliverance through the testing.[6]

This brings us to the second problem with this new army: It does not know its enemy, his tactics, and his power. Like many young recruits who go to war, many Christians have an unrealistic concept about their enemy, Satan. This type of ignorance will make a Christian soldier vulnerable and ready for defeat. The Apostle Paul made this statement to the Corinthians, *"Lest Satan should get an advantage of us: for we are not ignorant of his devices" (2 Corinthians 2:11)*. The problem is that many in today's church (including this new army) are ignorant of Satan and his devices, and as a result, he has gained a lot of territory into lives, homes, and churches.

Another downfall of this new army is that it does not know how to use the weapon provided by God to maintain the terrain. The only weapon that Satan respects is the Word of God, but this new army does not know how to handle it properly. Instead of putting Satan on the defense with it, these soldiers mishandle it, causing casualties within their own ranks and among the innocent.

Meanwhile, Satan sits back and has a good laugh about the farce that is taking place. He mocks as people sing about bringing down his

---

[5] Exodus 14:13; 1 Samuel 17:47
[6] Luke 22:31-32

domain because they are blinded to what the Word of God really says in such verses as *Romans 16:20, "And the God of peace shall bruise Satan under your feet shortly."* (Note, man will not put Satan under his feet; God is the only One capable of such a feat.) This capable foe jumps up and down as this new army turns a critical, judgmental eye on those who disagree with its tactics. He roars when this army arrogantly declares victory, knowing each time it is giving him a greater foothold into its various territories.

This brings us to another hard reality about the character of the new soldiers–they lack the fruit of the Spirit. This new breed of soldier lacks real love and compassion. When you look into the eyes of these soldiers, you see a hard glint that is ruthless and self-serving. They are prideful, militant, and aggressive. They have very little time or regard for the elderly or those who do not fit into their group. In fact, if you could describe the air they give off, it would be the same as fascism, which was prevalent in the days of Hitler and can be seen on all opposing fronts when it comes to true righteousness.

The time surrounding Hitler's reign of terror brought great darkness into this world, and sadly this new army will be no different. Jesus made this statement in *John 9:4, "I must work the works of him that sent me, while it is day; the night cometh, when no man can work."* I wonder how much daylight the real church of Jesus has before this great darkness tries to extinguish the real light?

Obviously, these soldiers' hearts have been surrendered to someone other than Jesus Christ. Jesus is humble, meek, lowly, and love personified. This is why Jesus was very clear regarding love, *"By this shall all men know that ye are my disciples, if ye have love one to another" (John 13:35).*

The only discerning fruit that identifies a person to Jesus Christ is love. The love of God is humble in attitude and benevolent in action.

Another problem with this army is that the soldiers have no idea where the war is. They suppose it is in the heavenlies when in reality it is closer than they think. In fact, many Christians will be surprised to find out just how close the war really is.

Where Is the War...?

Where does the spiritual war rage? Does it rage in the heavenlies, the courts of Congress or Parliament, our communities, next door, or maybe even in personal homes? The evidence of this war can be seen everywhere; it affects every area of our lives, but the Word of God tells us where the war is. The problem is few take note of what it says. The Bible also tells us what is really under attack. Since few understand what is on the line, they also fail to understand the dynamics of the war that invades every bit of their lives.

The Apostle Paul gives us a clear understanding as to where the spiritual war rages in *2 Corinthians 10:3-5,*

For though we walk in the flesh, we do not war after the flesh: (For the weapons of our warfare are not carnal, but mighty through God to the pulling down of strongholds). Casting down imaginations, and every high thing that exalteth itself against the knowledge of God, and bringing into captivity every thought to the obedience of Christ.

The first part of this Scripture tells us that our weapons are not fleshly. In other words, loud, repetitious "hyper" worship, unscriptural warfare, and brash declarations are nothing more than fleshly weapons that make Satan mock the most sincere and enthusiastic Christian soldier.

Secondly, our weapons are not for taking the domain of Satan but for pulling down strongholds, which can only be done through God. "Stronghold" means to fortify or the idea of holding ground or keeping safe.[7] These strongholds are so entrenched that only God can successfully bring them down.

And where do these strongholds exist? Look at *2 Corinthians 10:5:* **They exist in the mind.**

The greatest battle that rages today is taking place in the minds of people. This is where ingrained strongholds have taken root. *Ezekiel 8:12* gives us insight into these ingrained strongholds, *"Then said he unto me, Son of man, hast thou seen what the ancients of the house of*

---

[7] *Strong's Exhaustive Concordance of the Bible*; # 3794

Israel do in the dark, every man in the <u>chambers</u> <u>of</u> <u>his</u> <u>imagery</u>? For they say, The LORD seeth us not; the LORD hath forsaken the earth." (Emphasis added.)

"Imagery" in the previous text means imagination.[8] It is in the dark chambers of our minds that thoughts or imaginations construct an idea of God. These imaginations are made up of speculations that result in presumption or determination.

The Apostle Peter made this statement about presumptions in *2 Peter 2:10, "But chiefly them that walk after the flesh in the lust of uncleanness, and despise government. Presumptuous are they, self-willed, they are not afraid to speak evil of dignities."* We see that people who act within presumptions are walking according to perversion of the flesh and operating according to their own will. These presumptions will taint every thought and conclusion.

Ideas or concepts of God born out of perverted thoughts and imaginations of the flesh exalt themselves against the real knowledge of God. In fact, it is this exalted or idolatrous concept of God that ultimately rejects the real God of the Bible.

God describes the seriousness of this battle in *Genesis 6:5, "And God saw that the wickedness of man was great in the earth, and that every imagination of the thought of his heart was only evil continually."* Unless a person's thoughts are brought into captivity to the obedience of Christ, they remain continually evil.

This is why *Isaiah 55:8-9* tells us, *"For my thoughts are not your thoughts, neither are your ways my ways, saith the LORD. For as the heavens are higher than the earth, so are my ways higher than your ways and my thoughts than your thoughts."*

Arrogant fallen man has a hard time believing that his best "logical" conclusions are perverted to God. It is hard for a person to recognize that all unregenerate thought processes are nothing more than speculation. If a person fails to get a reality check about the depravity of his or her thought processes, this struggle will cause him or her to slip into a form of delusion. *Proverbs 14:12* explains this delusion,

---

[8] Ibid; # 4906

Battle For the Soul

"There is a way which seemeth right unto a man, but the end thereof are the ways of death."

The battle rages in minds, but what is the target the enemy is trying to destroy in a Christian's life? Jude gives us the answer to this question, *"Beloved, when I gave all diligence to write unto you of the common salvation, it was needful for me to write unto you, and exhort you that ye should earnestly contend for the <u>faith</u> which was once delivered unto the saints" (Jude 3,* emphasis added).

Satan's greatest target is the faith of a believer. If he can undermine a person's faith in God, he can cause that individual to stumble and fall into unbelief and skepticism. Unbelief will keep a person from entering into a place of confidence in God, and skepticism will cause a person to mock the truths of God.

How does Satan cause this type of destruction? He simply brings accusation against God, which causes a person to doubt and question the character of God. As more seeds of doubt take root, the more confused a person will become about God. This is where vain imaginations start filling in the blanks created by doubt and confusion, etching an image of an idol instead of upholding the character of God.

This image is a subtle lie, but it will undermine the spirit and truth of the Word and cleverly judge the one true God as unbelievable or undeserving.

God has provided weapons to bring down these idolatrous images, but the new army that is marching in churches today is void of these weapons. These weapons are not designed to take over Satan's kingdom, but to help the Christian stand and maintain his or her faith in God.

Throughout this book, we will be looking at these weapons, but the greatest one is truth.

Chapter Two

REALITY VS. TRUTH

Have you ever caught a glimpse into the mind of a person that actually made the hair stand up on the back of your neck? You have to wonder where he or she found his or her form of reality. You can clearly see that the person's conclusion is illogical and close to insanity, but to the individual it is sane, unshakable truth. In fact, this individual assumes his or her conclusion has to be obvious to any intelligent, thinking person.

You usually end up shaking your head at the person's reasoning, but you also find that some individuals are so convincing in their arguments you begin to question your own sanity. You wonder if you are the one who holds unrealistic perceptions of life and truth.

Over the years I have found consolation in the wisdom of a friend who helped me understand that when you are sound enough to question the validity of something in your own life or reasoning, you have not yet lost touch with reality.

For the last decade I have dealt with the issue of people's reality. My findings have brought sobriety as I had to face how vulnerable every individual is to embrace perverted perceptions. I also realized that people's reality can be easily manipulated without their knowledge.

The question is what is reality? According to my dictionary, "reality" is the quality of state of being real, the totality of real things, and the actual fact.[9] But in most cases, a person's reality is nothing more than his or her personal form of truth.

Scripturally speaking, truth is reality and this truth is able to make a person free. As you study the Word of God, you will find that truth is not

---

[9] *Webster's New Collegiate Dictionary,* G. & C. Merriam Co. © 1976.

a doctrine or a concept; rather it is the Person of Jesus Christ.[10] Jesus confirmed this in *John 8:36* after He stated the truth shall make you free, *"If the Son therefore shall make you free, ye shall be free indeed."*

Today people erroneously equate truth with doctrine or philosophy. I know that basic doctrines serve as boundaries to the Christian faith. But I also know that the odds of people possessing pure doctrine are almost close to impossible, especially in a society that is rampant with perversion and a church that has become worldly. The reason is that facts often become perverted as they are run through man's own perverted or worldly mind or logic. He will actually defile even the simple things of God.

This brings us to the character of truth. It is unchangeable and eternal in nature, which is why the Apostle Paul made this statement in *2 Corinthians 13:8, "For we can do nothing against the truth, but for the truth."* Therefore, truth is beyond the comprehension of finite man. He can never possess all truth because at best he sees through a glass darkly, but he can know the truth when Jesus becomes his standard of absolute truth.[11] If Jesus serves as truth, then everything in a person's life must line up to His characteristics, examples, and teachings.

Problems occur when people choose any basis of truth other than the Person of Jesus. They develop a reality outside of sound boundaries, as is obvious in people who maintain various forms of reality that are unrealistic and dangerous. This understanding has brought me to a startling fact: *Truth is always reality, but a person's reality may not be truth*.

Man's Reality

It is important to understand how people's reality works within them. Truth can only be found in the Person of Jesus, but everyday reality for people often consists of the things that are harsh and challenging.

---

[10] John 14:6
[11] 1 Corinthians 13:9-12

Rayola Kelley

These things serve as obstacles that can't be changed by any entity except God.

To change the face of any overwhelming obstacle, a person must first recognize his or her limitations. This is necessary if the person is ever going to come to the truth, and it entails accepting those things that can't be changed by personal intervention, intelligence, or strength.

The problem is that most people can't accept the type of reality that life brings. Since they can't personally resolve or change their unpleasant reality, they construct their own form of reality, which, of course, runs contrary to real truth. And whenever a person refuses to accept reality and sets out to change it, the individual will end up trying to play God by establishing his or her own form of truth. Note the following diagram.

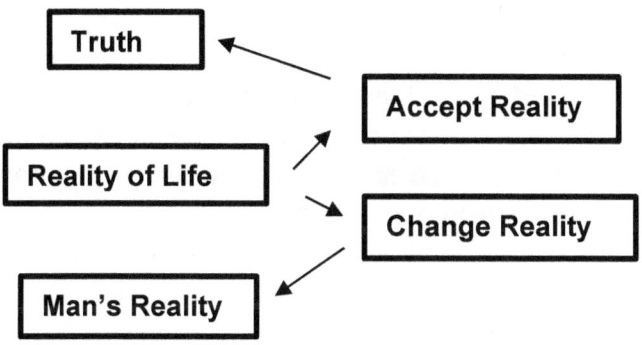

Man changes reality in order to adjust his world to his terms. This is a form of control, but it ends in failure because reality will not change; therefore, life will not adjust to mere man's manipulative attempts. This can produce feelings of hopelessness, anger, complacency, failure, rejection, incompetency, and loss of control.

When a person chooses to formulate his or her personal reality, he or she spirals downward into a dark and unrealistic abyss that produces destructive mental states. Individuals create their own reality in one of the four following ways:

1) Man ignores reality and hides in a reality conjured up in his mind, which often produces complacency or indifference towards present reality.
2) He refuses to accept present reality because it does not complement his world of feelings and emotions, so he sets out to adjust reality to his own terms, causing him to operate in a form of fantasy to avoid depression.
3) He refuses to take accountability for present reality, causing him to operate in an unrealistic state where uncomfortable situations are ignored and all personal participation that may be compromising and sinful is justified, making him right in his own eyes.
4) Or, he refuses to accept reality for what it is and sets out to create his own reality that he can control according to personal preferences and comfort zones.

The forms of reality that people adopt are illusive and unrealistic. They can cause people to operate in depression, anger, obsession, and insanity. Each of these states can serve as open doors for Satan, resulting in oppression or possession.

Oswald Chambers made this observation about the subject of reality or truth in his *Studies in the Sermon of the Mount*, "By *actual* is meant the things we come in contact with by our sense, and by *real,* that which lies behind, that which we cannot get at by our senses (compare *2 Corinthians 4:18*)." He goes on to make a distinction between these two groups of people by stating that the fanatic sees the real only and ignores the actual while the materialist looks at the actual only and ignores the real. He concludes that the only sane Being who ever walked this earth was Jesus Christ because in Him the actual and the real were one.

Jesus is truth personified. In His physical life He dealt in the actual world through practical means such as feeding the hungry, touching the sick, and reaching out to the rejected. He also dealt with the real world, which is unseen.

Although the real world is unseen, it is more real than the tangible world around us. It affects a person in greater ways than the actual world. Jesus knew the reality of both worlds and brought them together as He promoted an intimate relationship with God, confronted rebellion and demons, and supernaturally intervened on behalf of man in practical ways.

It is as you deal with different forms of reality in people that you begin to understand the real bondage that plagues man. As Oswald Chambers implied, man has a tendency to operate in extremes. He is either a fanatic that has no sense of the actual world around him, making him unrealistic at best and a fool at worst, or he operates in the material world, which makes him a skeptic of the unseen world at best and a mocker of God at worst.

Obviously, this bondage covers man's mind to keep him from seeing the truth. It justifies compromise, encourages tolerance, and applauds ignorance. It inspires conceit or an intellectual superiority that judges, scoffs, and mocks that which does not agree with its evaluation. And what is this bondage? It is called deception.

The Yokes of Men

Man carries one of two yokes: deception or truth. Jesus said of His yoke of truth that *"my yoke is easy."*[12] From the point of view of most people, truth is a grave yoke that can't be easily submitted to or carried. In a way, this is a correct conclusion. No one can bear the yoke of truth without the reality of Jesus, who makes the yoke of truth easy to bear and rewarding.

Another problem with the yoke of truth is that it is also very unattractive because eventually it forms a cross. If you follow Jesus, He leads you to a cross that requires you to make a clear choice between a narrow way or the broad road. Jesus' truth calls for people to deny their present perception or reality and embrace something that is narrow and contrary to their flesh and pride. It is at this crossroad that the courageous are separated from the cowardly.

---

[12] Matthew 11:30

Sadly, many people prefer to come under the yoke of deception, where they have many more choices. These choices give them more power or say over their lives, which is the real attraction to deception. Even though the yoke of deception becomes heavier with each lie or delusion, it serves a person's purpose because it justifies the flesh and feeds the pride.

This brings us to the author of the yoke of deception, Satan. In describing Satan, Jesus said in *John 8:44,*

> *Ye are of your father the devil, and the lusts of your father ye will do. He was a murderer from the beginning, and abode not in the truth, because there is no truth in him. When he speaketh a lie, he speaketh of his own: for he is a liar, and the father of it.*

To operate outside of Jesus automatically brings a person under Satan's domain. A person subjected to Satan can only display his characteristics—those of lust, hatred (murder), and deception. After all, his world is designed to create lust, inspire hatred, and cause its subjects to operate in deception.

John Owens said in his book *Sin and Temptation*, "Sin proceeds only when deception goes before it."[13] This is obvious in the world in which we live.

This brings us to another form of reality that can encourage delusion as well, the reality created by experience.

Experience vs. Truth

It is not unusual in Christianity to see experience take precedence over truth. Therefore, it is important to explain how experience confirms truth but truth must always be rightly used to discern experience.

Christians normally start their Christian lives by being taught doctrine. Pure doctrine represents righteousness, but knowledge or doctrine in its infant stage has no real substance. In fact, knowledge alone is not only limited, but it will also bring you to a crisis in your life when you discover there is a gap or great gulf in your understanding. Note the diagram on following page.

---

[13] *Sin and Temptation,* John Owens, © James M. Houston, pg. 36.

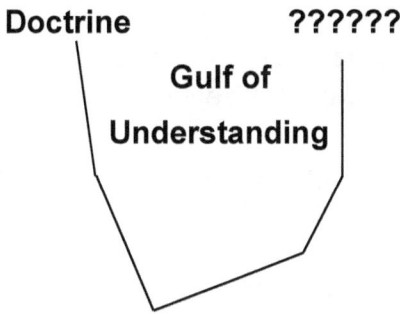

The question is what will it take to close this gap? The answer is experience. I discovered this fact on one of my many spiritual adventures.

One of the issues I struggled with was the Person of the Holy Spirit. For years He was at best a concept and at worse a subject you didn't pursue because of the controversy that surrounded His work and gifts. I had managed to skirt this subject until I came to a crossroad where I realized that I needed to make peace with the third person of the Godhead. After all, I had experienced the love of the Father and the beauty of the Person of Jesus, but the Holy Spirit still remained shrouded by my ignorance and limited by theology and speculation.

My first personal encounter with the reality of the Spirit of God was when I was overcome by sins and despair in my life. One night I was aware that God wanted to give me the power to overcome by filling me up with His Spirit. I remember thinking, "God, in my state I would probably abuse your gift."

Did I turn the gift down because I was afraid that I would defile it? All I can tell you is that nothing happened that night, but within a matter of days circumstances arose that forced me to face my sins and repent, coming back into a new and powerful relationship with God. It was at this time I encountered the incredible love of the Father and was touched by the loveliness of the Person of Jesus Christ.

The next thing I was aware of was that I was being shown things about future events. I shared the revelations with others, but they went unheeded. Eventually they materialized months later. Some people (including the Apostle Paul in *1 Corinthians 12)* would call this the gift of wisdom or prophecy. I personally never thought about whether it was a gift; all I knew at the time was that it appeared to be from God, and later it was confirmed by actual events.

I also found myself being drawn to those who understood the Holy Spirit. I had some biblical knowledge of the work and gifts of the Spirit. I knew He was real and necessary and that the church was not to forbid tongues and that believers were to covet the gift of prophecy over other gifts.[14] I also was aware of the abuses that seemed to follow the working of gifts, but I knew the Word clearly established proper boundaries, allowing me the freedom to be receptive. As you can see, I didn't have much of a basis to go on except that I chose not to be afraid of His work or gifts. As I surrounded myself with people who knew the Holy Spirit to be a Person and not a concept, I found myself being stirred up to know Him personally. Thus came my time of searching not only to know about Him but also to experience Him.

On another occasion I attended a retreat where there was a message in tongues. Four words went across my mind, and I could feel heat penetrating my body. I stood paralyzed by the idea that God could actually be giving me an interpretation to the strange message in tongues. I asked God that if He were giving me the interpretation, would He please confirm it by giving me more words. The same four words kept going through my mind.

After a long silence, another person gave a prophecy. I was relieved that none of the four words that I had seen were in the message. As I was about ready to pat myself on the back for not making a fool out of myself, another woman opened her mouth, and guess what came out of it? Her first four words were the exact same words that had gone across my mind numerous times.

From this point on, God used me in the gift of interpretation. I later learned that I could only remember four words at once and that anything past that limit would result in confusion. Once I was obedient to speak the first four words, the others came forth like water from an open faucet.

---

[14] 1 Corinthians 14:10

The next encounter I had in this area was with a friend. I was aware that my friend had experienced the power of the Holy Spirit. One day we talked about experiencing God in greater ways as we sat together at a graduation ceremony. As we were walking towards the exit after the ceremony, she suddenly took me by the collar, pushed me back up against the wall and practically lifted me off the floor. She looked sternly into my eyes and boldly declared, "You need the baptism of the Holy Spirit."

I understood my friend's frame of reference. She had been taught that there must be evidence of speaking in tongues to verify that one has truly been baptized with the Holy Spirit. Her intensity and her statement did not bother me in the least, but I began to evaluate my own life.

It was true I could not speak in another tongue, but I had been operating in gifts. I had to wonder if her experience or understanding of the subject invalidated my experience and deemed it insignificant. Over the years I began to realize that experiences, which can resurrect dead-letter doctrine into personal reality, can also be made into doctrine that is used unfairly to test other people's lives and experiences.

My next encounter happened at a missionary school. In one of our sessions the group was told to ask the Lord to show each of us our hearts. As I asked the Lord to show me my heart, He revealed to me that there were barriers in it that prevented His work. I immediately and humbly asked Him to bring those barriers down. As I was being prayed for, a prayer language came bubbling up out of the recesses of my spirit. According to my friend's theology, along with many others, I was now officially baptized with the Holy Spirit.

I realized my different encounters with the subject of the Holy Spirit through the years had constructed a bridge over the gap of understanding to create what I now knew to be reality. Note the diagram on the following page:

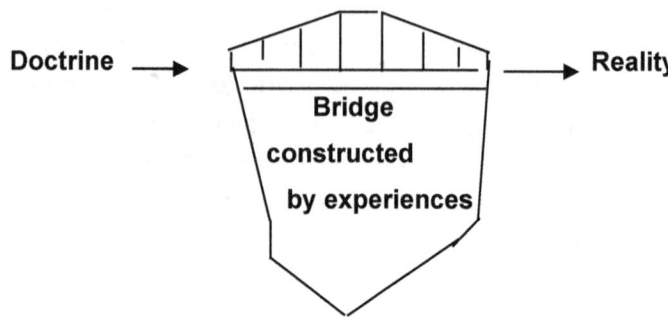

 I am aware that there is much debate over the baptism of the Holy Spirit. Each group has its own belief system, but others have a powerful experience to back up their understanding. Those who have theology alone are often afraid of the subject, while, on the other hand, those who have experience can make the experience a cause. Where is the balance?

 I have learned one important truth in my experiences with God, and that is that He is sovereign. God deals with people individually. He considers where they are and what they are receptive to when it comes to experiences or growth. When God was dealing with me, it was not according to acceptable doctrines of men or understanding but according to my personality and struggles. I can see where He gently worked around my barriers to do a work that was uniquely catered to and for me.

 Experiences with God are meant to be personal and not a matter of doctrine or debate. Those who lack experience and try to debate with someone to invalidate personal godly experiences simply reveal fear, arrogance, and ignorance on their part. On the other hand, experiences should never be used to test or disregard another person's experience.

 There is only one test that experiences have to pass, and that is the Word of God. All experiences must be scripturally validated before they can be considered truth. I tested all of my experiences according to the Word of God. I realized my experiences did not follow the order of some of man's popular doctrine, but they were found in the Word of God.

I have been around people who had spiritual experiences that penetrated every area of their being, but the practices and fruits that occurred were not scriptural. When an experience does not line up with Scripture to produce obedience and the proper fruit, then the experience is not of God but of a wrong spirit.

Experiences in the spiritual realm that are ungodly in nature can only create a reality that is nothing more than spiritual fanaticism and insanity. These experiences, which are inspired by the kingdom of darkness, set up the individual to be deemed an utter fool. Instead of bringing credibility to the person, such experiences will discredit an individual's testimony and make him or her a court jester in the circus arena of the world. Unbelievers mock what appear to be ridiculous religious performances.

It is important to realize that ungodly experiences are also designed to create delusion. This is why we must never allow experiences to determine our reality. We must avoid becoming a victim of delusion and regard experiences lightly until the Word of God substantiates them.

There are different forms of delusion operating in the world. Each form of deception brings an evil covering that will not only keep people in bondage to the lie, but will also keep them from perceiving truth. The result is an inability to see clearly the destructive path set before them.

There are only two paths that people can travel.[15] The path of truth is narrow and aligns the person to the character of Jesus Christ. The way of delusion is the broad road that allows the person to adjust truth to his or her own fancies.

Which path are you on?

---

[15] Matthew 7:13-14

Chapter Three

DELUSION OR TRUTH

Truth is a choice of the will while delusion is the consequence of deliberately *not* choosing truth. This is true for the whole Christian life. Rebellion is the consequence of not choosing obedience, unbelief is the product of not electing to trust God, and bitterness is the fruit of refusing to forgive.

Truth is also a sharp sword that causes offense.[1] This offense divides and separates family, friends, and religious bodies. People who are offended by truth are those who have erected a Jesus that is comfortable to their religious worlds, and they will easily become offended when the real Jesus is presented or lifted up in spirit and truth.[2]

The "t" in truth also represents the cross. A person can't embrace truth unless the individual first denies self and becomes identified with Jesus in the narrow boundaries of the cross. The narrow boundaries of the cross point to the narrow way man must seek in order to enter heaven.[3] Adhering to the truth cuts away the things that beset a person in his or her spiritual journey and lines a person up to God's way of doing—which speaks of the ways of righteousness. It also adjusts the person to enter into the narrow gate of life itself.

When people refuse to accept the truth, they ultimately adjust Christianity to their way of thinking. This enlarges the path to include that which is surface, insignificant, and controllable. It encourages a person to have a form of righteousness while denying the power of transformation that can only come by way of the cross and the Spirit.

---

[1] Matthew 10:34-39
[2] John 6:61-66
[3] Matthew 7:13-14

The cross is the only point of reconciliation between God and man.[4] The Apostle Paul talked about how Jesus as well as His followers have a ministry of reconciliation, but it can't happen until truth reigns through self-denial and the application of the cross.[5]

Because of our human nature, we see things in shades of gray, allowing for confusion, debate, and justification. These shades of gray often exist because we see spiritual truth as being too narrow and obsolete in regards to our present-day reality. As we regard truth as being insignificant, we begin to walk in the shadows instead of the light.[6] This is when we become prey to the consequences of refusing to make the right choices and going along with our natural preferences of darkness.

The irresponsibility of not making the right choices towards God often comes down to a person's attitude towards the Word of God. Few tremble at God's Word; therefore, they often ignore it or disregard it as insignificant. This lack of fear towards God's Word ultimately produces some form of delusion.

Delusion is often shrouded in confusion, but once a person gives way to it, it can produce a false peace. Although delusion may find its origins in various sources, its origin is the same because it is influenced by attitudes towards God and life.

For example, delusion can be a product of innocence, ignorance, neglect or abuse of truth, pride, or fear. It is attractive to the flesh, upholds fantasy, justifies sin, and exalts personal reality.

There are three forms of delusion in operation. The first form of delusion is *seduction*. The first seduction was recorded in the Garden of Eden when Satan seduced or beguiled Eve.[7] It is easy to be critical of Eve's foolishness to fall for Satan's line, but people who are flippant and critical toward those who have been seduced speak out of ignorance. Individuals who understand the dynamics of seduction know it can happen to anyone.

---

[4] Colossians 1:20-22
[5] 2 Corinthians 5:18-19
[6] 1 John 1:7
[7] Genesis 3:13; 1 Timothy 2:14; 2 Corinthians 11:3-4

Battle For the Soul

The Apostle Paul gives us insight into the dynamics of seduction in *1 Timothy 4:1, "Now the Spirit speaketh expressly, that in the latter times some shall depart from the faith, giving heed to seducing spirits and doctrines of devils."* Seduction is the work of Satan; therefore, its persuasive powers are supernatural in nature.

This seduction occurs when an evil covering is thrown over a person's mind. We read about evil coverings in *Isaiah 25:7, "And he will destroy in this mountain the face of the covering cast over all people, and the veil that is spread over all nations."* This Scripture shows us that nations as well as individuals are under wicked coverings.

Such coverings represent the type of spirit that a person succumbs to. This spirit will influence a person's perception. For example, a wrong spirit will dull the person's ability to rightly discern, ultimately erecting a different Jesus, and presenting a different gospel.

Sadly, within many churches evil coverings are adamantly being promoted. There is a teaching that every Christian should have a covering, meaning a spiritual leader overseeing him or her. This doctrine has become so popular I have often been asked who my covering is instead of whether I know the real Jesus. Obviously, people are becoming more comfortable with the idea that a person must be under some religious man or leader instead of the Son of Man. In reality no one comes under a man's influence; rather they come under the spirit that is motivating the individual. This is why seduction is predominate in the church.

The logic for having man as a covering is that the individual can serve as the person's protection, but in reality, the leader subtly replaces Jesus' authority.

Consider this scenario. Jesus is the head and His followers make up His body, but if an individual serves as a covering over another individual, where would you place that person in the picture of Jesus and His body?[8] Do you place this person over Jesus in your life? On this basis, one would have to admit that a human being will not fit properly over Jesus as the head. If you take the head away in order to place the covering of a person over you so that you can adhere to this

---

[8] Colossians 1:18; 1 Corinthians 12

teaching, what kind of picture do you have—a body that may have a covering but no head?

Covering and submission are two different concepts. I have no problem submitting to godly people out of fear of God.[9] I have no problem recognizing that others hold valid leadership positions, but all leaders in the kingdom of God are to be servants who are humble in attitude and submissive in action.[10] These godly leaders will never insist on becoming the head or covering over another person's spiritual life but rather through godly instruction and example will always lead the person back to Jesus Christ, the only head.

The problem with coverings is that men can abuse and destroy people in the name of godly leadership. Man in his fallen condition should never be entrusted with such a position. After all, a covering requires allegiance, not submission. It demands blind loyalty to a way of thinking and living. It encourages conformation rather than transformation. And most of all, such a covering can't change or save a person. There is only one Person who will keep people out of hell, and His name is Jesus. For this reason, I care only to be identified with the Son of God and not some man who could easily be subject to sin, the world, and Satan.

The Word of God is also clear there is only one mediator between God and man and that is the Man, Christ Jesus.[11] This is why *Isaiah 30:1* stipulates that the only acceptable covering for God's people is the Spirit of God. This verse confirms that it is spirit, not man that serves as people's real coverings.

A wrong covering of any type causes confusion that allows the enemy freedom to plant subtle errors into the minds of vulnerable people, shutting down their discernment. We can clearly see this in Eve's case.

In *Genesis 3:1*, Satan entices Eve into a conversation by falsely accusing God. He tells her that God said she was not to eat of every tree of the garden. Of course, she could eat of every tree except one,

---

[9] Ephesians 5:21
[10] Matthew 20:25-28
[11] 1 Timothy 2:5

but by twisting the emphasis of this truth in a small, subtle way, Satan was tempting Eve to set the record straight.

Her first mistake was trying to reason with the enemy. This mistake is not uncommon because man does not realize such an attempt is the initial lure into the spider web. We can't reason with Satan, and to try is to sign a death certificate.

The first small exchange between Satan and Eve served as the open door into Eve's mind that Satan needed. But it would be the second enticement that would allow Satan the opportunity to throw an evil covering over her by shooting a well-aimed dart at God's character through what appeared to be logic or reason.

Logical contradictions of God's Word or character always cause confusion that becomes a covering. Coverings cause unchangeable truths to become clouded or confused. This confusion actually keeps a person from seeing the real issue and robs him or her of the ability to rightly discern what is really going on.

Keep in mind how Eve explained to the devil that she and Adam could eat of every tree but one and if they partook of it they would die. Here comes the covering or confusion, *"And the serpent said unto the woman, ye shall not surely die for God doth know that in the day ye eat thereof, then your eyes shall be opened, and ye shall be as gods, knowing good and evil" (Genesis 3:4-5).* At this point I have no doubt that the serpent was beginning to sound logical to Eve. In fact, he was becoming more magnified as he threw doubt and suspicions on God's character and motive for depriving them of partaking of this one tree. In the end, Eve accepts Satan's presentation as truth, changing her former reality of truth to deception.

At this time we get some possible insight into why Eve was vulnerable to seduction, *"Ye shall be as gods, knowing good and evil."* The question is, what really enticed Eve? What was she hoping to gain in this temptation?

One reason many people are seduced is that they are looking for more of God. Instead of looking to God for the more they desire, they look elsewhere. Satan knows these vulnerable spots and seduces individuals to consider or pursue a pseudo avenue. Was Eve looking to be an actual god, or was she looking for a greater understanding or identification with God by gaining this knowledge of good and evil? This is speculation, but Satan knew her vulnerable point and used it to entangle her fully into his snare.

The next device Satan entices her with is lust. By this time Eve is thoroughly under his persuasion or covering and is entangled in his web. Now he is going in for the kill because once the desire takes root, the disobedient action follows. We can see how Satan defiled the purity of God's Word, blatantly lied about His character, and enticed her with perversion.

It is not unusual for people trapped in a web of seduction to sense that there is something wrong but to feel powerless to do anything about it. It is as though these individuals are being sucked down into a bottomless pit with such a force that they can't stop the impending destruction. This is why it takes God's intervention and His truth to snatch them out of this supernatural trap.

The second kind of delusion is that of *self-delusion*. We see this form of deception occurring in the life of Adam. Adam was not seduced when he partook of the tree of knowledge of good and evil. He was in charge of his faculties and knew the consequences of his action.

It is important to point out here that blatant rebellion serves as the springboard for all self-delusion. Adam was not deluded about his actions, but when God confronted him, his self-delusion started. Self-delusion is nothing more than justifying wrong actions. It is man's way of avoiding accountability and responsibility for his rebellious or questionable activities.

Although individuals usually know when their actions are unacceptable, they still must somehow either make it right in their own sight or become a victim of circumstances to avoid the consequences. When a person makes something right, he or she establishes his or her own form of truth.

In the case of the victim syndrome, a person simply adjusts the truth to make irresponsible actions look like they were beyond his or her control. Since the situation is being made to appear as being beyond the person's control, it logically makes the guilty party a helpless victim who is quick to point out the "real" culprits.

For Adam, he could not make his actions right no matter what he did, so he became the victim by blaming both God and Eve for his rebellion. He basically told God that He had made a mistake when He gave him woman because this woman forced him to sin (even though he was in full control of his actions); therefore, he was not responsible for his actions and undeserving of the consequences.

Self-delusion is the most insipid of all delusions. Seduction shows the insidious cleverness of Satan and the vulnerability of man, but self-delusion reveals man's rebellion and the foolishness of his own intellectual depravity and vanity.

Seduction throws a covering over its victim that conceals snares and pending destruction whereas self-delusion scrambles to hide behind a false cloak of innocence and ignorance through the means of self-justification. There are four such cloaks. They are the following:

1) The first cloak is that of *fig leaves*, which proud and rebellious man uses to cover pride and rebellion. This covering is used to try to hide a person's spiritual nakedness before God and is flimsy because it is not easy to hide a prideful attitude and its different forms of rebellion.[12]
2) The next cloak is a *religious cloak*. This cloak is not as revealing, for it hides a form of self-righteousness behind religious works and platitudes. It may be outwardly beautiful, but it lacks power and the fruit of the Spirit and is hypocritical in nature.[13]
3) The third cloak is *man's personal best*. It hides perversion that is made up of filthy rags.[14] Others can see the depravity of this cloak, but it gives a false sense of security to the one wearing it. The person wearing it truly believes he or she is spiritually acceptable because in the world's sight he or she is a good person.

---

[12] Genesis 3:7
[13] Matthew 6:1-18; Luke 20:46-47
[14] Isaiah 64:6

4) The fourth cloak is the *world's cloak*. This cloak covers man's spiritual condition with empty show and false pretense. It advocates success over righteousness, riches over morality, pleasure over holiness, and power over integrity.[15]

People quickly scramble to put on one of these cloaks when they are being exposed. *John 15:24* tells us men hate Jesus because He takes away the cloak, exposing the real core of their problem—that of a wrong heart condition.

Adam's actions did not originate with God or Eve but in his own heart. *Job 31:33* confirms this, *"If I covered my transgressions as Adam, by hiding mine iniquity in my bosom."*

Transgression means the breaking of the covenant. In this Scripture we see that Adam had it within his heart to break the covenant before he actually transgressed. This is true for all acts of transgression.

Jeremiah 17:9 tells us, *"The heart is deceitful above all things, and desperately wicked: who can know it?"* Adam had a heart problem that led to a treacherous act against God.

Hosea 6:7 gives us this insight, *"But they like men* (or like Adam) *have transgressed the covenant: there have they dealt treacherously against me"* (emphasis added).

It was Adam's choice to sin, but the real treachery of his heart was exposed when he blamed others for his actions. Eve stated truthfully that the serpent had beguiled her, but Adam actually bore false witness when he blamed both God and Eve.[16] The problem with self-delusion is that it can encourage greater deception by creating a frightening reality where there is no limit to wicked acts that will ultimately be justified at the expense of others.

God is the only One who can deliver a person out of seduction, but when it comes to self-delusion the person is the one who must stop the justification by agreeing with God's evaluation and repenting for his or her actions. This form of delusion is natural and very habit forming; therefore, it is hard for a person to break but not impossible if the

---

[15] Matthew 22:8-14; James 4:4
[16] 2 Corinthians 11:3; 1 Timothy 2:14

individual humbles self, confesses to God, and cries out for mercy. Reliance on God, submission to His truth, and insistence on personal integrity will break this destructive habit of self-delusion and result in victory.

The third form of delusion can be found in 2 Thessalonians 2:11, *"And for this cause God shall send them strong delusion that they should believe a lie."*

It is hard to fathom that God would send a delusion since He is all truth. My perception of this Scripture is that God simply removes all restraints from one of Satan's religious delusions, allowing him to move unhindered among God's people. I believe this conclusion is upheld by the incident found in *2 Chronicles 18* when a lying spirit was allowed by God to entice King Ahab into a battle that would mean his demise.

Obviously, when God allows a delusion of this nature to freely reign, truth will also be presented to bring a contrast. For example, Ahab chose to believe the lie after the truth was presented by a real prophet of God.

This brings us back to a very important truth about delusion sanctioned by God. Its main goal is not to deceive but to test the hearts of men.

I have watched religious delusion expose the hearts of people. The Word of God warns us that such a delusion will be predominate in the end days. This delusion will be a strong, enticing, powerful religious deception that those who justify sin, deception, and unrighteousness at any level in their lives will find irresistible.

This type of delusion also serves as a covering, but unlike the covering of seduction that is thrown over unsuspecting victims, people will actually choose to submit to it willfully. Once they do, it will consume their souls with greater darkness, deception, wickedness, and judgment.

This brings us down to a scary prospect. We know God must deliver a person from seduction and that only through godly repentance and truth can a person be snatched from the consequences of self-delusion. But since it is God who is sanctioning the third type of delusion, who is left to save a person from its strong tentacles? Frightening thought, but I have seen God deliver people from such a delusion. However, they must become totally broken by their arrogance and fall on their faces in repentance, thereby throwing themselves totally upon God's mercy and grace.

The problem you will encounter in this delusion is that it is devastating to a person's pride, making it very hard for the person to seek and accept God's forgiveness and restoration. For this reason, many people self-destruct because of this delusion rather than experiencing forgiveness and restoration.

Have you come under a wrong covering? Or perhaps you are hiding behind a cloak. The truth (Jesus Christ) is waiting for you to turn around and face Him. Like Bartimaeus in *Mark 10:50*, you need to cast off any garment or cloak that keeps you from being transparent before Jesus and come to Him in humility so you can be made whole.

Now let us consider how people view truth.

Chapter Four

A SAD COMMENTARY

There is no greater tragedy than watching man reject truth. Truth is so liberating. It is the way to eternal and abundant life, and yet man prefers delusion.

Over the years I have dealt with all three forms of delusion that were discussed in the last chapter. I have come to the conclusion that delusion is a form of *insanity*.

Insanity means unsoundness of mind, but to me it is best defined as refusing to deal honestly with the present reality. The problem with delusion is that it creates an insane world for those who must contend with it. People I have encountered who insist on their particular delusion are the most frustrating and unrealistic individuals to be around. They are not only unteachable, but their reality is absurd and unbelievable.

It is my observation that most people avoid the present reality by hiding in the past or by living in the future. For example, many people cling to the past in order to justify present-day actions or live in the future to avoid facing the harsh reality of life. Living in the past will cause complacency, self-pity, or apathy while living in the future causes frustration, anger, and disillusionment. And those who do live in present-day reality outside of Jesus often live in despair because they can't change or control reality. Eventually they give up on life and give in to anger, self-pity, or being a hopeless victim.

Rejection of truth will harden a person's heart. The more the truth is discarded, the harder the heart. Once individuals begin to create their own reality, they will become confused. As they struggle to maintain their reality, they give way to delusion that becomes a form of insanity.

Eventually, they will crucify the truth whenever they encounter it. Note the diagram.

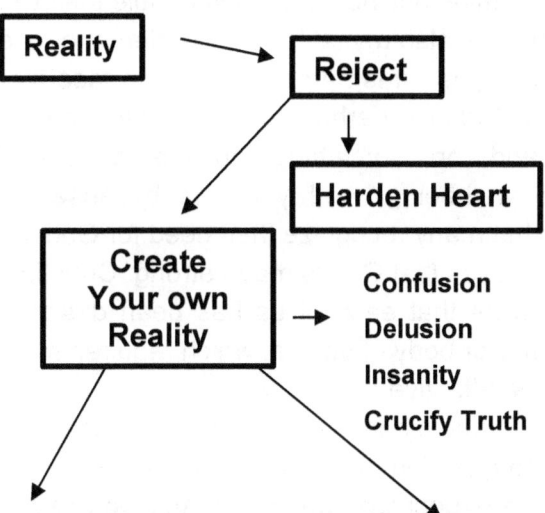

Past	Present	Future
Excuses	Can't control reality	Fantasy
Hopelessness	Close down: despair or anger	Disillusionment
Anger	Self-pity; Martyr	Anger

By facing the present reality with integrity and graciousness, a person gets a reality check. It is also the only means of coming to the truth, which alone is able to change our present reality. Yet the change does not necessarily come with a change in circumstances but a change of disposition, attitude, and perspective concerning present-day life.

In life four types of realities will cause a person to create his or her own personal reality. It is important to understand that each of these realities of life is also meant to try hearts, enlarge people's capacity towards spiritual truths, and cause them to grow spiritually. They are:

1) *Limitations*: Limitations not only show people their weakness or inability, but they also reveal how dependent they are and how fragile life really is. It is hard for people to face the truth that they are not God or superhuman. They hate the idea that they must depend on something outside of themselves to experience well-being. And yet it is because of personal limitations that many recognize their need for God. It is through such weaknesses that God is made strong. Christians also will come to realize that each of us has been designed to work within a family or body of people, which requires submission on our part to be effective.[1]

2) *Drudgery*: Drudgery is hard on people because it causes individuals to question their worth in the scheme of things. As Christians we expect God to use us, and we imagine not only great things for ourselves but also exciting times in the way of mountain-top experiences.[2] When nothing of significance happens, questions and doubts begin to formulate in our minds. Of course, Satan effectively uses this because we can't change our particular present lot without sinning or creating a fake reality.

   Oswald Chambers made this comment about drudgery: "The height of the mountain top is measured by the drab drudgery of the valley; but it is in the valley that we have to live for the glory of God." He also stated that it requires the supernatural grace of God to endure drudgery and live an ordinary, unobserved, ignored existence as a disciple of Jesus....Chambers went on to say: "We have to be exceptional in the ordinary things, to be holy in mean streets, among mean people, and this is not learned in five minutes."[3] It is important

---

[1] Ephesians 5:21; 1 Corinthians 12; 2 Corinthians 12:5-12
[2] Jeremiah 45:5
[3] *My Utmost for His Highest*, October 2nd and 21st devotionals.

to keep in mind that the mundane times are not only times of testing but of preparation. Do not allow drudgery to cause you to conjure something up in your spiritual life. Not only will you be outside of God's will, but you will also set yourself up for defeat. If God is not convicting you of something in your drudgery, be faithful with what is in front of you until God tells you to change direction or leads you down a different path.

3) *Crises:* Crises prove we are not in control of the events that affect our lives. This reality can cause a person to fall into a pit of hopelessness and anger. Jesus tells us not to fear crisis or tribulation, for He has overcome the world and is in control.[4]
4) *Trials:* Trials prove we can't change anything. This is hard on pride because we have high opinions of our capabilities. We have endless plans of how to change things that are unpleasant and tedious. *James 1:2-4* tells us these trials are to establish godly character in us and not to avoid or try to resist them.

As you consider delusion and its consequences in light of the hope we have in Christ, it is hard to believe that people would not flee from that which is questionable. But the truth is people prefer delusion over truth. Jesus summarized this harsh reality in *John 3:19-21,*

And this is the condemnation, that light is come into the world, and men loved darkness rather than light, because their deeds were evil. For everyone that doeth evil hateth the light, neither cometh to the light, lest his deeds should be reproved. But he that doeth truth cometh to the light, that his deeds may be made manifest, that they are wrought in God.

Man's preference for darkness is a sad commentary on the soul.

Granted, people are vulnerable to deception, but truth is made available to those who are on the path of deception. Man has a choice. My past experience in confronting people who were in deception or cults or operating on the fringes of questionable doctrines and teachings has been that 90 percent of them chose to continue in their delusion regardless of legitimate concerns and proof of their error.

---
[4] John 16:33

Obviously, the reality of these people has been changed to embrace the lie as a truth. Their attitude towards those who show concern or disapproval is that of arrogance, pity, or tolerance.

Since my close-up encounter with people's perverted reality, I have striven to understand why a high percentage of people choose to drink the poison Kool-Aid of deception (like those at Jonestown) rather than partake of Jesus' banquet table.[5] The reasons vary, but they all spring from one main problem.

Before we can fairly understand the core of the problem, we must consider the reasons for preferring delusion over truth. The reasons alone serve as an indictment against man, but the core of the problem seals his doom.

One reason people avoid truth is because it calls them to personal accountability. Whether we like to face it or not, most people can't stand being wrong or weak. Because of our great pride, we hate to face our fallibility and vanity; therefore, we come into delusion about our capabilities, limitations, and weak status. We bluff our way through uncharted territories, become experts in our ignorance, justify our failures, and avoid facing our errors. This unwillingness to be honest about our imperfection is one of mankind's greatest downfalls.

This downfall is what keeps man from coming to God for a full and abundant life. As Jesus stated, *"Blessed are the poor in spirit: for theirs is the kingdom of heaven."* Salvation can only come to a soul who recognizes his or her spiritual poverty, is honest about sins, is humble because of weakness, and is aware that spiritually he or she is nothing more than a worm in the scheme of things. In short, real salvation is the greatest type of demotion that can occur to any self-sufficient, arrogant soul, but it is also the most liberating.

Likewise, spiritual growth hinges on whether this demotion continues to take place in an individual's Christian walk. It simply means a person is giving way to the Lordship of Jesus Christ daily instead of to his or her fragile pride.

---

[5] Jim Jones, a charismatic leader, indoctrinated his people to blindly drink poisoned Kool-Aid upon his command. As a result, about 1,000 people died because they believed a fanatic.

Another reason people avoid the truth as the standard for their reality is because it won't allow for fairytale endings in our present life. People in countries that have abundance have a tendency to regard life as a big fairytale. Life is far from being a fairytale. It is comprised of harsh realities that shake every foundation.

I remember watching a woman being interviewed after her home was destroyed by a tornado. Because of it, one of her children had spent days in a coma. The woman implied this destruction should not have happened to any family, but she was really saying that it should not have happened to her family because it shattered her American fantasy of happiness, prosperity, and utopia. The truth is, devastation had been happening all around this woman for years and in various forms all over the world but she remained indifferent to it. But all of a sudden, this type of devastation was wrong and unacceptable because it had personally touched her life instead of some stranger's.

Like many Americans, this woman lived in a false reality, a fantasy, until a storm tore up her world. It is hard for people to realize that life is not a fantasy but instead is tragic. But when people live in fantasy, they can ignore the plights of others because tragedy is not a reality in a world of fairytales.

Sadly, fantasy produces not only an unrealistic world that is self-centered and self-serving but also fragile. Such a world hinges on the idea that life is a bowl full of cherries and that everything will work out in the end. After all, bad things only happen to bad people.

In this imaginary place the person serves as a director of his or her own world. He or she can avoid growing up, facing the tough reality that shakes other people's worlds, and remain aloof, indifferent, or unrealistic about those who have great struggles. Needless to say, this type of world is popular because it allows the person to be god of his or her world.

But life has a way of popping the plastic bubble by proving man is not God. Probably the harshest reality of all is when people find they are not really in control of their worlds. It is also a harsh reality to discover that life has no favorites—the sun shines on the evil and the good, and rain falls on the evil and good.[6] No one is exempt from the different blessings or tragedies of life.

This is why the Apostle Paul tells Christians they must think on things that are real (or true), which keeps a person from operating in an unrealistic and indifferent world.[7] A world that promotes fantasy and indifference makes an individual foolish and ineffective in the kingdom of God. In fact, such a person is quickly viewed as being out of touch with reality, causing him or her to lose credibility as a minister of Christ.

Another reason truth is not appreciated is because it calls for discipline. Truth sets up immovable boundaries for people to operate within. Because rebellion lies in the heart of man, he has a tendency to reject, move, or change boundaries that do not originate with him or prove to be beneficial to his cause.

Because of this rebellion, people adamantly reject the idea that truth can only be realized within one boundary: that of the character of God. They want the freedom to determine their own form of truth. After all, if they chose to seek greater avenues of so-called insights other than the limited one of God, they should have the right to do so without being judged a fool by a narrow perspective. They mock the concept that truth comes down to a person instead of some great intellectual philosophy. But Jesus said in *John 14:6*, *"I am. . .the truth."* He is the visible expression and example of God. He is the essence of eternal reality, and all truth will ultimately be judged according to His character, teachings, and examples.

This brings us to the bottom line or motivation as to why people prefer delusion over truth. *2 Thessalonians 2:10-11* states, *"And with all deceivableness of unrighteousness in them that perish because they received not the love of the truth that they might be saved. And for this cause God shall send them strong delusion that they should believe a lie"* (emphasis mine).

The reason people do not prefer truth is because they *do not love* it. In short, a person does not really love God. They might be in love with their personal idea, concept, creed, or interpretation of God but not

---

[6] Matthew 5:45
[7] Philippians 4:8

in love with the Person of God. As you can see, there is a big difference between these two perspectives; one is based on a fantasy and the other one is inspired by the real Person. Sadly, to offer truth to a person who does not love it is to give more reasons for misinterpretation or perversion of it. As Jesus clearly stated in *Matthew 7:6*, *"Give not that which is holy unto the dogs, neither cast ye your pearls before swine, lest they trample them under their feet, and turn again and rend you."*

Ravi Zacharias, in his book *Jesus Among Other Gods*, talked about the struggle people have with reality. He stated there are a couple of reasons why people fail to respond to truth: It is not being preached and there is also an inability to receive it, producing an acute loss of reality.

It takes a love for God and a love of God working in a person's life to favor God and His truth over personal reality that prefers and condones deception and works of darkness.

In order to embrace truth, one must deny self. People live in some type of denial. In most cases they live in denial about personal failures, responsibilities, and reality. This is made evident by the destruction of relationships as people refuse to face their part in the breakdown. It is easy to see this in people's spiritual lives. For example, if a person does not deny self to embrace the way, the truth and the life, he or she will ultimately deny reality and the lordship and life of Jesus Christ.

Because of man's preference for darkness, most people live in denial about their spiritual condition rather than deny self to know the essence of real life that can only be found in Jesus. They flounder, flop, and fall in their struggles, but in spite of their failure to experience a satisfying life, they still refuse to accept the truth.

Truth will never serve self-centered purposes. It will always expose self-delusion for its insipid ways and expose pride for it idolatrous claims. It will shake all fantasies and lies as well as prove man to be vulnerable and small in the scheme of things. It will always bring a person back to the reality that truth is narrow and is summarized in one person, Jesus Christ.

I believe God has been allowing various religious delusions to test those who do not love the truth. This lie will force a decision, causing those who prefer darkness to get off of the fence and openly chase after deception with its many compromises and philosophies. This lie will eventually swallow up those who prefer personal reality over the eternal truth. It will expose a rebellious heart and arrogant attitude as well as bring silence on the Day of Judgment.

The question every God-fearing, blood-bought saint must answer is, am I a lover of the truth? This is the only motivation that will keep a person from falling for the great delusion now sweeping the face of the earth.

The next question is, what must I do to ensure that I am able to stand no matter what comes against me? The answer to the last question is simple: I must overcome.

Chapter Five

OUT OF BALANCE

What must a Christian overcome? Again, we must understand what happened in the Garden of Eden to answer this question. We must also come to terms with man's dreadful plight before we can grasp the means to overcome.

God formed Adam and Eve to exist in an innocent state. This innocence was not a product of ignorance but a state determined by what both knew experientially. For example, Adam and Eve knew that there was a difference between good and evil, but all they had experienced was God's goodness and perfection; therefore, they did not experientially know evil.

Satan's enticement to Eve was that she could reach the same status as God by simply experiencing both good and evil. But to experience something, a person must actually partake of it; hence enters the attraction to the tree of knowledge of good and evil. This attraction translates into the first known temptation leveled at man. As *James 1:14-15* states, *"But every man is tempted, when he is drawn away of his own lust, and enticed. Then when lust hath conceived, it bringeth forth sin: and sin, when it is finished, bringeth forth death."*

Satan tempted Eve by arousing her imagination. The imagination thinks along the lines of unknown possibilities that will tantalize the appetites of the flesh, stir up the ego, and awaken the fantasies of the eyes. The problem with these types of possibilities is that they do not constitute present reality or give a realistic picture of future consequences. These possibilities often turn out to be nothing but vain, useless imaginations.

Satan knows how to use possibilities effectively because at the core of them are lies. For example, when I consider my fallen nature I can see why I could be considered a miserable failure in every aspect of my life since the possibility to sin is present. But such possibilities are void of one element: Jesus Christ. Jesus as truth changes the equation by reminding me of the cross.

The cross reminds me that the possibilities must give way to reality, and now my life and truth is Jesus. Because of Jesus in me and me in Him, God does not consider what might be or what could be but He looks at what is—Christ in me the hope of glory.[1] This is where my truth and hope rests, and any other perspective is going to bring delusion or condemnation to my life.

When the enemy of God enticed Eve to consider the possibilities, she opened up the elements of her soul to explore the benefits of evil. The elements of the soul are the *emotions, intellect,* and *will.* As Eve's imagination became subject to the exploration of evil, her soul became more focused on the tree of knowledge of good and evil.

For example, she noticed that the food of the tree appeared to be good. This enticed her desires to partake of all it possessed. She also saw that it was pleasant to her eyes. In other words, the possibilities of greater pleasure stirred up her emotions. As she thought about the possible wisdom available through the fruit, her mind became enticed to experience all that was conceivable.[2] It all seemed so right because the possibilities were there for greater fulfillment, pleasure, and wisdom.

We know that Eve's conclusion to the matter was not right but deadly wrong, but by this time there was no sense of wrong and no reality about the dangers or consequences that could bring a reality check. Her mind had become darkened to truth and impending results. But, the ultimate extent of this deadly pursuit was not fully realized until Adam willfully disobeyed. This was when both of their eyes were opened to their real spiritual state.[3]

It was in Adam's willful act of disobedience that the real consequences were sealed for man.

---

[1] Colossians 1:27
[2] Genesis 3:6
[3] Genesis 3:6-7

How Far Did Man Fall?

As we will see, the very area that was tempted in the Garden of Eden now reigns. But before we can understand the operations of this new god that was erected due to man's rebellion, we must understand what kind of environment was produced to encourage this god to rule with great authority and power in each succeeding generation.

Because of his rebellion, Adam fell into a total state of darkness. This spiritual darkness meant the light of God went out of Adam, allowing darkness to invade every area of his being. When man fell into this darkness, the one great lie— "ye shall be as gods"—not only remained intact but also penetrated every area of his soul. The summary of this lie can be found in *Isaiah 14:13-14*,

> *For thou hast said in thine heart, I will ascend into heaven, I will exalt my throne above the stars of God: I will sit also upon the mount of the congregation, in the side of the north: I will ascend above the heights of the clouds: I will be like the most High.*

For man this lie translates in this manner: "I will reign! I will exalt my throne (of self) above all else when it comes to my world. I will rule in all spiritual matters that I encounter, and I will control the circumstances that come my way. I will be as God."

As a result, man often tolerates God in his world as a religious gesture while behind closed doors he pursues, attempts, and plays at being God. When life proves that he is not in control, he might run to God, but it is often with the idea that he will be able to control God if he plays his spiritual cards right. It is when God refuses to be man's puppet that this fallen condition raises its ugly head in anger and unbelief to bring forth accusations against God.

When Adam fell into this darkness, he took on the very disposition of darkness. We know the pattern of this disposition is Satan. This is why Jesus said in *John 8:44, "Ye are of your father the devil."*

It is hard for people to realize how far Adam fell because the darkness of every soul is a normal state. Therefore, there is no way we could envision the depth of this darkness; we have no contrast when it comes to this world. In fact, people often think their darkness is light.[4]

The way that we convince ourselves of this is by considering the "good" things we do rather than who we are—creatures that prefer darkness.[5] Because of kind or generous acts, many people believe that there is some good in them, something redeemable. But in reality nothing redeemable is within man. He is miserably lost as well as deluded about his real spiritual condition. Hence this warning in Proverbs 14:12, *"There is a way which seemeth right unto a man, but the end thereof are the ways of death."* [6]

No human knows the depth of man's dark disposition except the Man, Christ Jesus. He had a contrast to the depth of man's fall because He came from the glories of heaven. He was pure—the light of the world that exposed darkness everywhere He walked. But I believe it was on the cross that Jesus experienced the real depth of man's fall.

Man's spiritual state put Jesus on that cross. The spit, hatred, and mocking directed towards Jesus showed just how opposed man is to being ruled by the God of the universe. The darkness that covered the earth while Jesus was on that cross represented the darkness of man's soul which continually tries to distinguish the true light of the world.[7] But it was the cry on the cross that gives a glimpse of the depth to which man had fallen, *"My God, my God, why hast thou forsaken me?"*[8]

Jesus experienced that depth of darkness in His own soul, and it made His whole being cry in utter despair. We can't understand it, but we can catch valuable glimpses of it as we walk in the light of Jesus. At times we become humbled as we sense the great length to which His mercy went to quench judgment and how deep His grace reached to offer each of us eternal life.

Because of this dark environment of man's soul, he is forever trying to get around God's holy character. He tries religion instead of the cross

---

[4] Matthew 6:22-23; Luke 11:34-36
[5] John 3:19
[6] See Matthew 6:22-23.
[7] John 1:9-12
[8] Matthew 27:46

of Jesus because grace does not allow for self-glorification. He replaces the salvation of Jesus with intellectual pursuit because the cross seems too foolish and insignificant. He hides behind religious creeds so that he can maintain some kind of control of his spiritual life. Ultimately, man refuses to concede, submit, repent, and humble self before God Almighty and accept God's terms of salvation. Because of this rebellion, darkness grows. And where darkness resides, bondage exists.

This dark environment not only causes bondage but has also caused man to taste the bitter sting of his new god.

The Results

Due to Adam's blatant disobedience, all men would taste the consequence and bitterness of darkness—that of death.[9]

Adam's action brought death upon mankind in two ways. First, physical death entered the scene and began to work its deadly influence at the conception of life. This relentless enemy plagues physical life until life succumbs to its embrace. The second death is spiritual death. All men are born in this death, which is summarized as a separation from God.

Man's relationship with God was broken when Adam disobeyed. Sadly, people have a hard time understanding how the breaking of fellowship between man and God produced spiritual death unless they realize it is God alone who constitutes spiritual life or well-being. Therefore, man's only link to real life is found in a relationship with God. Without God, man is spiritually dead, condemned to live a life of ruin, emptiness, and hopelessness.

When man sinned in the garden, he fell from his innocent state into a darkened condition where his soul, and not his spirit, began to define life. This new state was opposite to how God formed man because in the beginning man was made a living soul by the breath of God. The living part of the soul was made possible by the presence of the spirit or breath of God that resided within him.

---

[9] Romans 5:18-19

God put the spirit or breath of life within man so he could relate and interact with his Creator on a spiritual level. After all, God is Spirit, and man must worship him in spirit and truth.[10]

The soul of man had been formed to serve as an avenue for his spirit to express worship and adoration to God. The mind was to consider and meditate on God's greatness and ways. The will had the freedom to show worship by choosing to love and obey God. Emotions were the means to reach out and experience God in a personal way.

When the fellowship was broken by Adam's disobedience, the light which is the life of man went out in his spirit. Watchman Nee dealt with this subject in his book, *The Normal Christian Life*. He pointed out that when Adam chose the wrong tree, he determined the lines of his development. He would now command a knowledge he knew because the elements of his soul became over-developed. With his emotion touched, his reasoning power developed, and his will strengthened, he could decide which way to go. Nee summarized it with this statement, "The whole fruit ministered to the expansion and full development of the soul, so that not only was the man a living soul but from henceforth man will *live by the soul.*"[11]

This over-developed soul caused a change in leadership. God no longer reigned in man's life, but rather man now called the shots from the providence of his will. Man ceased to be directed by the spirit that was subject to God and became controlled by the whims of his over-developed soul. This caused a great separation between man and God. *1 Corinthians 2:14* confirms this, *"But the natural man receiveth not the things of the Spirit of God: for they are foolishness unto him: neither can he know them, because they are spiritually discerned."*

Watchman Nee put this over-developed soul in perspective. He pointed out that when the body becomes our life we live like beasts and when the soul becomes our life we live as rebels and fugitives from God. Even though we may be gifted, cultured, and educated, we are still alienated from the life of God.[12]

---

[10] John 4:23-24
[11] *The Normal Christian Life*; Watchman Nee; © Angus I. Kinnear; pg. 152
[12] Ibid; pg. 178

The breaking of fellowship with God not only broke the only link of life between man and his Creator, but it also broke the heart of God. This was made evident on the cross of Christ when His side was pierced by a sword and blood and water came forth, signifying a broken heart.[13]

In the Garden of Eden, normalcy for man was the reality of God and His goodness. But, in the world where the soul of man reigns, normalcy represents sorrow, despair, tragedy, and death.

The first man blew it in the Garden of Eden, but man continues to travel this rebellious path as he avoids the sovereign reign of God and gives way to the various appetites and desires of the soul. But you can see at times that in the deepest recesses of man's mind he has a knowledge that his own kind once possessed something that was beautiful and perfect. You observe how he tries to develop a perfect society outside of God without success. He strives for some kind of normalcy only to find disillusionment.

It is vital that man resolves what he has lost and regains it. But before he can resolve and regain a lost utopia, he must realize that all imperfection begins and remains with his own personal rebellion.[14] In other words, the imperfection of man's world does not rest with a God who may appear to be harsh or with those who share his environment. This imperfection thrives within his own insistence to call the shots in his life, or in other words, to be god in his world.

It is man and not his world that is out of balance. Man's out-of-balance condition has managed to throw the rest of the world into utter chaos.[15] This chaos will remain for man until God takes His rightful place in his life. But before this restoration can take place, man must understand the nature of this chaotic condition and come back to God on His terms.

---

[13] John 19:34
[14] Romans 3
[15] Romans 8:19-22

The Normal Man

Christians must overcome the over-developed soul to bring order back into their worlds. The scriptural terms that refer to the over-developed soul are "the flesh" or "the old man." The over-developed soul also points to the fallen man's disposition that expresses the attitude and works of Satan. As Jesus elaborated in *John 8:44*, *"Ye are of your father the devil, and the lusts of your father ye will do."*

The works of "the flesh" can be found in *Galatians 5:19-21*,

> Now the works of the flesh are manifest, which are these; adultery, fornication, uncleanness, lasciviousness, idolatry, witchcraft, hatred, variance, emulations, wrath, strife, seditions, heresies, envyings, murders, drunkeness, revellings, and such like: of the which I tell you before as I have also told you in time past, that they which do such things shall not inherit the kingdom of God.

These works are evident in today's world, revealing how much the flesh is in operation and the extent of the war that rages between the flesh and the Spirit and between good and evil.[16]

Colossians 3:9-10 states, *"Lie not one to another, seeing that ye have put off the old man with his deeds; And have put on the new man, which is renewed in knowledge after the image of him that created him."*

Ephesians 4:22-24 commands,

> That ye put off concerning the former conversation the <u>old man</u>, which is corrupt according to the deceitful lusts; And be renewed in the spirit of your mind; And that ye put on the new man, which after God is created in righteousness and true holiness (my emphasis).

The problem with the old man is that he operates in total rebellion and darkness. He has no desire to come under the leadership of another. He wants to experience the works of the flesh without hindrances or consequences. He is driven by lust, deluded by pride,

---

[16] Galatians 5:17

and subject to desires and whims. His ways are perverted, his thoughts vanity, and his preferences the ways of death.[17]

Today people try to clean up the old man or rehabilitate him, but the Word of God is clear: You can't make peace with the old man without declaring war on the Spirit of God. The flesh is at war with the Spirit, and like any enemy in wartime situation, the flesh must be subdued in order to be ruled by the Spirit of God.[18]

The Word of God tells us the old man must be mortified or put to death for the new man to be resurrected. Who is the new man? It is Jesus Christ.[19] But what does it mean to have the life of Christ being manifested in and through us? This brings us to the subject of normal Christianity.

It is the goal of many to be considered normal instead of abnormal, but what constitutes a normal individual? What kind of rulers do we need to use to make such a judgment call? After all, normalcy means different things to different people. For this reason, it is not unusual to test normalcy based on our own personal lives. Our pride cleverly convinces us that we understand that which is normal, wise, practical, logical, or factual. Because of this high opinion of self, we feel that we can properly judge what is normal. This is why the Apostle Paul made this statement, *"...not to think of himself more highly than he ought to think; but think soberly, according as God hath dealt to every man the measure of faith" (Romans 12:3b).*

In God's sight man's normalcy often represents the ways of destruction. Man's ways fail to measure up to God's ways because His ways are higher than man and constitute the essence of eternal life.[20]

With this in mind, we must ask who or what serves as a standard of normalcy in God's economy. Oswald Chambers stated that Jesus Christ is the only man considered normal in God's kingdom.[21] He serves as an

---

[17] Proverbs 16:25; 21:8
[18] Romans 8:4-14
[19] Romans 6; Colossians 3:1-17
[20] Isaiah 55:8-9
[21] *Bringing Sons Into Glory & Making All Things New;* Oswald Chambers; © 1990 by Oswald Chambers Publications Associated Limited, pg. 116

example of what God intended for the first man, who because of disobedience failed to reach this state before God.

But what was this state that Adam failed to reach? You must keep in mind that Adam was formed in the image of God; therefore, he was to serve as the unhindered reflection of God in the midst of His creation. The second man, Jesus, confirmed this when He said, *"...he that hath seen me hath seen the Father" (John 14:9b)*.

Adam was formed in an innocent state, but he never reached his potential to reflect the glory of God. This brings us to the conclusion that God never intended for him to remain in his innocent state because it made him vulnerable. The question is, what was Adam's potential, which he failed to reach in the Garden? According to Oswald Chambers, Adam's potential was to be transformed or transfigured as Jesus was at the Mount of Transfiguration. [22]

On the Mount of Transfiguration, Jesus' glory was unveiled. From the very beginning God's design for man was to bring him to a place where He could unveil His glory through him. But for Adam to reach this stage, he would have to be transfigured. Adam failed to make the decision to come higher to reach his ultimate potential by choosing the tree of life. As a result, he lost his innocent state to rebellion, separation, and death.

The Word of God tells us the mind, which has occasionally been known to be interchanged with the word "soul," must be transformed or transfigured in order for the new man or new life to be resurrected.

Romans 12:1-2 says,

> *I BESEECH you therefore, brethren, by the mercies of God, that ye present your bodies a living sacrifice, holy, acceptable unto God, which is your reasonable service. And be not conformed to this world: but be ye transformed by the renewing of your mind, that ye may prove what is that good, and acceptable, and perfect, will of God.*

Ephesians 4:23 states, *"And be renewed in the spirit of your mind."* And *Colossians 3:10* tells us, *"And have put on the new man, which is renewed in knowledge after the image of him that created him."*

---

[22] Ibid, pg. 115-116

A transfigured mind means the unveiling of the image of Christ in our lives. His attributes and life will shine forth in and through our lives. This is why the Apostle Paul instructed Jesus' followers to, *"Let this mind be in you, which was also in Christ Jesus" (Philippians 2:5).*

He also made this statement to the Romans, *"For whom he did foreknow, he also did predestinate to be conformed to the image of his Son, that he might be the firstborn among many brethren" (Romans 8:29).*

How can an individual reach this potential in God's kingdom? A person must be led there by the leading of the Holy Spirit. Being under the control of the Spirit speaks of meekness and results in self-control or discipline.

Jesus said of Himself that He is meek. In other words, He was under control because He did nothing unless the Father ordained it. Before we can be in control of our dispositions and actions, we must come under the control of the Holy Spirit, where the flesh will be mortified and where we are ruled by the power of God. We must learn to do nothing unless the Holy Spirit ordains it. As we come under control, we will be able to respond in a controlled or disciplined manner.

Romans 8:1 and *14* says, *"There is therefore now no condemnation to them which are in Christ Jesus, who walk not after the flesh, but after the Spirit. ...For as many as are led by the Spirit of God, they are the sons of God."*

Galatians 5:16-17 states,

> *This I say then, walk in the Spirit, and ye shall not fulfill the lust of the flesh. For the flesh lusteth against the Spirit, and the Spirit against the flesh: and these are contrary the one to the other: so that ye cannot do the things that ye would. But if ye be led of the Spirit, ye are not under the law.*

The Spirit of God will lead us into revelations of Jesus that will transform our disposition as to the way we look at things and the way we do things. We will literally become the new creations that the Apostle Paul talked about in *2 Corinthians 5:17.*

As one can see, the battle for the soul begins in the mind. The mind must be transformed to overcome the enemies that so easily beset each of us. A transformed mind means a soul that no longer reigns according to its lusts, desires, and preference of darkness, but rather is being led by the Spirit of the living God.

It is important to note that in this battle God first goes after the mind and not the heart. I must point out the mind in this text represents our attitude or disposition. Our disposition is determined by how we perceive God. Our perception of God determines how we process information, which often points us to the soul. This is why the word "mind" can be interchanged with the word "soul".

The heart represents the spirit of man and determines the spiritual quality of a person's life. Spirit is considered the higher state of man for it can only be influenced by spirit, while the soul is considered the lower state of man because it is influenced by environment, temptation, and the world. The heart can be touched by the things of God, but for transformation to occur it must be regenerated by the Holy Spirit, which can't happen until the mind comes under the control of the Spirit. Because of this I have learned the mind must be brought under control in order to reach the heart. In other words, God can't possess the heart until the mind is under the control of His Spirit.

Is your world out of balance? Do you feel you are out of control? If so your soul could be reigning instead of being ruled by the Holy Spirit. Examine yourself and see whether the Spirit of God is leading you up to the Mount of Transfiguration or the natural man is leading you down the paths of destruction and death.

Chapter Six

TESTING THE SPIRITS

As stated in the previous chapter, to overcome the "old man" a person must be led by the Spirit of God. As an individual submits to the Holy Spirit, He transforms or regenerates the person. *"Not by works or righteousness which we have done, but according to his mercy he saved us, by the washing of regeneration, and renewing of the Holy Ghost" (Titus 3:5).*

Regeneration points to the new life. Therefore, we can see that the Spirit of God is responsible to bring forth a transformed or new life. Our response to His work should be that of humility and submission.

First John 4:1 takes us one step further, *"BELOVED, believe not every spirit, but try the spirits whether they are of God: because many false prophets are gone out into the world."* This Scripture serves as both a warning and a command. Christians' spiritual well-being and destiny, hinges on blood-bought saints protecting their souls by testing the spirits and bringing them under subjection to the Holy Ghost.

The problem is that many people who do bother to test something do so according to their particular doctrines and not by the Spirit of God. Of course, these people consider their doctrines to be the Word of God, but these two sources are distinctly different.

The subject of doctrines has the potential of creating bloody wars in the kingdom of God. Much of the doctrine I encounter is not the fundamental doctrine found in *Hebrews 6:1-2* but man's theology. The doctrine of Christ is to establish upright living, but man's doctrine is used to interpret Scripture and determine reality. It allows him to put God in a nice, controllable box or package. Sadly, the reality that man's doctrine creates is just another form of man's reality. It is often idolatrous, arrogant, and erroneous in nature and motivated by a wrong spirit. This type of reality usually reeks with self-righteousness or super-spiritual religion but is minus the reality and attitude of the Person of Jesus Christ.

This is why the Word of God should not be the only source people use to test spiritual teachings or activity. In my spiritual journeys, I have met people who had sound doctrine but a wrong spirit. I have also encountered people who had wrong doctrine but a right spirit, and still others who had both wrong doctrine and spirit. The distinct differences and conflicts between these groups never come down to doctrine but to spirit.

If people have a right spirit, they are teachable and open, but if they have a wrong spirit, they are bent on protecting and upholding their theology as a sacred cow—no matter whom they sacrifice or crush in the name of their doctrine. In fact, when you get past their beliefs, you encounter people who are not only in bondage to a narrow, surface world, but who are often fearful, skeptical, and angry because this world is very fragile and lacks substance.

Doctrine creates a fragile world because it has no power to save a person. Even though these people act as if your very salvation hinges on agreeing with them, underneath they know that eternal life is determined by the presence of one particular Person, Jesus Christ, being in an individual's life and not by some vain, petty theology of man.

It is important to point out that there is a spirit behind the Word of God. That spirit is the Holy Spirit. When using Scripture to test something, it is vital that you are not looking for technicality as much as the spirit or intent of something. I believe this is what the Bereans were doing in *Acts 17:11*. They were searching the Scriptures to see if Paul was correct in his teachings. In other words, they were comparing Scripture with Scripture to see if Paul's presentation was consistent with the spirit or intent of the whole counsel of God.

Jesus stated in *Matthew 7:16* that we shall know people by their fruits (not doctrine). To determine fruits you must examine the doctrine of a person in light of the spirit. Sound doctrine without a right spirit kills revelation knowledge of Jesus, undermines genuine faith, and creates a false religious light in which all scriptural truths will not only be judged but also perverted.[1]

The Word of God is limited in its ability to test because it is influenced by the spirit of the person who is handling it. It is only the Holy Ghost that brings life to the written word as He enlarges man's capacity to gain a higher perspective that will bring a greater revelation of Jesus within Scripture.[2]

I remember when theology reigned in my life. I not only had erected a god I could understand and control in my mind but a god that fit nicely into my religious games and fantasies. God had to break the stringent boundaries of my belief system so He could become my reality. I realize that God is revealed in Scripture, but He is not contained within all of Scripture. The spirit behind my handling of the Word will determine if I discover the deep truths of God or erect an idol.

This is why testing the spirits is a vital responsibility for Christians. Not only do we need to test the spirit behind those we submit to in the kingdom of God, but we must also test the spirit that is prompting us.

First, we must answer these questions: What spirit can influence people, and what actually constitutes a spirit? There are three main spirits operating in the world. They are the *Holy Spirit*, the *natural spirit,* and the *spirit of the world*.

We know that the only right spirit is the *Holy Spirit*. He is the third person of the Godhead. He is not a force but a being. He has distinguishable characteristics and will not move outside of His attributes as God. He is gentle; therefore, He can be grieved, quenched, and rejected.[3]

The Holy Ghost is the representative of God in the world. His main responsibility is to lead people to the salvation of Jesus. Therefore, He lifts Jesus up and draws people to His character, love, and grace. He is the gift and promise to believers from the Father who, through Him, empowers followers to live victorious lives. The Spirit convicts of sin, righteousness, and judgment. He is the living, active breath of God in

---

[1] 2 Corinthians 3:6
[2] Romans 7:6; 2 Corinthians 3:6
[3] Ephesians 4:30; 1 Thessalonians 5:19

the believer, working to reconcile and restore the person back into a complete, growing relationship with God through Jesus Christ.[4]

Another spirit that is a prevalent influence in the world is man's *natural spirit. Proverbs 25:28* states, *"He that hath no rule over his own spirit is like a city that is broken down, and without walls."* Man's natural spirit is nothing more than the "old man" or the flesh ruling. As Watchman Nee pointed out that the flesh is still the flesh whether it is good or bad. The difference between the good the flesh produces and the good that flows from the new life is that the flesh always has self at its center. He goes on to explain that flesh sees no need to trust in the Holy Spirit.[5]

The old man's spirit can be summarized as unruly, unyielding, undisciplined, or unmanageable. The flesh must be mortified or put to death in order for the soul to be ruled by the Spirit of God.

The old man's substitute for the Holy Spirit is self-righteousness. This righteousness is a fake light that focuses on the old man's so-called goodness, which is nothing more than filthy rags before God.[6] It expresses itself in theology, religious standards, practices, rituals, and traditions that have been devised by man. This arrogant facade is only a cloak that covers the filthy rags of man's best. It is deceptive because it gives a person a false sense of righteousness while establishing the individual on sifting sand rather than upon the immovable Rock of Jesus.[7]

If the natural spirit is not properly ruled, it actually makes a person an unwalled city.[8] This is a serious spiritual condition because it means that the individual is not protected from enemies of the soul, such as Satan, but is susceptible to attack and defeat.

This is why Jesus told those who are serious about following Him to deny self and pick up the cross. William Law made this statement about

---

[4] John 14:26; 16:7-14; Luke 11:13; 24:49; Acts 1:4-8
[5] *The Spiritual Man,* Watchman Nee, © 1968 by Christians Fellowship Publishers, Inc., pgs. 112-113
[6] Isaiah 64:6
[7] Matthew 7:24-28
[8] Proverbs 25:28

this subject, "...self-denial is our capacity for being saved; humility is our savior."[9]

If the natural spirit is not dealt with up front, the follower will be vulnerable to the influence and bondage of the third spirit.

The third spirit is Satan, who is known as the *spirit of this world*. *Ephesians 2:2* states that this enemy of the soul "works in the children of disobedience." He finds footholds or openings in the vulnerable areas of people's lives. *Ephesians 4:27* confirms this when it commands, *"Neither give place to the devil."* These vulnerable areas allow him to influence, oppress, and exploit the people who fall victim to his devices.

James 4:7-10 gives this clear instruction,

> *Submit yourselves therefore to God. Resist <u>the</u> <u>devil,</u> <u>and</u> <u>he</u> <u>will</u> <u>flee</u> <u>from</u> <u>you</u>. Draw nigh to God, and he will draw nigh to you. Cleanse your hands, ye sinners: and purify your hearts ye doubleminded. Be afflicted and mourn, and weep: let your laughter be turned to mourning, and your joy to heaviness. Humble yourselves in the sight of the Lord, and he shall lift you up* (emphasis added).

James clearly tells us that submission, repentance, humility, and sanctification will not only cause Satan to flee, but also will keep him at bay.

Satan counterfeits the Holy Spirit and His works through religious spirits, familiar spirits, and an anti-Christ spirit. A religious spirit causes a person to major in religion while denying Christ in attitude and action. The anti-Christ spirit is a pseudo-religious spirit that rides on the reputation of Christ while denying there is one true God and avoiding submission, accountability, and testing by other saints in the Body of believers. The familiar spirit gives information to the so-called "prophet" or "minister" that can be very detailed—full of condemnation as well as general or half-truths.

The Holy Spirit leads while the other two spirits strive to manipulate, pressure, or control. The Holy Spirit warns while the other two spirits unmercifully judge and threaten. The Holy Spirit never exalts Himself, but rather exalts Jesus Christ as He gently attracts people to the lover

---

[9] *God's Best Secrets;* Andrew Murray; © 1998 by Whitaker House; pg. 272

of their souls. On the other hand, the ungodly spirits flatter, exalt man, and insist on blind loyalty to causes and agendas in order to receive the desired worship.

As you can see, it is not difficult to discern the spirit behind something, but many fail to do so. They are ignorant about the real character and work of the Holy Spirit and are often led by the old man into Satan's camp.

Christians must make sure they do not have a breach in their lives with God.[10] They have been given an armor that covers wholly their spiritual lives and a weapon that is able to keep Satan at a respectable distance. But a breach in the wall of their lives will make them vulnerable to the lion who is ready to devour the weak, lonely, and foolish.[11]

Testing the spirits is also imperative due to the different strategies required to overcome the natural spirit and the spirit of the world. For example, if you discover the natural spirit is influencing you, you must repent or make an about face and submit to God's authority to close any gaps. If Satan is behind a situation, then a person must take authority over him.

Instead, many people try to repent for Satan's activities and take authority over their natural spirit. This is definitely a wrong strategy. The problem with the natural spirit is that he works from within; therefore, his deeds must be repented of and put to death so that the soul can be properly *ruled*. On the other hand, Satan operates from the outside; therefore, he needs to be *subdued* and *pushed back* to ensure victory. As *1 John 4:4* reminds us, *"...greater is he that is in you, than he that is in the world."*

Obviously, the hard part is discerning between a natural spirit and the spirit of the world. It comes down to the heart. If a person is toying with a sin in his or her heart, the old man is in operation and the individual needs to repent and draw close to God. If an evil thought or impulse that does not exist within a person's heart suddenly comes upon him or her, then it is one of Satan's darts and the individual must take authority over him.

---

[10] Isaiah 30:26; 58:12
[11] 1 Peter 5:8

The type of spirit that influences us also determines the type of spiritual law we are operating under.

The Two Laws

Romans 8:2 tells us that there are two spiritual laws in operation in the world, *"For the law of the Spirit of life in Christ Jesus hath made me free from the law of sin and death."*

People operate according to one of these two laws. These laws are an unseen phenomenon that determines the natural order of things in a person's life. The Apostle Paul confirmed this in *Romans 8:5, "For they that are after the flesh do mind the things of the flesh; but they that are after the Spirit the things of the Spirit."* It is natural for a person to operate under one of these laws without recognizing that he or she is automatically adhering to a spiritual law that is in operation.

As we can see, these two laws stand on opposite poles from one another. One law brings life while the other one results in death. Keep in mind that the law we subject ourselves to is determined by the spirit that we are giving way to.

The natural spirit and the spirit of the world make us subject to the law of sin and spiritual ruin. If a person is operating according to his or her flesh, he or she will naturally be operating under the law of sin, which results in death. It will be natural for this individual to rebel against God, justify wrong dispositions and actions, and pursue after every whim and lust that entices the flesh. This is why the Apostle Paul made this statement, *"For if ye live after the flesh, ye shall die..." (Romans 8:13a).*

Operating according to the law of sin and death simply means you are under Satan, the author of death. *Hebrews 2:14-15* says,

> *Forasmuch then as the children are partakers of flesh and blood; he also himself likewise took part of the same; that through death, he might destroy him that had the power of death that is, the devil; and deliver them who through fear of death were all their lifetime subject to bondage.*

The enemy of our souls entices us to sin so that he can bring us under the judgment of death. People who subject their souls to the spirit of the world already stand condemned by the law of sin and death. This is why we must recognize Satan and take the authority given to us by the One who has all authority to overcome him and put him on the run.[12]

Being under the Spirit of God ensures life. He actually leads a person to life that can only be established in a growing relationship with God. The Apostle Paul put it best, *"For as many are led by the Spirit of God, they are the sons of God" (Romans 8:14).*

The Holy Ghost is the essence of resurrected life and possesses righteousness. He is our seal and upon salvation takes residence in our spirit to begin to work out the salvation that has been put in us by faith in what Jesus did on the cross.[13]

You must ask yourself which law are you operating under. If you're unsure, Jesus gave the means by which to test yourself. It is found in *Matthew 7:16, "Ye shall know them by their fruits."*

The fruits are the products of the spirit that is in operation within you and the law to which you are naturally subject. For example, if you are influenced by the wrong spirit and operating under the law of sin and death, your attitude and actions will tell on you. Therefore, when was the last time you honestly evaluated your fruits to see which spirit you are of and which law you are under?

Identifying Your Spirit

Most people have a vague concept of what constitutes "spirit," and when they hear the word, they think of something that is supernatural, spiritual, or an unexplainable phenomenon.

In all honesty, it is hard to define spirit. But what we can understand is how spirit works in our lives. By grasping how spirit influences man, we can begin to discern properly the spirit in operation within our lives and in the lives of others.

Spirit affects three areas of man: *motivations, intentions,* and *goals.*

---

[12] Matthew 28:18
[13] Romans 8:8-13; 1 Corinthians 3:16; Ephesians 1:13-14; Philippians 1:6

Proverbs 16:2 states, *"All the ways of a man are clean in his own eyes; but the LORD weigheth the spirits."* In the New International Version the word "spirits" is translated "motives."

Motives are often determined by influences such as personal desires, priorities, and agendas. The emphasis or direction of these pursuits is based on the spirit that is influencing the individual and the law that the person is operating under.

There are only two motivations that compel or drive man to respond. They are the *love of God* and *the pride of man.*

The motivation behind the right spirit is *the love of God*. This love has only one source, God Himself. Man can only please God when He is motivated by His everlasting love. The Apostle Paul stated that he was constrained (or compelled) by the love of God.[14] In *Romans 5:5* he declared that *"the love of God is shed abroad in his heart."* Therefore, anything done outside of the love of God will be considered wood, hay, or stubble and will be burned up on judgment day.[15]

The other motivation behind man is his *pride.* Satan is the king of pride, and man is forever being set up by it to be deemed a fool of fools and be discarded like rubble.

Pride is idolatrous and deceptive in nature, vain in disposition, and foolish in practice. It is what gives the old man his identity, purpose, and rights. It is in competition with God, for it demands homage. It is the total opposite of God's love.

In *1 Corinthians 13,* we see that the opposite of love is pride in operation. For example, it is impatient, cruel, competitive and rude, and it demands recognition. It is selfish to the core, touchy, judgmental, hypocritical, unteachable in spirit, and quick to sacrifice others.

Pride is a monster that can cleverly influence and pervert every desire and need creating appetites of lust. To the onlooker visible pride can be repulsive, unreasonable, and cruel. As for God, He resists the pride of man and will eventually judge it with all of the other works of darkness.[16]

---

[14] 2 Corinthians 2:14
[15] 1 Corinthians 3:12-15
[16] 1 Peter 5:5

We must deny pride any access into our lives. The only way we can overcome this monster is to recognize how it works in our lives and ask God to give us a perfect hatred for it and then nail it to the cross.

The next area affected by spirit is our *intentions*. You have probably heard the term "the intents of the heart."[17]

Intentions point to purposes or determinations. This is where a person finds the inclinations or incentives to carry something out. For example, if you are inclined to do something, it means you are leaning towards that direction. The right circumstances will automatically cause you to go according to your inclination or determination. Intentions of this type involve the *will* area of a person.

It is important to point out "good intentions" do not fit in this category. Intentions without the inclinations are nothing more than wishful thinking or false pretenses. I say this because Christians have a tendency to hand out "good intentions" like candy with no incentive to carry them out. This practice reveals an individual who is all talk and no show, which equals a bona fide hypocrite.

The challenge for Christians is to line their tongues up with the godly inclinations to avoid emotional, unmindful, impulsive statements that are nothing more than foolish or false intentions. Impulsive intentions of this nature have been known to ruin the credibility of many people.

Intentions that are influenced by spirit and subject to one of the laws have already been established in the will and will be carried out in some manner. This is why *Hebrews 4:12* says, *"For the word of God is quick, and powerful, and sharper than any two-edged sword piercing even to the dividing asunder of soul and spirit, and of the joints and marrow, and is a discerner of the thoughts and intents of the heart."*

The Word of God not only exposes the spirit and type of law motivating a person but also the true inclinations of the individual's heart. The problem is that many dissect the Word with their intellectual conceit instead of allowing it to become a sword to their souls.

This sword is capable of cutting away the religious cloaks, stripping away the Christian masks, and unveiling all false pretenses and delusion to reveal the spirit and intent behind a person's life.

---

[17] Hebrews 4:12

There are two distinct intentions that determine a person's inclinations. They are to *glorify God* or to *honor self.*

The Holy Ghost main intentions in this world are to bring glory to the Father and honor to the Son. *Matthew 5:16* instructs us to, *"Let your light so shine before men, that they may see your good works, and glorify your Father which is in heaven."*

If a person loves God, his or her main inclination will be to bring glory to Him in everything that is done. This intention can only become a natural inclination through constant submission to the Spirit of God and obedience to His Word.

The people who are motivated by the natural spirit and/or the spirit of the world will have only one inclination, and that is to *receive personal honor*. This intention causes tremendous bondage, insecurity, and fear. It also produces extreme reactions in people who either become complacent (because this honor eludes them) or are driven by lust for more recognition, love, or power.

This brings us to *goals*, the third area that is affected by spirit. Many people have devised goals for their lives, but the goals I am talking about have to do with focus.

Focus is what keeps a person on a particular path. This focus is influenced by spirit. It is not unusual for a person to have noble goals but for reasons beyond his or her control be unable to reach them due to being motivated by different influences. Such influences are unseen and will cause a person confusion or double-mindedness, making the individual unstable in every area of his or her life.[18]

Focus goes back to personal priorities and agendas. These priorities and agendas may be good, but the motivating spirit will define how a person will fulfill these pursuits.

For example, a person's goals may be godly, but if the individual's priorities and agendas are self-centered, he or she will be pulled in two different directions. Even though this individual may attempt to head in the right direction, he or she will eventually give way to self-centered priorities by submitting to the natural spirit or the spirit of the world's

---

[18] James 1:8

methods to finding fulfillment in pursuits such as love, acceptance, and recognition.

People may or may not be aware that they are striving for one of two main goals, depending on the spirit in operation. Either their focus is to *lift up Jesus* or *to make self God.*

The Holy Spirit has one goal, and that is to *lift up Jesus.* Jesus said in *John 12:32, "And I, if I be lifted up from the earth, will draw all men unto me."*

Like a committed matchmaker, the Holy Spirit woos people to Jesus. Like a great teacher, He leads people to the reality of the precious Son of God, for His whole focus and ministry is about Jesus. There is nothing as wonderful or as glorious as Jesus being lifted up above the world's philosophies, man's lifeless traditions, and the world's business so that one lost individual is able to see the loving, caring Jesus who is full of grace and truth.

Therefore, one can only reason that if the Lord Jesus Christ is missing from any form of truth, religious activity, or man's best, the Holy Spirit is absent as well. If the Spirit of God is not behind or involved in an activity, movement, or doctrine, Christians must not participate in, support, or partake of it. In fact, they must quickly separate themselves and flee.[19]

The goal of the wrong spirit goes back to the lie in the garden. It is to make man God in his own eyes. Deification of man ultimately means Satan receives the worship. This has always been Satan's plan—to take the worship away from God and heap it on himself. Sadly, man is willing to oblige him.

Note the following diagram to see how these spirits operate.

Spirit	Right Spirit	Wrong Spirit
Motivation	Love of God	Pride
Intention	Glorify God	Honor self
Goal	Lift Jesus up	Make self God

---

[19] 2 Corinthians 6:14-18

This brings us to the end results these spirits produce in the spiritual life of a person.

The Results

2 Corinthians 3:17 tells us, *"Now the Lord is that Spirit: and where the Spirit of the Lord is, there is liberty."* Liberty is everything when it comes to Christian growth and maturity. *2 Corinthians* tells us if the Spirit of God is in our midst, we will have the *liberty* to grow in our lives with God.

Spiritual freedom is more evident as we have the liberty to receive each new revelation of Jesus Christ. In fact, there are three stages of gaining godly insight into the character of God. They are *knowledge, revelation,* and *enlightenment.*

Knowledge grows when you start gaining truths or facts about God. Revelation comes when the Holy Spirit makes the learned knowledge a personal living reality, and enlightenment occurs when you apply that reality to your life so it becomes truth. Change will take place when truth becomes alive, manifesting the life of Jesus in and through you.

As Jesus comes forth in a person's life, he or she will display the *fruit of the Spirit* found in *Galatians 5:22-23.*

Many times, people have a hard time accepting greater truths about Jesus because they do not fit in their nice little doctrinal boxes. This inability to receive is a form of unbelief, and it will keep God from being God in their lives and cause them to operate in a wrong spirit.

The other two spirits produce *bondage.* Not only do these two spirits justify and condone the very things that will put an individual in bondage, but they also maintain the bondage with deception, pride, and fear. This deception and pride exalt a person as God.

It is not unusual to see this bondage escalate when there is an aggressive, controlling person present. When someone other than the Holy Spirit is trying to control you or call the shots in your life, you will experience bondage as well.

Note the completed diagram.

Battle For the Soul

Spirit	Right Spirit	Wrong Spirit
Motivation	Love of God	Pride
Intention	Glorify God	Honor self
Goal	Lift Jesus up	Make self God
Results	Liberty & Fruit of Spirit	Control/ Bondage

People need to test whether they have liberty to grow in Christ or whether there is an unseen bondage that prevents them from moving forward.

Sadly, rather than testing the spirits, people go on the basis of whether something appears supernatural or religious or makes them feel good. These evaluations are nothing more than fleshly and, in the end, will cause people to accept delusion over truth.

Are you testing the spirits? If not, you need to know that you are not only in disobedience to God, but you are also opening up your soul to destruction.

Chapter Seven

Frame of Reference

The next step in understanding the battle for the soul is realizing how a person's frame of reference operates. This frame of reference can be illustrated with a football goal post.

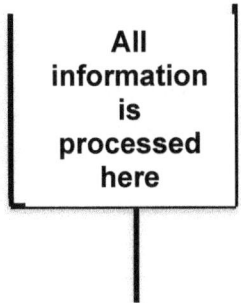

All the information a person obtains is processed within the confines and boundaries of the frame of reference that has been established in his or her mind. This frame of reference is not always based on truth but usually on what other influential people have taught the individual during his or her childhood or other vulnerable times. Such teachings are *assumed truths* that rest on shaky foundations.

These foundations are shaky because people's form of reality is usually not based on the unshakable truth of the Jesus of the Bible. For example, many people will assume their parents' religious preference is correct and will never really test or challenge it. This is not to say they won't rebel against it at some point in time, but in the back of their minds they remain loyal to their childhood teachings or influences and will fall back on them in times of trouble or devastation.

The problem is that people whose form of reality is based upon assumptions can't really defend or explain why they maintain the views they possess. When people frame of reference is challenged, they will become confused, defensive, or angry.

As you begin to recognize how limited and shaky a person's frame of reference can be you will see why the Apostle Paul says, *"For we know in part."*[1] You can also begin to understand why man's conclusions are very limited or perverted: Information never enlarges a frame of reference but rather the frame of reference adjusts the information to fit within its limited perspective.

Therefore, a person's world is only as large as his or her frame of reference. For example, individuals who operate in a small world do so because they are full of self. Self confines a person to a world that must revolve around the individual's needs, whims, and purposes, making his or her world quite narrow. You will also find if an individual's view is small, his or her ability to deal with anything that may clearly challenge that outlook will be met with confusion, fear, anger, or rage.

On the other hand, you meet people whose understanding of the world is wide and all embracing. It is not that they easily accept any new concept or information, but they have a freedom to explore any new possibilities. They are not afraid of their views being challenged, changed, or adjusted if it means embracing greater truths. In fact, these people's greatest fear is they may become stagnant, comfortable, complacent, or unteachable towards any enlargement that truth would bring to their limited world.

As you observe people, you will be able to discern three attitudes towards the truth. The type of attitude displayed towards the truth determines the depth and size of a person's frame of reference. Consider these different attitudes in a sober, prayerful manner.

1) **False Seeker**: This individual's form of truth is based on the latest fads or popular movements of the day. He or she is easily persuaded by anything that looks, sounds, or feels good. The

---

[1] 1 Corinthians 13:9

approach of this person is very fleshly in nature. We can read about this type of individual in *Ephesians 4:14*, *"That we henceforth be no more children, tossed to and fro, and carried about with every wind of doctrine, by the sleight of men, and cunning craftiness whereby they lie in wait to deceive."*

2) **Pseudo Seeker:** People who fit in this category give you the impression that they want the truth. They are very religious and appear to be teachable—that is until you hit one of their sacred cows. A sacred cow consists of something that the person has put spiritual confidence or value in. It can be a belief system, person, or practice. As soon as you touch their cow, you will realize that all information is tested according to their sacred cow and not according to truth. This approach is idolatrous in nature and reeks with self-righteous pride. Jesus best described this individual in *Matthew 15:8-9*,

> *This people draweth nigh unto me with their mouth, and honoureth me with their lips; but their heart is far from me. But in vain they do worship me, teaching for doctrines the commandments of men.*

3) **Truth Seeker.** This type of individual wants to know and possess the truth no matter what it costs him or her. He or she will search for it with the whole heart, knowing that it will be found.[2] This individual is like Zacchaeus, who was ready to climb above all obstacles just to see Jesus. As a result, salvation came to his house.[3] This type of person is ready for all sacred cows to be exposed and destroyed. He or she will take lightly preconceived notions, personal ideas, and religious speculations and opinions. You might find this person in a religious crowd, but he or she will not be a part of it. The truth seeker may be involved in a movement but will be walking according to a different drum, like the woman with the issue of blood. She was not following Jesus to be part of the crowd;

---

[2] Jeremiah 29:13
[3] Luke 19:1-10

Battle For the Soul

rather, she was in the crowd to touch Him, and as a result she was made whole.[4]

This brings us to the main source that determines whether a person's frame of reference is immovable or adjustable. It is determined by the spirit that motivates the individual. Note the following diagram.

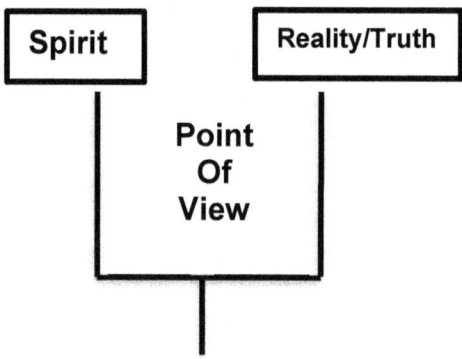

The Holy Spirit is forever adjusting man's frame of reference. He does this through the work of transformation or regeneration of the mind.[5]

The natural spirit simply justifies or confirms a person's established frame of reference while Satan reinforces it with such devices as lies and fears. This is why it is easy to discern if a person has the liberty to embrace truth or if he or she is in such bondage that rejection of any truth contrary to the individual's frame of reference is a given fact. This is where the real dilemma begins, for if a person rejects the truth, he or she is discarding the very key that can set him or her free.[6]

---

[4] Matthew 9:19-22
[5] Romans 12:2
[6] John 8:32

Defining Reality

It is vital to understand how spirit motivates or influences the reality people adopt as truth.

If the Holy Ghost is the spirit defining truth, He will do so through the Word of God. The Word of God serves as a "spiritual washing machine" that cleanses man from perverted thought patterns that will defile the truths of God.[7] Then the third Person of the Godhead will take that which has been purified and line it up to the complete Word of God to bring both liberty and life.

Ultimately all truths will adjust and line up to the person of Jesus for He is the truth.[8] He alone will be lifted above all human conclusions as the only absolute standard of truth to any matter or conclusion. Note the following diagram.

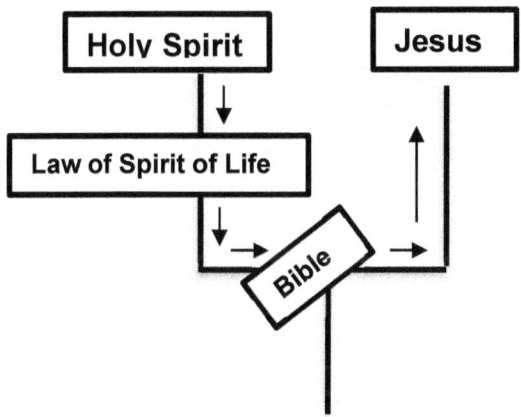

What happens if the Holy Ghost is not defining truth for a person? After all, every individual (regardless of age) must come to some type of conclusion or understanding about a matter.

This is where the pride of man comes into play. The pride of a person who is not subject to the Spirit of God is the source that determines that person's reality. This simply means that the "old man" is ruling without

---

[7] Ephesians 5:26
[8] John 14:6

any hindrance or opposition, giving way to the influences of the spirit of the world. And any time the "old man" rules, he will determine his own reality.

Pride in this area operates according to four distinct rulers: *concepts, standards, images,* and *ideas*. Note the following diagram.

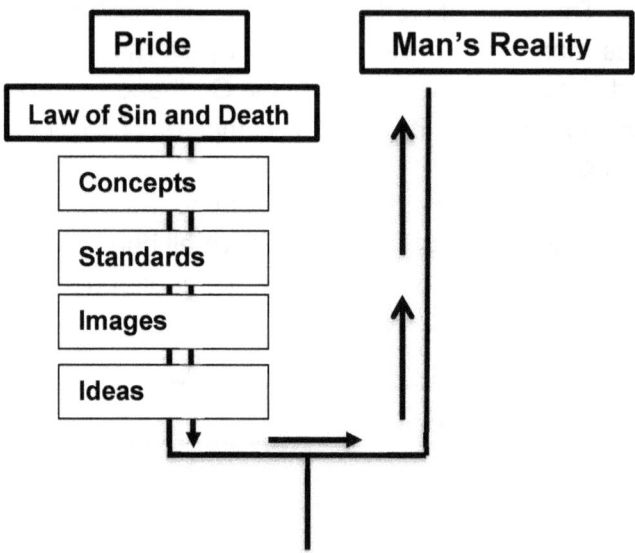

Unlike God's love which has been made available to all who comes to His Son, these rulers are conditional, making them tough taskmasters. They actually serve as man's means of earning or winning approval and ultimately will cause bondage and condemnation because they are not always obtainable.

These rulers vary in terms of the type of pursuit or goal they strive to reach to gain understanding. For example, *concepts* are general notions that determine the *way* things should be. *Standards* determine *how* things should be while *an image* establishes the *way* something *must* be. *Ideas* are concrete boundaries that determine how something is *going* to be in the scheme of things.

These rulers serve as ladders and bridges to connect senses, knowledge, experiences, and understanding in order to draw wise, practical, logical, or factual conclusions. *Ladders* in this case represent the *control* and *order* we want to establish or ensure in our worlds while *bridges* represent *understanding* and *perfection* that make us feel like we are on top of things in our lives, homes, and activities. The Word of God's reference to these types of ladders and bridges are "precepts" and "lines."

Isaiah 28:10 states, *"For precept must be upon precept, precept upon precept; line upon line, line upon line; here a little and there a little."* In Isaiah lines represent truths and precepts point to revelations of God. Isaiah is talking about establishing an unshakable foundation that is complete, sturdy, and balanced. This foundation has no gaps because the lines of truth establish or uphold revelations of God that are complete and life changing. *1 Corinthians 3:11* identifies that spiritual foundation to be none other than Jesus Christ. In fact, the apostles Paul and Peter make various references for our need to come to the knowledge of Jesus Christ in their epistles.

Jesus is not only the spiritual foundation, but He is also the chief cornerstone that must sit at the center of the church and all spiritual beliefs and practices. All other stones (Christians and their beliefs) must line up to Him in spirit and truth.[9]

The problem with pride's rulers is that they rest on shaky foundations such as assumed truths and the popular beliefs and philosophies of the world. (See *Colossians 2:8*.) They are very limited in information and unable to adjust to any truths that challenge their foundation and credibility.

Each of these ladders or bridges is a counterfeit of the ladder and bridge God provided. God's ladder was the cross of Christ, and the bridge is Jesus Himself. These two avenues are the only way to gain truth, reach heaven, and touch the heart of God. Any attempt outside of God's ladder and bridge will miss the mark, causing deception, destruction, and death.

Each of pride's ladders and bridges has its own slants or ways of collecting information. For example, *concepts* work as an ongoing bridge. The person must bring all conclusions down to his or her level of understanding, where the individual will fit everything into his or her form of truth. The problem with this bridge is that it has neither height

---

[9] 1 Peter 2:5-9

nor a heavenly perspective, leaving the person to struggle with a limited or immovable perspective that becomes a rut, pit, or prison. As a person struggles to build each bridge, he or she becomes more closed in because of the mental speculation and introspection.

Oswald Chambers said of introspection that we are built in such a way that we are obliged to examine ourselves. Introspection is the direct observation of the processes of our minds. This process causes one to realize he or she is incalculable causing the person to seek to understand self, which is introspection. Chambers concluded the matter with this statement, "Introspection without God leads to insanity."[10]

Standards serve as ladders that reach for order and purpose. These ladders are very straight and require the person to reach a pinnacle to find understanding, ensure order, and fulfill purpose. The problem with these ladders is that they may have height but they lack width. In other words, they allow no room for adjustment or error. People who operate within standards find their world becoming smaller and smaller as they climb upward into a realm of bigotry, judgmentalism, and skepticism.

Images utilize both ladders and bridges. The ladders of control slant towards the bridges of perfection. The problem with this construction is that the individual ends up with a biased lopsided form of reality because it can only go in one direction. This limits people's peripheral vision, keeping them from seeing around them. There is no room for error or change, which causes frustration, anger, and delusion because the desire for perfection continues to elude the individual as his or her world plummets out of control.

Ideas also establish personal reality with both ladders and bridges. People who operate with ideas have very straight ladders of control, and at different points these ladders will connect with narrow bridges of understanding. The problem with these ladders and bridges is that they are cemented in, leaving no room for adjustment or exploration. These people will lack dimension and insight because they can only operate within the limited area in which they have been established.

---

[10] *Biblical Psychology*, © 1995, Oswald Chambers Publications Association Limited, pgs. 138-139.

These different ladders and bridges put stringent conditions on those who operate within them. They subtly replace the Word of God with rituals or traditions of men, forcing individuals to perform or conform to unbearable yokes. They allow no room for human frailty or error. They demand perfection and infallibility. In the end, they weigh a person down into the miry depths of fear, despair, hopelessness, and condemnation.

This is why Jesus made this statement in *Matthew 11:28-30*, *"Come unto me, all ye that labour and are heavy laden, and I will give you rest. Take my yoke upon you and learn of me: for I am meek and lowly in heart: and ye shall find rest unto your souls. For my yoke is easy, and my burden is light."*

The Spirit of God does not put unbearable conditions or yokes on an individual. He only asks a person to love God with everything in him or her for doing so will humble and bring the person into proper submission. As a person submits to the work and power of the Holy Ghost, Jesus becomes the only standard of truth in his or her life, giving the individual a balanced perspective and the liberty and power to walk in victory.

The question is, how do I get rid of harsh rulers in my life? There is only one instrument that will take the power away from these unbearable dictators: the cross.

Application of God's ladder (the cross) to the rulers actually takes all power and credibility from these harsh taskmasters. Once the cross is applied to the rulers, Jesus will automatically bridge the gap between you and God through reconciliation and restoration.

Consider the diagram on the following page.

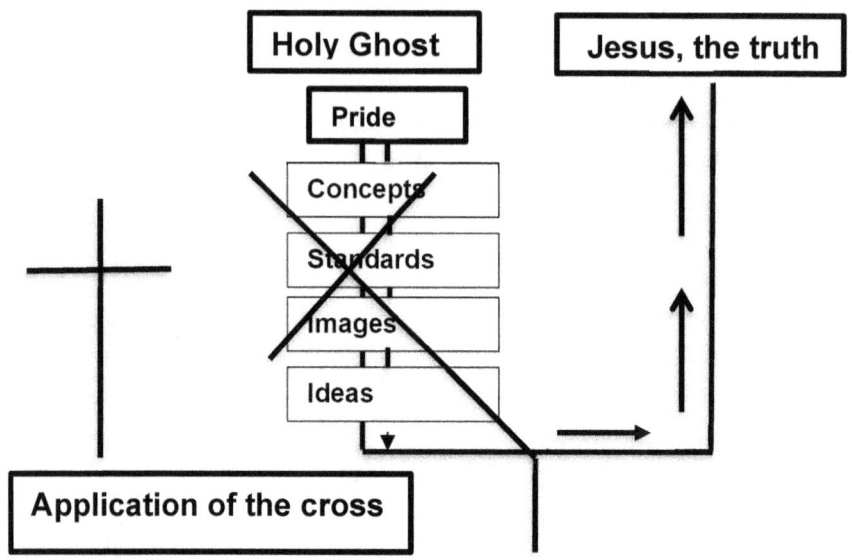

As the cross crosses out the power and influence of pride's rulers, the Holy Spirit will begin to reveal Jesus Christ in the Word of God. As Jesus is unveiled, He will be gloriously lifted up as the only standard of truth and present reality. He will overshadow the insignificant and add height, width, dimension, and depth to a person's frame of reference. He will enlarge a person's vision, thereby enlarging the individual's perception to embrace the unknown, the impossible, and the incredible. It's no wonder that the psalmist penned these words, *"I called upon the LORD in distress: the LORD answered me, and set me in a large place"* (Psalm 118:5).

The "large place" represents freedom, enlarged boundaries, and the ability to move forth to discover greater territories of liberty and truths of God.

What is presently influencing your form of reality? Is it being established by the Holy Spirit or by one of pride's rulers? Is your foundation based on the person of Jesus Christ, or is it founded on assumed truths firmly incorporated by the cultural and religious philosophies of man and the world?

Chapter Eight

PATTERNS!

It is not unusual to observe destructive patterns in a person's life. Once again, these patterns can be traced back to the person's frame of reference. Three different types of patterns can be observed in a person's life. They are *behavioral, emotional,* and *lifestyle* patterns.

As all things pertaining to the mind or soul area, these patterns are greatly influenced by the type of spirit in operation. For example, the right spirit (Holy Ghost) will stop destructive patterns and establish godly habits. The wrong spirit will justify or reinforce destructive patterns.

As we are about to see, there is more to man's frame of reference than spirit and reality. It is important to understand what makes up our frames of reference. The frame of reference is comprised of the *will, intellect,* and *emotions* of man. In short, the frame of reference also constitutes the essence of man's soul. Note the following illustration.

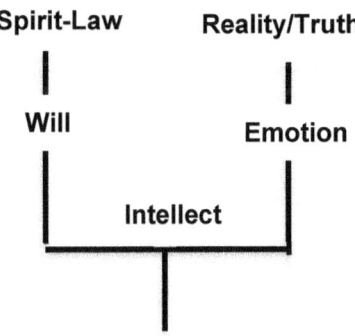

Notice how the intellect works *within* the boundaries of the will and emotions. Everything that happens to an individual is automatically processed between these two boundaries to gain understanding. If understanding eludes a person, he or she can begin to get into a mental or emotional rut.

If this rut is not resolved, it can cause a person to fall into an *emotional pattern*. This pattern begins with some form of fear.

Hebrews 12:3 says, *"For consider him that endured such contradiction of sinners against himself, lest ye be wearied and faint in your minds."* Man faints as *fear* invades his mind. This happens when understanding or control eludes a person.

Understanding a situation is associated with a person's need to belong or find purpose in life. This need is often determined by how a person perceives love. People interpret love in one of three main ways: experiencing emotional love, feeling accepted, or receiving recognition.

The opposite of this need for purpose is fear. When a person is not able to make peace with a trying or traumatic situation, fear of failure, rejection, incompetence, or losing control can bring forth insecurities, accusations, and shame.

After fear begins to paralyze or drive a person, *anger* follows. Fear taunts the person about his or her so-called personal failures, but anger usually turns around and accuses God of failing.

It is important to realize that man's rulers (concepts, standards, images, or ideas) are what condemn the individual because of his or her inability to live up to them. Keep in mind, these rulers are opposite of God's incredible love. They are very conditional, and they bring on the fear of consequences because a person can't live up to the rulers' conditions. This is why the Apostle John made this statement, *"There is no fear in love; but perfect love casteth out fear: because fear hath torment. He that feareth is not made perfect in love" (1 John 4:18).*

These very same rulers that condemn man will also quickly judge God's handling of a matter if the situation is not changed according to a person's standards. After all, if we are trying to do something right and yet God fails to recognize our deeds by adjusting the situation to our way of thinking, God becomes unfair and cruel in our minds.

Anger towards God or bitterness towards the situation finds its origin in what a person considers to be his or her *rights*. After all, if a person is performing a certain way, he or she has the "right" to expect benefits from good deeds or actions.

Many people are unknowingly angry with God because of these rights. Some have walked away from Him while others have decided that He does not exist because He failed or offended them in times of need and distress.

Unchecked anger in this stage often ends in rage, bitterness, vengeance, and unbelief. Once a person reaches this stage, he or she will feel out of control. This is where the person will stuff the anger and isolate self in order to gain control of his or her world.

At this level a person can become complacent, moody, apathetic, or full of self-pity. This individual will feel invisible, lonely, and out of control. As he or she struggles to gain some form of understanding, order, or control, *depression* will overcome him or her.

Depression is a deep emotional pit that can express itself in various ways. Spiritual oppression, unresolved issues, physical illness, and anger can create this pit. It can harbor its own personal *fears* and *rights*. For example, many fear depression and as depression invades the soul, the fear of it will heap more depression upon the individual, causing a deeper pit. Others harbor rights because of depression.

Over the years I have personally encountered bouts of depression. It creeps upon me when I least expect it. When it finally makes itself known to me, I resort to eating the most enjoyable but unhealthy foods to try to make myself feel better. Needless to say, this is a vicious cycle that causes condemnation and more abuse of the body. I finally realized that my depression harbors a destructive right, and I was able to readjust my perception by voiding my right. This actually changed the power my depression had over me.

It is important for people to realize that when they hit the depression stage, their perspective is totally untrustworthy. In fact, this is when many become lost in a maze of introspection that will leave them deluded and feeling hopeless and weary. Consider the diagram.

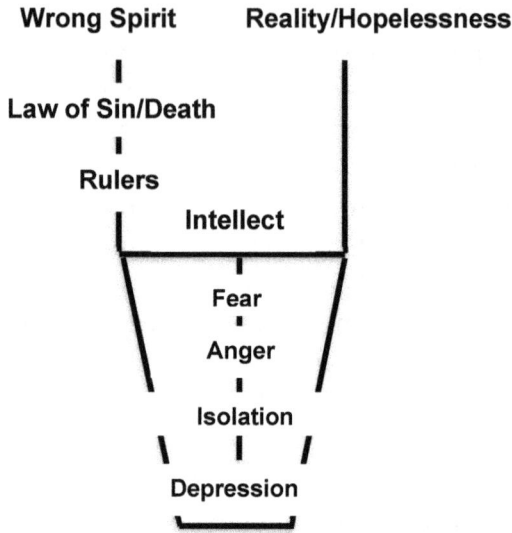

The next area we must consider is the *will* of man. It is here in the soul or frame of reference that man makes determinations. These determinations can also be referred to as the inclinations or intentions of the heart.

All wrong determinations begin when people try to fill in the blanks with vain imaginations or speculations in situations that are void of resolution. The problem with speculations is that they seem so logical or right, and yet their origins go back to pride. In fact, speculation ends in presumptions.

The Apostle Peter made this statement about presumptions, *"But chiefly them that walk after the flesh in the lust of uncleanness, and despise government. Presumptuous are they, self-willed, they are not afraid to speak evil of dignities" (2 Peter 2:10).*

The chief characteristic of presumptions is its refusal to submit to authority. People who operate from presumptions sincerely believe they are right and will not consider their error or bow to truth when challenged to do so.

Wrong determinations can come out of traumatic experiences, unresolved issues, or self-centered agendas. They can set up people for failure and destruction in every area of their lives. For example, a person who has been greatly hurt or traumatized by a terrible experience with family or friends can make the determination never to trust anyone again, creating fear and erecting mistrust as a means to dictate or control the type of relationships he or she may have in the future.

This cycle becomes ingrained as pride's rulers justify all wrong decisions by confirming that people are untrustworthy due to the fact that they forever fail to meet the unrealistic standards of a person's ruler. The failure to comply with these harsh rulers justifies unhealthy actions, confirms presumptions, and exalts personal rights.

Satan reinforces these determinations with lies or suspicion. He constantly uses pride's rulers to implant lies or suspicions about the real motives of people in the minds of those who harbor these inclinations.

For example, it is not unusual that a person who has a destructive determination will misread people out of fear or insecurities and draw judgmental and wrong conclusions. Satan simply comes in with a lie or false accusation to confirm the individual's worst fears or speculations.

Wrong determinations eventually become immovable walls in the will area as they begin to serve as a means of self-preservation. These blockades keep both people and God out of their inner core. These walls can be constructed with bricks that indicate that pride's rulers built the wall one brick at a time.

For example, each brick represents a different concept, standard, or idea. These different bricks can actually represent the rulers of other people such as spouses, parents, churches, or friends. This point was firmly established when I ministered to a woman who had such a brick wall. She was shocked to find out all the bricks belonged to her family and not to her.

These walls can also be solid. Solid walls imply that Satan has helped establish it with lies, fear, loneliness, or control. In some cases there are walls that can be comprised of both bricks and demonic influences.

These blockades also force a person to play god in his or her world as he or she strives to direct everything for self-protection. This not only

Battle For the Soul

creates bondages of fear, frustration, and anger but also sets up *behavioral patterns.*

Behavioral patterns are a person's means of keeping people at bay, unsuspecting, or under control. In short, it is a way of preventing people from threatening or challenging the individual's fragile state of vulnerability that is being hidden behind the wall of protection.

Note the following illustration.

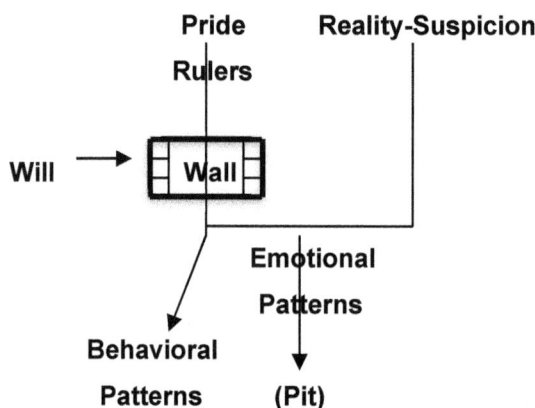

One more important notation concerning the wall in the will area: Many unsuspecting Christians have these walls. In many cases these walls were erected before these people came to Christ. Unless the walls are brought down, they will keep these Christians from realizing their place in Christ. This will cause frustration, despair, and condemnation.

The next area of the soul we must understand is the *emotions*. Our emotions represent our senses. These senses are used to *interpret* what is going on around us.

The problem with our emotions is that they interpret situations we encounter according to the determinations or inclinations of the will.

This brings us to a hard fact; emotions can do nothing outside of the will. Therefore, if there is a wrong determination the emotions will interpret everything according to pride's rulers, which simply justify and confirm any destructive decisions of the will.

As you can see, the emotions can be blinded towards truth if the will is enslaved to ungodly or fleshly inclinations. If there is a wall erected in the will area, the person will not be able to see truth because the wall will cause their emotions to bow down to the inclinations of the will.

This creates an inward perspective and not an upward focus. This will cause idolatry as well as stifle a person from seeing the real light of Jesus Christ.

The only way this destructive perspective can change is if the wall is brought down so the will can come into submission to the Holy Spirit. As the will lines up to the Holy Spirit, the emotions will be brought under the control of the Spirit, who in turn will interpret and define Jesus Christ as light, truth, grace, and glory. Note the illustration.

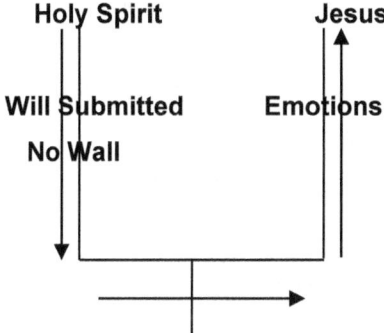

When the emotional level is bowing down to a person's will, it can create *mindsets*. A mindset is a definition of self and God. These mindsets serve as concrete walls in a person's frame of reference.

For example, let's say there is a wall in the will area of a Christian. The Christian has striven to get beyond the wall with no avail. It seems as if he or she is hitting this unseen barrier at the same place in his or her spiritual growth. Since this person can't get past the wall, he or she begins to speculate why a greater life in God eludes him or her. Pride's rulers quickly become judges while Satan shoots darts of lies, accusations, and doubts at the person about his or her salvation and God's love and character.

Battle For the Soul

As the person begins to see the possible logic to the accusation, he or she begins to agree with the unbending rulers and the half-truths of Satan. This agreement causes a definition to take shape, which will eventually close the mind down. After all, something must be wrong with this person, for God seems to be ignoring his or her plight. Hence enters a definition of self.

Popular definitions I have encountered are, *"I am unworthy or unlovable."*

This type of definition becomes a mindset that sets a person up to fall into *lifestyle patterns*. For example, a person who sees self as unworthy or unlovable is unable to accept anything of value or worth. This individual will actually shun or abuse people or things that he or she feels are more honorable or better. In the end, this person will end up accepting less in his or her life. Note the diagram.

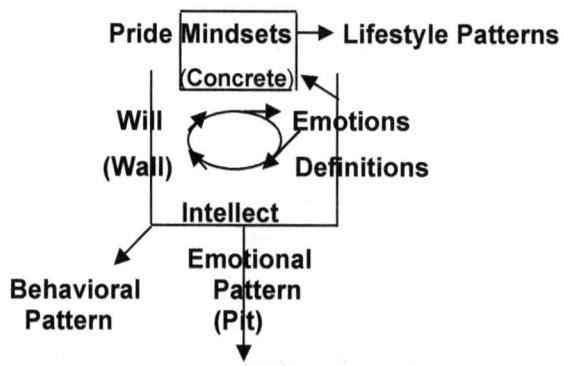

I have watched both men and women who had mindsets accept losers over winners. I have witnessed Christians with these concrete walls be unreceptive towards God's blessings. It is as though these people have closed arms towards anything decent. They find themselves in the same type of relationships and involved with the same caliber of people.

Another problem with mindsets is that they not only define the person, but they define God as well. People with mindsets define God according to self because they are unable to see Him beyond their concrete perception.

Perceptions of God that are tainted by mindsets are based on the fleshly rulers of concepts, standards, images, or ideas. These rulers not only humanize God in a perverted way but also cause a person to embrace another Jesus Christ.

There are many different Christs being presented today. It is not unusual for people to sincerely declare their love and devotion for Him, but in examining their faith, you find that they are in love with or devoted to their idolatrous concept of Jesus and not with the Person of Jesus. This is why the Apostle Paul had this warning in *2 Corinthians 11:3, "But I fear, lest by any means, as the serpent beguiled Eve through his subtlety, so your minds should be corrupted from the simplicity that is in Christ."*

These mindsets that are directed at self and God often complete the limited but vicious mental cycle many people become enslaved to. It can cause some people to feel as if they have no room to move or breathe.

Obviously, all mindsets have to come down. They usually serve as Satan's last assault on truth and the final line of defense against the glorious light of Jesus and His Gospel. Once a mindset is brought down, Jesus needs to take His rightful place and serve as the final line of defense by becoming the bridge between the Holy Spirit and reality.

This godly bridge is not a concrete wall that keeps people and the essence of real life out but a passageway in which a person can experience reality by embracing real life, the life of God. Consider the illustration.

Battle For the Soul

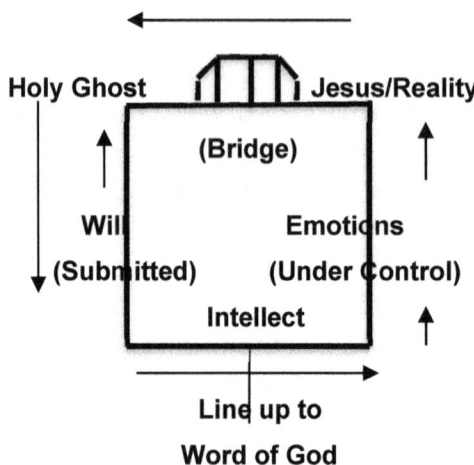

When Jesus opens the way to truth about all matters, instead of a mindset cemented in your mind that stops you, there will be a bridge. Jesus Christ actually connects our emotions to the Holy Ghost, allowing the Spirit to interpret the happenings around us. This connection is free flowing like unleashed waters flowing through the soul, tearing down formidable walls, filling up empty pits, cleansing and washing away residues of the old life of bondage.

This is why Jesus referred to the Holy Spirit as Living Waters.[11] It is only Jesus who can uncap this water into our souls as He connects each of us to truth and liberty in a relationship with the Living God.

Are you in bondage because walls and pits are keeping you from experiencing the real Jesus and His Living Waters? If so, you need to know the Lord Jesus Christ is your only solution. He is the only One who can deliver you from the bondage incurred by your frame of reference. Accept His invitation right now by coming to Him with a humble heart, on bended knees, and with hands lifted up. He will not reject you.

---

[11] John 7:37-39

Chapter Nine

WORLDVIEW

It is hard for us to fathom how our frames of reference could serve as formidable prisons. After all, our conclusions seem so right. We have looked at every angle; therefore, how could God not be in agreement with our final evaluations?

Isaiah 55:8-9 shows how our thoughts rank in light of our all-knowing God, *"For my thoughts are not your thoughts, neither are your ways my ways, saith the LORD. For as the heavens are higher than the earth, so are my ways higher than your ways, and my thoughts than your thoughts."*

Our thoughts do not begin to hit the mark of truth. Even as God's followers, our conclusions work on a limited plane that lacks eternal perspective. The works of the flesh and the influence of egos plague our understandings with perversion and foolishness. Oswald Chambers summarized this matter well when he stated, "Darkness is my own point of view."[1]

Obviously, man's point of view is the essence of darkness and deception. This is why God's ways and thoughts are so much higher than human understanding. They are above man's best-calculated conclusions, and yet God's truths are simple enough that they can be found close to the ears of those who are childlike in faith and are clearly established in the hearts of the pure.

God must step on the scene of our lives and deliver us from the darkness that shrouds our minds. He does this by bringing down all walls, demolishing mindsets, and lifting us out of our emotional pits so we can see His truth by embracing His Son Jesus Christ in His fullness.

---

[1] *Biblical Psychology*, pg. 124

We have painstakingly looked at how the boundaries of the frame of reference affect us, but now we must understand how we process all information that influences the will and the emotions. Therefore, the last area we must explore and understand in our frame of reference is the *intellect*.

We have already noted how the intellect operates between the will and the emotions of a person. It is in the intellect that the will and emotions are brought together in agreement by means of mental evaluations and conclusions.

These evaluations and conclusions, unless inspired and sanctified by the Holy Spirit, are nothing more than vain imaginations that exalt themselves against the real knowledge of God.[2] These imaginations find their reinforcement because of strongholds (*walls, mindsets, and pits*) that create unbearable bondage.

The intellect represents the guts or core of the frame of reference. Within the makeup of the intellect you will find *perception*, *subconscious*, and *conscience*.

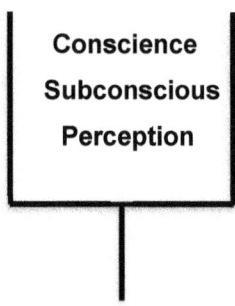

It is important that we understand how these three factors work because they will ultimately determine how we look at life and how we perceive God. It is also in this area where discernment is fine-tuned. For example, if our intellect is subject to the right spirit, it will be able to discern the wrong inclinations of our will and the state of our emotional level. If it is under the wrong spirit, the will and emotions will subdue the intellect and dictate its understandings or conclusions.

---

[2] 2 Corinthians 10:3-5

Our *perception* represents our foundation or what we call *worldview*. Our worldview is our value system. It is where we make distinctions between right and wrong, and it serves as a foundation to all of the judgment calls we make.

Parents, teachers, religious upbringing, and God establish the perception people possess. God actually established the initial foundation of this value system, according to *Romans 1:18-20*. These Scriptures state,

> *The wrath of God is being revealed from heaven against all the godlessness and wickedness of men who suppress the truth by their wickedness, since what may be known about God is plain to them, because God has made it plain to them. For since the creation of the world God's invisible qualities—his eternal power and divine nature—have been clearly seen, being understood from what has been made, so that men are without excuse* (NIV).

God has given an inward knowledge or truth of Himself to every individual formed in the womb. This inward knowledge is in accordance to His character, which means it is moral, upright, and holy.

As a child grows, parents, teachers, or religious influences either tear this initial foundation apart or they properly build upon it, making the child aware that there is a Holy God that deserves his or her devotion, service, and worship. Jesus made reference to this building up or tearing down in *Matthew 5:19*,

> *Whosoever therefore shall break one of these least commandments, and shall teach men so, he shall be called the least in the kingdom of heaven but whosoever shall do and teach them, the same shall be called great in the kingdom of heaven.*

It is in the *subconscious* where we *interpret* the information that we witness or process. This interpretation is based on our worldview while its attitude toward infractions is influenced greatly by the type of spirit and law we are operating under.

For example, if we see someone steal, we subconsciously interpret it as theft because of our value system. It is not something we have to think or debate about because it has already been judged by our foundation.

The problem with our subconscious is that is can be quite indifferent when it comes to personal actions. In fact, it can be very judgmental towards others while being impersonal and tolerant towards the very same sins and practices in its life. This is where the judgmental board is located that Jesus talked about in *Matthew 7:1-6,* which keeps a person from seeing his or her own discrepancies.

This brings us to the third area of our intellect, our *conscience*. It is our conscience that connects our personal actions with our subconscious thoughts, and we feel guilt or remorse over those personal actions. Here lies another problem; our conscience is often perverted, which causes it to operate in extremes.

For example, the conscience can be *extroverted,* which means it has been blinded to self (the "old man") by self-righteousness that is often inspired by concrete doctrine or a religious spirit. This type of conscience is insensitive and cruel because it only deals with surface matters and never gets down to the heart or spirit of something. The reason for this cosmetic emphasis is quite simple; self-righteousness will automatically put blinders upon those who are operating within its limited and judgmental confines. This type of conscience has its religious agendas and is quick to serve as a religious conscience to others rather than to the individual who holds to its perverted perception.

The other type of conscience is *introverted*. This is where the conscience is actually *oversensitive,* but most of its judgments are turned inward on self. This type of conscience in a Christian is often the product of legalism. It produces fake nobility and condemnation in a person and is often the product of an antichrist spirit because it makes the person responsible to be perfect or a personal god in his or her world. Both extreme consciences operate in unbelief because they put their confidence in man rather than God.

Our conscience operates within the boundaries of *principles*. Principles operate according to the spirit and the law we are under. They determine how we will apply or handle the information we process. There are two main principles in operation, those of *iniquity* or *godliness*.

For example, if a person is operating under the principle of iniquity, it simply means the individual will hold truth in unrighteousness.[3] The application or handling of information determines the type of fruits that will be evident in a person's life.

While the subconscious area discerns the outward, the conscience deals with personal activities based on subconscious interpretations.

Our conscience is also the place where we *define* the value or quality of our lives. The quality of a person's life hinges on two different definitions.

The first definition comes down to how we actually perceive ourselves. The problem is that many people have betrayed themselves by trying to *ignore, silence,* or *justify* away their worldview.

This was made evident when I dealt with a young woman who had an abortion. She was in a situation that allowed her to justify her act, but later on she found herself suffering from depression. She was newly married and her relationship with her husband was caving in. She had been to a counselor for more than a ten-month period with no relief.

As I dealt with her, we finally came to the subject of her abortion. I asked her about her religious affiliations. She confessed that she was raised Catholic. I asked her what the Catholic stand was on abortion. She admitted that the church viewed it as murder.

I began to explain to her about her worldview. Her worldview, which was initially formed by God and confirmed by the moral teachings of her church and family, declared that abortion is an act of murder. When she justified her actions, she temporarily drowned out her conscience by making her act justifiable in her subconscious mind, but her value system remained untouched and intact.

Her value system eventually revived her conscience when it started judging her action. The final judgment ended up defining the type of person she was in her mind. I asked her how her worldview was judging her. With haunted eyes, she had to admit she saw herself as a murderer, unworthy of life and happiness. Needless to say, she could not receive her husband's kindness and was in a silent prison of sorrow, despair, and hopelessness.

---

[3] Romans 1:18

This brings us to the second source that gives meaning to our life: our definition of God. If our conscience is not clean, we have a hard time seeing God in any other light than His holiness, anger, and judgment. We are unable to believe that He could love and forgive us for despicable actions that we personally condemn. Since we stand hopelessly condemned in our own minds, we have no hope of forgiveness, deliverance, and change. Without such hope, life ceases to be meaningful. After all, we all know what happens to people who are not forgiven and stand condemned without any recourse.

There are only three ways to silence the judgments of a moral worldview. The first way is to agree with God's evaluation of personal attitudes or actions and confess it so that you can receive forgiveness for your actions. *1 John 1:9* verifies this, *"If we confess our sins, he is faithful and just to forgive us our sins, and to cleanse us from all unrighteousness."*

And *Hebrews 9:14* says, *"How much more shall the blood of Christ, who through the eternal Spirit offered himself without spot to God, purge your conscience from dead works to serve the living God?"*

The second way you can subdue a moral worldview is to sear your conscience. *1 Timothy 4:2* says, *"Speaking lies in hypocrisy; having their conscience seared with a hot iron."*

It is easy to sear a conscience. If you simply justify wrong actions long enough, you will delude yourself, drowning out the conviction of your conscience. Justification of this nature is nothing more than self-delusion, exchanging the truth with lies and operating within darkness. If the conscience is not functioning, neither a present reality check to discern personal actions nor any avenue for the worldview to revive the conscience is left.

The third way to silence an ethical worldview is to change it. There is only one way to completely change a worldview, and that is through *indoctrination*.

Indoctrination

It is important to understand how indoctrination works. It is the oldest and most effective means of changing a person's worldview. Leaders such as Adolf Hilter employed it along with college professors, teachers, and cults, cult leaders, television, and newspapers have used it and continue to do so with an alarming success rate.

If you understand how people process information, you can easily indoctrinate individuals and change their worldview without them even knowing it. As *Matthew 15:14* pointed out, *"Let them alone: they be blind leaders of the blind. And if the blind lead the blind, both shall fall into the ditch."*

God always works from the foundation of truth upward, but indoctrination works from the top down. God works from the foundation in order to enlarge a person's limited perception of Him so that the Holy Spirit can define life according to His character or nature. A godly foundation actually represents His ways being upheld as all information is properly interpreted according to His truth, the Person of Jesus Christ, which ensures a healthy quality of life. (See *John 14:6.*)

Indoctrination, on the other hand, has to change your definition of what constitutes life in order to change your perspective of God. By changing the definition of something, you can change the spirit or intent behind it. Once you change the spirit behind something, it will determine how a person will apply it. Note the diagram on the following page.

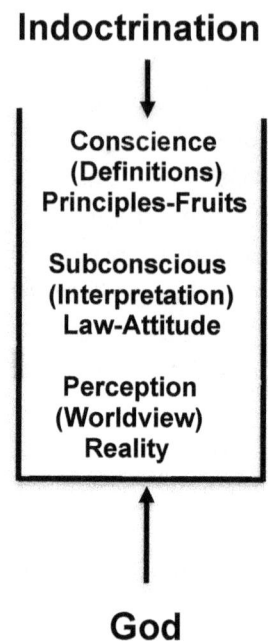

By redefining how you apply information, you redefine life and God. As your definition changes about life and God, your interpretation will change. As the interpretation changes, the worldview will adjust accordingly.

Indoctrination of any kind, no matter how religious, will bring people under the law of sin and death and subject them to the wrong spirit. In the end, they will be paying homage to the god of this world as their will and emotions submit to the new worldview being subtly established.

The indoctrination that often takes place in the Christian realm is very clever. It appears to be holy and righteous but it has the wrong spirit behind it. It is hard for people to accept the fact that it is easy to bring people under another spirit. As previously stated, all a person has to do to subtly change the spirit is to change the intent or meaning of something.

For example, take the world "meek." When most people look at the word "meek," they do so in light of the world's definition. The world's definition for meek makes us think of a wimp or a weak person. The emphasis or intent of this meaning leaves a wrong impression when it comes to spiritual truths because the spirit behind the word in this context belongs to the spirit of the world and not the Holy Ghost.

The best definition I have heard concerning meekness in the kingdom of God is "controlled rage." In other words, it means our strengths and capabilities are all under control of the Holy Ghost. Now compare the different meanings of the word "meek" in light of this statement, *"Take my yoke upon you, and learn of me; for I am meek and lowly in heart: and ye shall find rest unto your souls" (Matthew 11:29).* Can you begin to see that by changing the meaning of a word, you can change the spirit of something and redefine God?

In situations where a person has a wrong definition, he or she will ignore a word such as "meek" or brush over it because it causes confusion.

This is why to protect the truth we must understand the spirit or intent of even a word in order to discern the spirit behind something properly. Every time the right meaning of a spiritual truth is exchanged for a lie, it becomes a means to change the interpretation of how we view life and God.

Indoctrination works in small ways by nibbling at our definitions, silently changing our interpretation, and eroding our foundation. The end result of this indoctrination is a reprobate mind. *Romans 1:28* says, *"And even as they did not like to retain God in their knowledge, God gave them over to a reprobate mind, to do those things which are not convenient."*

This verse shows us indoctrination can bring a person to a place where he or she no longer retains the knowledge of the one true God. In this state, a new god or Christ is erected, often in the form of a religious leader, creed, or cause. This will change the principle of a truth, causing discernment to go out the back door. This is when a person will call good "evil" and evil "good." There is neither present reality nor any boundaries to safeguard a person. In fact, an individual in this state will be working in total darkness and deception. Such a person will fall into the same trap that many in Israel did during the days of Judges, *"In those days there was no king in Israel, but every man did that which was right in his own eyes" (Judges 17:6).*

Of course, when you fall into this trap it means the "old man" is reigning instead of the only true King, Jesus Christ.

Note the following illustration.

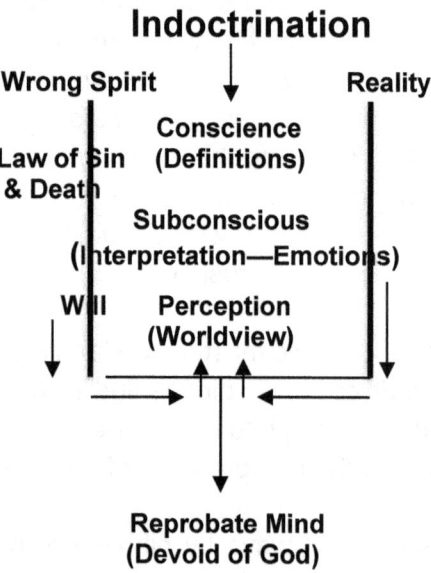

How is your perception of God? Are you succumbing to indoctrination or searing your conscience by justifying sins in your life? Once again, the fruits of your life will tell on you. Honestly examine them.

Chapter Ten

THE BOTTOM LINE

The webs that people weave for themselves are entangling and overwhelming. These emotional and spiritual webs complicate the simplicity of Christ, drown out the obvious, and cause people to dig deep pits of deception and depression. They also cause people to run around the same mountains of frustration and anger over and over again.

Wading through the web of a person's perception can be both time-consuming and unsuccessful, but sadly it has proven to be financially beneficial to some who take advantage of miserable and hurting souls. Is it any wonder that psychologists, therapists, and counselors are in demand?

Over the years I have realized that no matter how much you may want to help someone, unless the individual wants to get real about what actually ails him or her, any attempt to help is nothing more than a game that wastes valuable time.

In one incident I tried to help a woman whose life was a sordid mess. Each time she came to me for ministry I would wade with her through her emotional web. After each session she seemed relieved, but by the next session she was back to her same old pathetic state.

That is when it dawned on me that some people don't want to overcome; they just want enough relief from the stench and mess of their pigpens so that they can peacefully live in them. These people are usually seeking attention, confirmation for wrong attitudes and actions, sympathy, or emotional hype. In fact, sessions often serve as nothing more than a sick fix or provide a false hope that one day some form of magic will somehow change their pathetic existence. Obviously, these types of individuals want everything to change around them to meet their needs but are unwilling to change personally. Such people would prefer to feel sorry for themselves or be noble martyrs rather than taking responsibility for the shambles of their world in order to become open to change.

I also realized that I had to discern such individuals. Satan is a time robber, and this type of person is doing nothing more than his bidding.

At this time, I discovered what I call "the bottom line." The bottom line is the motives behind a person's attitudes and actions. This line is often buried under various layers of denial, excuses, and symptoms.

Denial of something is a person's way of wishing away a problem, traumatic events, or emotional wounds. Excuses represent self-delusion while symptoms represent wrong attitudes or sins. For example, alcoholism is a sin, not a disease as our politically correct society would have us believe. This destructive habit is the symptom of something that has never been confronted or brought to the light and has become so addictive it now controls the person.

The problem is that many waste their time on the symptoms rather than getting to the bottom line. Even though combating such things as alcohol is a noble cause, it only chips away at the tip of the iceberg. In my experience I have learned you can subdue a symptom but until you confront the bottom line, the symptom will express itself in other destructive ways.

In a way, a symptom serves as grave clothes. Even though the person is living, he or she will reek with the stench of decay that has been taking place because the individual has not really been exposed to life. Real life eludes such a person until he or she is resurrected. It is only after a person is made whole that the grave clothes can be loosed.

The question now is what constitutes the bottom line? There are two main bottom lines that motivate or compel people in their cycles and life. They are *rebellion* and *unresolved issues*.

Rebellion is a culprit you often encounter when dealing with people in destructive cycles. When you trace rebellion, you find that it is caused by something called ungratefulness and is made up of rights. Ungratefulness refuses to recognize God's blessings and intervention while rights are quick to bring accusation against Him for not honoring them. These rights cause the person to operate in unbelief and will ultimately justify the person as he or she moves out from under God's authority.

Unresolved issues are losses, hurts, wounds, or issues that have never been properly resolved in one's mind. These issues keep a person in bondage to the ill treatment or issue that continues to taunt and haunt him or her. Both of these bottom lines are self-centered and involve introspection.

When trying to help this type of individual, people usually end up contending with the symptoms rather than the actual bondage. They try to wade through endless excuses. This simply means that the helpful or concerned individual is trying to outlast or out-logic the excuses, thinking the problem will be solved. But the truth is people never run out of excuses because there is no resolution that will satisfy their logic.

In other situations, people feel if they just ride out the emotional roller coaster with an emotionally wounded person it will eventually come to an end. They learn about the 50th time around the track that not only does the roller coaster never stop, but it also gains momentum. By the time these well-meaning people have tried to survive the emotional ride repeatedly, their emotions become frayed and they are ready to abandon the ride just to regain some sanity.

In other cases, people try to wade through the layers of hurt, disappointment, and anger. But as they spiral downward they begin to realize that there is no end to the pit and that the darkness has become thicker and is now trying to engulf them.

Each attempt to help a person in any of these ways often leads to a dead end. This is why I discovered that in order to preserve my own mental well-being, I had to cut through the endless excuses, avoid getting on the roller coaster, and stay away from dark pits. As I avoided the traps and went for the bottom line, I learned there was a way to cut through the games people play, keep my sanity, and be effective at the same time.

The bottom line is devoid of excuses and reveals the real reason for a person's attitude and actions. It has no tracks or pits to run around; therefore, there is no game-playing going on. It brings truth to the emotionally hurting and sheds light into deep pits.

Battle For the Soul

As you can see, it is important to discover the bottom line because it is the real cause behind a person's plight. For example, I dealt with an individual who was in blatant sin.

This person blamed circumstances in her life for the sin she was involved in. As I cut through her veneer and excuses with truth, she finally confessed she was in her present sinful lifestyle because she felt she had the right to be happy. In her mind, God would understand.

By getting an individual to the bottom line, you cut out the game-playing and justification and often reveal the real culprit behind many of the destructive cycles. The main culprit is the sin of selfishness. This sin always leads to introspection and unbelief.

William Law pointed out that; "self is the whole evil of our fallen nature...for self is indeed both an atheist and idolater. It is an atheist because it has rejected God, and it is an idolater because it is its own idol."[4]

Once the bottom line is revealed, rebellion and unresolved issues are brought to the forefront and the person is brought to a place of making a decision. Will the individual continue to demand the perception he or she now processes, or will he or she allow God to step on the scene and make it right?

It is important to realize that unless the bottom line is changed, nothing will change in the person. To change the bottom line involves the following godly virtues and actions.

1) *Integrity* is the virtue that accepts reality or truth, and truth is a must for any bottom line to change. Integrity is a combination of honesty and humility. No one is born with integrity, but rather it is willfully formed in an individual's character. Depending on the individual, integrity must be applied at different points of one's character. For example, integrity must be up front in order to stop the process of justification before it starts for the individual who weighs all matters. For another type of person it must win over emotional fervor, while another individual must end with integrity after walking through all of his or her concepts. The final

---

[4] *God's Best Secrets*, pg. 272.

type of person must consider all of his or her ideas in light of integrity or he or she will make even the deception of sin right in his or her sight. As you can see, integrity does not allow the person to accept reality based on personal conclusions, emotions, images, or ideas. This virtue actually challenges individuals to get above the reality determined by the "old man" to seek God's perspective. Ultimately, it can be described as the first step of faith after the "old man" is declared limited and perverted in his reality.

2) The second stage of restoration is to *agree with God's evaluation.* It takes integrity to admit rebellion or face what one would consider spiritual failure, but a person with integrity is willing to take accountability by lining up to God's evaluation of his or her condition. A good example of people who needed to line up to God's evaluation was in the church of Laodicea in *Revelation 3*. This church thought it was rich, possessed much goods, and had need of nothing when in fact the Lord saw it as wretched, miserable, poor, blind, and naked. Talk about thinking more highly of self than one ought to think! But this is typical in many cases. The main way of lining up to God's evaluation is to agree with the spirit and truth of the Word of God about your plight or spiritual condition.

3) *Brokenness* is the next stage. Agreeing with God about one's spiritual state will always lead a person to this third stage. Brokenness is necessary for both healing and restoration. Bondage always implies the person is enslaved in an area of life. This brokenness implies that all barriers are down, allowing for the healing work of God. The problem with brokenness is that if there is no resolution (healing) and commitment for restoration, the person remains a cracked vessel. This state will keep a person from receiving and responding. For example, a person in this state can't receive forgiveness from God or extend real forgiveness to others.

4) *Repentance* is the next step to restoration. The bottom line reveals why bondage exists in the first place. Repentance

means changing the bottom line, but such change can't take place unless one understands the reason for his or her condition, agrees with God's evaluation about his or her spiritual state, and is actually broken over it. True repentance does not involve some apology without action but a complete change that takes place in the heart (no longer inclined in wrong direction), mind (evaluation of something is changed), and action (an about face).

5) Now that you have changed direction, the final level of restoration is *walking* in it. *1 John 2:6* says: *"He that saith he abideth in him ought himself also so to walk, even as he walked."* The Christian life is a walk that involves walking out this new life and embracing its liberty and victory.

Getting a person to the bottom line is easy. You must be ready to enter in according to the person's perception, patiently instruct, uphold truth, and point people to Jesus in meekness. Truth presented in this attitude has an uncanny way of putting pressure on a person in denial or giving someone hope who is broken and wounded. But keep in mind, all truth must be upheld within the framework of love for the person's soul, with commitment to his or her well-being, and in a spirit of meekness.

The problem with confronting people who are close to us is that we confront the situation from our perspective. In other words, the confrontation centers on how it is affecting me, myself, and I and not what is really going on with the person who is struggling.

Over the years I have learned that the greatest hindrance to real ministry is the individual ministering. I can't tell you how many times I have stood in the way in a situation and as a result caused an escalation of problems rather than regress.

Here are a few things to keep in mind while ministering:

1. It must never be about you but about the reality of Jesus. Get out of the way and let His Spirit shine through.

2. It is never about what the individual is doing but about who he or she is before God. All bondage begins in a person's life because something is amiss in his or her relationship with God.
3. Do not get caught up with symptoms, emotional roller coasters, or pits of depression. People need to understand the bottom line, and so do you if you are going to properly minister to them.
4. Do not waste your time on people who insist on playing the game. There are plenty of people who are truly looking for a way out of their bondage. Make yourself available and learn to redeem the time by not letting Satan rob you.

I will be dealing in more detail with many of these subjects, but now this brings us to our next important subject, *the powerless church*.

Chapter Eleven

THE POWERLESS CHURCH

Recently, I encountered a testimony that not only brought some sobriety to me but also confirmed some of my worst fears about what I call "the visible church."

A woman was searching for the truth about Jesus and His salvation and had gone from church to church to find it. In one of the churches she attended a person recognized her as a woman with an unsavory reputation. The pastor told her if she continued to come to church, she was to come late and leave early. In another church she found the courage to pass along a prayer request to the pastor, only to watch him make a performance of wadding it up in his hand and putting it in his pocket, with the comment that it was not worth praying for. This woman's search lasted 14 years before she ever found someone who would not be intimidated by her past or consider her insignificant in the scheme of things and would actually answer her questions.

This woman is a Christian today—not because the church was faithful to its commission but because Jesus is faithful to every searching, lost soul.

I am sure we would like to think that we would respond differently if we found ourselves in a similar situation. But the truth is that I have heard many such horror stories.

Before I bring an indictment against the church, I must establish what the real "church" is. There are three entities within the world that we call "church." The first entity is the religious system. This system was organized by man and is man-centered and man-operated.

This system is the most visible entity today and is the most influential in setting trends and conditioning people in how they view present-day Christianity. The problem with this entity is that it is very carnal and has subtly replaced Jesus with personal righteousness and moral and political emphases while pursuing the world with a justified vengeance. It is moving towards the one-world religious system that will eventually give way to the antichrist system.

The second entity that is called "church" is comprised of religious edifices that can be seen of men. These buildings are set apart by the doctrines and denominations of man. Although most of the doctrines or creeds can be based on sound scriptural doctrine, these beliefs often become defiled and useless because man exalts them over Jesus. In essence, man exalts his interpretation of doctrine rather than seeking to know Jesus, making the doctrines idolatrous in nature and devoid of a right spirit.

This exaltation of theology becomes the breeding ground for cult mentality and practices. It produces elitism, fear, intimidation, and condemnation. It is out of this environment that the religious system has been given life, authority, and power. The system is often intertwined and influences people's interpretation of what constitutes doctrine.

Churches that are based on denomination, beliefs, or man's interpretation are fragile. These interpretations actually set followers up for disillusionment and disappointment because buildings can be destroyed and man's interpretation of doctrine will ultimately prove to be vain and foolish. In fact, these beliefs serve as the shifting sand that Jesus warned about in *Matthew 7:24-27*.

This brings us to the "real church." It can be found amongst the religious system, alive within buildings, and functioning in the midst of doctrinal elitism.

This "church" is universal in nature. It may be in the system but not part of it. It may agree with doctrines but refuse to be limited by them. This entity may be active within buildings but will not be committed to them.

The real church does not see success in light of numbers, big buildings, or worldly popularity but as to whether truth is upheld and the presence of God is a reality. This entity can't be control by a system, contained by a church building, or represented by doctrines or denominations for it is made up a body of people who stand distinct in purpose, commitment, and focus.[1]

The true church walks to a different drum beat because it realizes it is blood-bought and can only find life, hope, and direction from the head of the church, Jesus Christ. As a result, those who are part of the true church are often hated by the world, rejected by those who are religious, and avoided by those who operate in carnality.

Since these substitutes are conditioning people's perception of Christianity, it is important for the real church to understand how agreement and involvement with both the system and doctrines of man can render it powerless.

The first two churches discussed in this chapter often "play church" rather than serve as a visible expression of Jesus. This often causes these two entities to operate under an antichrist spirit that serves as a substitution of Jesus. These entities often rob from God's real servants and destroy real faith and the testimony of Christ in the hearts of many.

These antichrist or religious substitutes hide behind various Christian titles and activities but can be devoid of the heart of Christianity, Jesus Christ. They use the right language but are empty of the right fruits. They have an appearance of righteousness but deny the power. Because they can be a blatant counterfeit of Jesus, the Apostle Paul gave Christians this instruction, *"...come out from among them, and be ye separate, saith the Lord, and touch not the unclean thing; and I will receive you" (1 Corinthians 6:17).*

I say all of this because the real leaders and body of Jesus are dispersed throughout these entities. The real church is trying to make a difference in many ways by changing the emphasis of these organizations, but the problem is that these entities are changing the face of Christianity without many of the followers of Jesus being aware of it.

Sadly, the real church is being exposed and inundated by this antichrist system because many well-meaning Christians are trying to find leaders and bodies within these two entities to support and be in fellowship with. They are trying to be obedient to what they know, and

---

[1] Ephesians 4:4; Colossians 1:18; 1 Corinthians 12:12-14

yet many feel drained after partaking of the fruit of these religious counterfeits.

It is important that the saint realizes that these religious substitutes are not only trying to change the face of Christianity but its foundation and cornerstone as well. Therefore, it is vital that the saint discerns the spirit behind these two entities to determine whether separation is necessary. Here are some ways to test any system, movement, or church body to discern if it truly represents God or whether it is promoting another Jesus, gospel, or spirit.[2]

Counterfeits of God lack a heavenly *vision*. Religious substitutes have brought so much of the world into the church that the heavenly vision of the real church has become hidden beneath worldly pursuits for material wealth, prestige, and purpose. As a result, these antichrist substitutes promote, function like, and act like the world. There is no distinction between the ways of the world and the ways of these visible organizations.

Since much of the heavenly vision has been clouded by the pseudo teachings and emphases found in these entities, many in the church have also lost a clear reality of hell. They are no longer able to look up or down but find that their vision or focus is straight ahead, causing many to be enticed by the attractions of the world that are now tantalizing their eyes and affections.

Sadly, all these religious substitutes can see is what will benefit them, and as they become more self-absorbed and self-serving, they become more worldly, rendering those in their midst as powerless. The Christians who are being influenced by this idolatry become spiritually dull, confused, disappointed, or deluded. Those who have become deluded are now striving to put roots down in the world instead of setting their affections on heaven, where Jesus is sitting on the right hand of the Father and real pleasures await them ever more.[3]

The beauty about the heavenly vision was that it gave people hope as they looked heavenward and fervor as they looked downward to the reality of hell. This godly vision is what keeps the real saint from looking

---

[2] 2 Corinthians 11:1-14
[3] Psalms 16:11

to the world and being mesmerized into a state of luke-warmness in their love and commitment to the Lord Jesus Christ.

Today it seems as if much of the real church is subtly coming under the bondage of the world as it gives in to the pressure of others and bows down to the ways of these religious substitutes. As sincere people innocently give way to these substitutes that embrace the world's ways, they become blind to eternal truths, a heavenly destination, and an eternal judgment. This is why the warning of *Proverbs 29:18* continues to echo through the corridors of time, *"Where there is no vision the people perish."*

This brings us to another problem that arises when God's people cease to be heaven-bound and become earth-entangled. One of the casualties of this type of spiritual condition is the Gospel. The Gospel is the power of God unto salvation.[4] Here is where the true church's power really lies, but if this message is changed or watered down in any way to fit the world's ways or downplayed to make it acceptable to fleshly appetites and worldly philosophies, it is rendered ineffective. Anytime this message is nullified, the real church will immediately become powerless in situations as many become defiled and carnally minded in their perception of God. This condition will open the church up to have its foundation undermined, the cornerstone replaced, and the heart and mind (head) made susceptible to a transplant.[5]

This exchange of these major areas in the church means that innocent people are being prepared to accept another gospel, embrace a different Jesus, and uphold another spirit.[6] We actually can see where this is happening today.

The gospel of today is a worldly gospel that measures godliness in light of the world's definition of success. The idea that people could be promoting or accepting another gospel should put fear in their hearts. After all, in *Galatians 1:6-9*, the Apostle Paul warned that anyone who would preach another gospel would stand accursed, but those who promote this gospel lack fear of God, which makes them fools.

---

[4] Romans 1:16
[5] 1 Corinthians 3:11; 1 Peter 2:6-8; Colossians 1:18
[6] 2 Corinthians 11:1-3

This prosperity gospel is gaining inroads into the various churches because it promotes worldly wealth and indulgence over personal identification with Jesus that comes through self-denial and suffering. This new gospel has been cleverly changing how many within the church look at holiness. Worldly prosperity rather than godly character now determines holiness.[7]

Because the measuring stick for holiness has been changed from a heavenly level to an earthly plane, the real foundation and cornerstone of Christianity is being chiseled away with lies. Instead of testing everything to the immovable foundation of Jesus, which was first laid by the first apostles and prophets, many are being tossed to and fro by various winds of doctrine.[8]

A new breed of apostles and prophets are now reconstructing the foundation that has withstood every attack for the last two thousand years. This reconstruction not only disbars the old foundation, but it has also removed the cornerstone and put in its place those who claim to be appointed to usher in this new age of the church. Likewise, these leaders are also replacing the real head of the church by claiming preeminence over it.

This new breed of leaders claims the old will no longer do. As a result, their revelations supersede the Word of God, fleshly sensationalism replaces the fear of God, emotional hype becomes a sick substitute for real worship, and worldly pursuits and riches overshadow preparation for eternity.

Instead of this new type of church wanting to add souls to the kingdom of God, it wants to add money to its coffers and establish the kingdom of God on earth through political maneuvers, religious coups within church bodies, doctrines of demons, and lying signs and wonders.

Instead of seeing the world as a harvest field, this false church sees it as something that must be conquered and possessed for the good of its causes. Instead of seeing itself as a co-laborer with God in this great harvest field of humanity, it sees God as someone who can be controlled

---

[7] See Luke 12:15
[8] Ephesians 4:14

by using His promises as a whip over His head and by verbally proclaiming the right things in the name of faith.

This brings us to a serious warning from Jesus: *"For what is a man profited, if he shall gain the whole world, and lose his own soul? Or what shall a man give in exchange for his soul" (Matthew 16:26)?*

Since this visible church is more earthly and worldly in its agendas and presentations, it has become increasingly fleshly in its pursuits. These pursuits put this new church on the opposite pole from the real church.

The goal of the real church is to seek to know God. To know God and His will serves as the real believer's treasure, meat, hope, and power. But this false church, which is gaining momentum within local bodies as well as becoming brasher in its claims and teachings, is pursuing after new revelations and signs and wonders. These new revelations and signs and wonders not only appeal to fleshly sensationalism, but they are also a vital part of the lustful entertainment this antichrist system specializes in to draw people into its tentacles.

Some in Jesus' generation sought after visible signs. Jesus said this about them, *"An evil and adulterous generation seeketh after a sign; and there shall no sign be given to it, but the sign of the prophet Jonas" (Matthew 12:39).*

The problem with becoming fleshly in the pursuit of spiritual greatness is that the person fails to recognize the greatest miracle that ever took place—**Jesus' resurrection.**

The faith of the true saint hinges on this one miracle. Clearly, all miracles and supernatural acts pale in light of this one great supernatural occurrence because Jesus' resurrection clearly states that death has no sting, the grave has no victory, and the Christian faith is valid and alive.[9]

If this antichrist system is worldly and fleshly, then one must conclude it is also sinful to the core. The Word of God is clear that all sins in any camp will weaken the body or group; therefore, they must be taken care of.

---

[9] 1 Corinthians 15:54-56

But in many cases sin is reigning within this new church and is greatly overlooked. Sins such as pride, fornication, lust, greed, slander, abortion, fraud, idolatry, and witchcraft are being practiced by those within this entity and are often disregarded by the leadership, which is weighed down with sin as well.

As a result, innocent seekers of God are falling through the cracks of condemnation and becoming lost in despair because they are powerless to overcome personal sins. They find themselves becoming vulnerable to skepticism and mockery, not only towards their own testimony of Jesus, but to those around them as well.

We know it is a serious offense to be subject to the works of the flesh because, *"...they which do such things shall not inherit the kingdom of God"* (Galatians 5:21c).

This brings us to another fruit of this false church, and that is the move for all to come under one covering. The emphasis on *unity* among all churches has become not only another gospel but also a religious and social cause that ignores spirit and truth.

This religious unity promotes peace in place of the right Spirit. It is being subtly presented through the humanistic, New Age philosophies that advocate tolerance, self-esteem, and political correctness at the expense of truth, self-denial, the cross, the real Gospel, and the character of God. In other words, it is throwing out all godly boundaries to have this illusion of false peace.[10]

We know this move for peace can be compared to the counterfeit rider on the white horse in *Revelation 6*. Instead of holding a sword of judgment as Jesus will when He comes back in power and glory as the King of kings and Lord of lords, this rider holds a bow without an arrow.[11]

This call for unity at any cost is moving the church towards the one-world religious system. This one-world religious system will appear righteous and will even have its own prophet who will be able to do miraculous signs, but it will be under the complete dominion of Satan.[12]

---

[10] 1 Thessalonians 5:1-3
[11] Revelation 6:2 compare to Revelation 19:11-19
[12] 2 Thessalonians 2:3-9

Today, lives, marriages, homes, and churches are falling apart at the seams because there is no spiritual authority and power to overcome the darkness that is invading this world and encroaching on the lives of Christians. The real church is being rendered powerless by the mixture of spirits, gospels, and various Christs and the result is that many innocent, uninformed, unprotected people are falling prey to the kingdom of darkness.

The question is, how can the real church stand even in the midst of this invasion of humanism, heresy, lying signs and wonders, and wolves in sheep's clothing? It is simple: We need to get back to our source of authority in order to be imbued with the power of God.

The Christian's source of authority is Jesus Christ. Christians do not need more formulas and seminars; they just need to come to the knowledge of the real Jesus and begin to walk their lives out according to His character. The real church does not need more revelations or prophecies to experience change and power, but rather it needs just one revelation—that of the Jesus of the Bible. The body of Christ does not need more religious leaders; it just needs the King of kings and Lord of lords to take His rightful place in lives, homes, and congregations.

Once Jesus' authority is established in a person's life, the power will come through the indwelling presence of the Holy Spirit. He will have the freedom to land as the dove did after the waters of judgment on wickedness abated during Noah's time. He will be able to flow freely when all of the dams of self are removed. But right now the Spirit of God is being grieved by the sin, hypocrisy, and religious compromise of the real church with this antichrist system. False doctrines, wrong spirits, and gospels are quenching Him. He is being rejected by unbelief and ignorance, abused by counterfeits, feared by the ignorant, mocked by skeptics, and pushed aside by the self-righteous.

Are you devoid of real authority and power? You can blame it on a lot of things, including Satan or God. It is true that Satan is a foe capable of defeating and destroying a person, as you will see by the devices he uses. It is also true that God allows the testing and adversities in our lives. But it is important to know that the real key to defeat or victory does not lie with Satan or God but with the individual and what he or she embraces to be truth.

It is time for the real church not only to stand for truth, but also to come out and be separate from this antichrist system. This religious system is as doomed as the Titanic, and each Christian must escape from its idolatrous ways before this doomed system meets the Immovable Rock.[13] As Jesus said, *"...if it were possible, they shall deceive the very elect" (Matthew 24:24c).*

---

[13] Matthew 21:44

Chapter Twelve

OPPRESSION OR POSSESSION?

Since we understand the place of bondage, it is important that we now come to terms with how the enemy works and the devices he uses.

There has been a long-standing debate going on about Satan and how he works. As with many subjects in the Word of God, man has striven to put Satan and his devices into a nice, understandable package. The truth of the matter is Satan is not a doctrine but a powerful, living entity and his devices are facts, not fables or a matter of man's theology.

The theology man has developed about the enemy of souls has reduced Satan into an indifferent or controllable fantasy and his devices into a source of jesting and mocking. This reduction of Satan has clouded his nature and activities and put him into the arena of debate rather than in the battlefield where he must be confronted.

This debate has caused people to operate in extremes about Satan. Some deny that he exists while others accredit him with far too much influence. A. W. Tozer summarized these extremes in his book, *Born After Midnight:* "If he cannot make skeptics of us, he will make us devil-conscious and thus throw a permanent shadow across our lives." He goes on to say that there is a hairline between truth and superstition.

Each extreme is dangerous and shows people's ignorance and speculation about this enemy. As *Hosea 4:6* declares, *"My people are destroyed for lack of knowledge..."*

Since the Word of God does not present Satan as a doctrine but as a powerful enemy, we must avoid putting him in a nice, comfortable religious box. After all, Jesus confronted and contended with him. He didn't pretend, ignore, or act like he wasn't there. He silenced him in the wilderness and cast his cohorts out of people. He rebuked him when he was using Peter to stop His journey to the cross and submitted His will to the Father to overcome him in the Garden of Gethsemane. He ultimately defeated him when He obeyed His Father by offering Himself up as the Passover Lamb on the cross.

Jesus' encounters with Satan were not to show His supernatural powers over him, but to show us how to overcome the enemy of our souls. We must tread the same path as Jesus did to put this enemy at bay. We must overcome him with the Word of God, take authority over him in our lives, and contend with him in the lives of others. We must submit to God's perfect will and apply our personal cross to defeat his attacks and inroads into our lives.

As we consider the world around us it is clear to see the battle with Satan is real and raging in the spiritual realm. Since the Bible speaks of him, we as fundamental Christians have no other choice but to come to terms with him. But Christians must avoid stuffing him in some comfortable theology as a means to keep in accordance with the Bible. Such attempts means a person is tacking Satan onto theology, which will inevitably deny his existence altogether and make him into a fable.

Make no mistake; we must be able to recognize our enemy and beware of his devices if we are going to be effective soldiers in the kingdom of God. Satan's goal is to become our personal god in order to receive worship. He is a capable foe, a lion seeking whom he may devour. He has no original lies or ideas; therefore, he counterfeits everything of God except godly love and uses the same lies with each new generation. He understands the weaknesses of man's mind and is an expert flatterer and liar who does not play fair.[1]

Another debate that rages over Satan is just how much influence he can have in a Christian's life. The fact that we are referred to as soldiers in Scripture, fighting a battle and given armor, implies it is no small matter.[2] In other words, our encounters with Satan can't be simple little games or skirmishes where there are no victims.

The answer to how much influence Satan can have in a Christian's life depends on how much right or territory he or she gives him. Like all

---

[1] Matthew 4:10; 1 Peter 5:8; John 8:44.
[2] Ephesians 6:10-18

enemies, Satan is after territory, mainly the minds and hearts of men. If he can gain access into any area of man's soul, he can cause bondage.

The amount of territory Satan gains determines whether his influence in a person's life is *oppression* or *possession*. It is important that people understand there is a difference between these two words.

Oppression is nothing more than bondage in the *soul* area. This bondage manifests itself in confusion, depression, fear, and complacency. The Word of God is often rendered useless and the love for God will grow lukewarm. It seems that instead of the person's life being full and satisfying with the things of God, the Christian life becomes a burden too great to bear.

Oppression keeps the person from moving forward in his or her relationship with Christ, often causing confusion, frustration, and condemnation. This individual may keep up a facade to keep people from suspecting his or her spiritual struggle, but the struggle is real and disheartening.

Possession occurs when Satan actually possesses or controls a person's spirit, soul, and body. Unlike an oppressed person who is able to maintain control of his or her faculties, a possessed person can't control his or her actions. In dealing with possessed people, a Scripture or reference to Jesus as God Incarnate or His blood can set demons or spirits off into uncontrollable tirades.

The next question is, can a Christian be possessed? The answer is no, but a believer can be oppressed. We have encountered Satan's influence in Christians' lives. The problem with many Christians is that if you mention Satan has some kind of inroad into a believer's life, they balk because their frames of reference have been established by man's interpretation of Scripture. They automatically perceive that such an implication means a Christian is possessed.

Whether a person is oppressed or possessed, we must not ignore or reason away Satan's influence. The individual must be delivered or set free from Satan's claims or rights in his or her life in order to experience the fullness of salvation and victory.

Over the years we have encountered the same manifestations of Satan in oppressed people as we have in possessed people. We have watched Christians being slam-dunked onto the floor by an unseen force. We have witnessed uncontrollable shaking, body parts contorting in unnatural ways, foaming at the mouth, supernatural strength, and blue or brown eyes changing into a murky green. We have heard demonic screams and voices along with smelling a sulfuric odor being emitted from the person going through deliverance.

At times I have tried to accredit some of these bizarre behaviors to the individual playing some sick game until something of a supernatural means happened, such as the person's eye color changing. Satan is bizarre and gross in nature. There is nothing as sobering as meeting him face to face. You know he is playing for keeps and will use every device to keep a person within his grasp.

The Main Entrance

Satan uses various means to make inroads into a person's soul, but there is only one main entrance into the soul of man, and that is through his will.

We have talked a lot about the will of man, but it also serves as the main entrance for Satan to oppress a person. In fact, the will can be like a revolving door that can cause a person to operate in confusion.

Man has no control over his life except in one area: who is going to rule his life. The one who reigns in man's life will determine where man will spend eternity—heaven or hell. Eternal destination is the most important issue of life, and it rests in man's hands. Otherwise, man is subject to the circumstances that life hands him.

Life is designed to bring man to choose who will rule in his life. For example, life teaches us two important facts: 1) Man is not God, and 2) man needs God. Destruction occurs when man allows life to cause him to become hard towards God instead of turning to Him in need.

It is in the will area that man chooses whom he will believe and serve. This decision may take place many times during the day. Every time man is faced with issues that concern life, truth, sin, direction, and change, he must decide at each point whether he is going to look to God or to his natural preference of relying on self, the world, or Satan.

Who or what the person submits to will determine if the person is in blatant idolatry or acting in obedience. Submission to the wrong god will become the entrance to oppression. This oppression simply means Satan will begin to take territory as the individual gives way to his devices.

Each time a person gives way to Satan, he makes greater advancements by taking more territory. His goal is to tightly enfold people into his delusion.

Let us consider how Satan gains inroads into our lives and some of the spirits that he uses to plague people today. If you are oppressed, maybe you will identify the source that is doing Satan's bidding in your life.

Doing Satan's Bidding

There have been discussions about the possible difference between spirits and demons. According to some leading authorities in this area, the main difference between spirits and demons is that demons need a body to do their bidding, while spirits may use a person as a vessel but they are not solely dependent on a body to operate effectively. Demons mainly affect the individual they are influencing while spirits uses their vessels to afflict, torment, and push others who come in contact with them. (Compare *Matthew 8:28-32* with *Acts 16:16-18.*)

The main entities I will be dealing with are spirits. Demonic spirits can push, prod, and motivate a person into all works of darkness. The spirit often receives its name based on the fruit it produces. For example, a spirit of anger produces rage, fear will paralyze or drive a person, while unbelief creates skepticism and mocking.

The most oppressive spirit we encounter in people is a spirit of fear. Fear is nothing more than worship because a person usually bows down to this entity without even being aware that he or she is succumbing to it.

I will be discussing such subjects as fear, unbelief, and anger in the following chapters due to the fact that they serve as open avenues for Satan. The spirits I am concerned with in this particular section are those that are often ignored, condoned by our Christian, worldly culture, or serve as a substitute for the work of God.

Self-righteous spirit: This spirit can be described by *Romans 10:2-4:*

> *For I bear them record that they have a zeal of God, but not according to knowledge. For they being ignorant of God's righteousness, and going about to establish their own righteousness, have not submitted themselves unto the righteousness of God. For Christ is the end of the law for righteousness to every one that believeth* (emphasis mine).

Self-righteousness comes from pride and justifies ungodly attitudes and actions. Jesus didn't come for those who perceive themselves to be righteous because He knew their hard-heartedness would not allow them to receive Him.[3] This form of righteousness is based on a person's ruler and is very hypocritical in nature and cruel in judgment.

When people look at their own righteousness, it becomes a pseudo light that blinds them to the real light and righteousness of God. It calls for conformation and not transformation, which keeps a person's righteousness surface and outward, causing delusion that ultimately serves as a judgmental board.

People with this spirit have replaced a relationship with God with religious activities and display a pride that is on a religious trip or cause. They are looking to self to be right instead of to God, who is the only one who can make individuals right.

Anytime self-righteousness is in operation, the work of mercy and grace is replaced by religious zeal that lacks wisdom and compassion. This zeal is ignorant towards what constitutes real Christianity and righteousness.

The Word of God is clear that a person's only source of righteousness is Jesus Christ. When Christians fail to realize this, it is because they have forgotten that they stood level with every other sin-laden person at the foot of the cross in need of forgiveness and salvation.[4] In fact, these people act as if they have spiritually arrived.

---

[3] Matthew 9:12-13
[4] 2 Peter 1:8-13

Self-righteousness finds its origins in the reign of the "old man" and is clothed in a religious cloak. In the end, it produces rebellion as the self-righteous individual must rely more and more on self to become acceptable. Any time such reliance exists it is rebellious in nature and hard-hearted in attitude.

Religious Spirit: This spirit is popular among wannabe ministers who want to be a somebody in the kingdom of God, but who are not willing to pay the price. This spirit becomes a substitute for spiritual preparation that produces the experience and growth every bona fide minister needs to properly serve Jesus in the right spirit and attitude.

Religious spirits delude the individual into thinking he or she is something special in the kingdom of God and has something of value to offer. Super spirituality replaces maturity and devotion. Fake nobility is exhibited in the place of humility, and prideful piousness becomes a sick substitute for experience and godly wisdom. In fact, this religious spirit fakes everything from love and truth to righteousness.

Individuals who are driven by this spirit usually desire attention. They think highly of their spiritual abilities but are only full of dead religious platitudes that are used to give the appearance of wisdom. They will interrupt meetings and become obnoxious when the spirit is vying for attention with other religious spirits. When you get more than one religious spirit in a meeting, it can be like a free-for-all as they try to outdo each other with "gifts," "prophesy," or "words of knowledge and wisdom."

The greatest accomplishment of religious spirits is that they not only turn people off from God but they drive them away from the real Jesus. To the mature Christian, they are an irritation that can only be tolerated for so long before being confronted or rebuked.

Antichrist Spirit. This spirit denies that there is one true God with the goal of deifying man. It uses the idea of Jesus to erect a different Jesus, therefore changing the Gospel and standard of holiness.

The self-righteous spirit creates its own delusion about righteousness while the religious spirit deludes the one who has given way to it, but the antichrist spirit wants to deceive the masses. It is the main spirit behind cults, heretical teachings, and the New Age. Leaders who operate under an antichrist spirit have had some religious teachings but have their own agenda, which is not the cross of Christ or lost souls.

This self-serving agenda can vary with the leader, but the result is the same: The leaders will be exalted as gods in the lives of their followers. Their followers will become so seduced that they will sacrifice all to blindly follow their god into the very fires of spiritual ruin and hell.

Familiar Spirit: This spirit serves as a substitute for the Holy Spirit and opens the person up to the kingdom of darkness and witchcraft. I can't tell you how many pastors' wives I have encountered over the years operating with this spirit.

This spirit is the one that gives information to its subject about someone, causing the individual to accredit his or her insight to the Holy Spirit. The open door for this spirit is wickedness because the individual does not want to get real in his or her life before God. Getting real with God simply means giving up control of one's world.

The people who are open to this spirit want the things of God without humbling self and coming to repentance for their wicked, independent ways. The people I see with this spirit walk in some kind of perversion in their life, whether it be sexual or in the area of truth.

I remember a pastor's wife who admitted to automatic writing and accredited it to the Holy Spirit and her "so-called" above-average spirituality. Automatic writing is one of the products of a familiar spirit.

It is important to realize the kingdom of darkness takes pride in the information it feeds its devotees because it is very detailed and leaves vivid pictures.

On the other hand, the Holy Spirit only gives you a sense of something but never the details. The reason for this is that details create a picture that can be etched in the recesses of a person's mind. These etchings can taint and defile that which is pure. This is why the Holy Spirit only gives a person a sense of something and never the details. He does not want to erect something in the imagery of person's mind that will taint the purity.

The familiar spirit is the one who gives mediums their information. The idea that such a spirit is prevalent in the church today should not only cause us to get on our faces and cry out for mercy, but we should be ashamed that we have allowed such a disgrace to darken the doors of our churches.

Perverted Spirits: Perverted spirits operate on various levels, but their main goal is to pervert anything that is pure and acceptable to God. They pervert truth, sex, language, vision, hearing, and motives.

I remember a Christian woman who admitted to practicing sexual perversion at the request of her husband. She confessed that her mind even perverted a beautiful flower because of how perversion made her regard the things around her.

This spirit creates its own pigpen that people not only wallow in but also attempt to get others to join them in. These people are miserable in their dirty pens, but they will delude themselves to it because of pride. This delusion causes them to ignore their misery as they become complacent in their mire and offended when others confront them or refuse to join them in their sick perversion. Therefore, it is not unusual to encounter a complacent spirit or spirit of self-pity when you encounter perversion.

I have personal knowledge of how a perverted spirit operates. This spirit has been prevalent in my family due to heretical teachings that have been passed down from generation to generation. If truth is perverted, then there are no limits to perversion as it makes various inroads into a person's life. I was finally set free from its influences, but I can remember how my encounters with it made me feel dirty and unclean. I so wanted to wash it off, but I needed others to stand in the gap for me. As truth unveiled this spirit's destruction in my life, I was set free from it.

Since my liberation from this spirit, I am able to discern it in others. Every time I encounter this spirit in people, I recognize its tentacles and will rebuke it for trying to find some kind of opening into my life.

Perverted spirits find openings through erroneous teachings, disobedience to the Word, and toying with and practicing sexual sins. The problem is that perverted spirits will cause people to toy with sin, thinking they can handle it, but in reality, perversion is capable of becoming a sick addiction that entangles the mind, will, and emotions. Deviant sexual sins such as fornication (all illicit sex outside of the marriage bed) along with pornography are the products of this spirit's reign.

It is important to point out seduction walks hand in hand with this spirit. People are often seduced into perversion before they actually practice it. Once they are seduced and begin to practice the sin, the perverted spirit takes hold of their emotional makeup by gaining inroads into their feelings and affections. As they give way to this spirit, it entangles them into its web of lies and unfulfilled fantasies. As the victim sets out to fulfill their sick fantasies, their emotions are greatly heightened, the imagination is stirred up to the exciting possibilities, and their desires become focused on fulfillment.

I must state that most of the excitement of perversion is that which is conjured up in the imagination, more than the action of it. Once people act out the fantasies, they find themselves falling into a pit that leaves them feeling empty, dirty, and guilty. This seems to be the emotional and mental cycle of those who get caught on this insidious merry-go-round.

Spirits of Lust: Perversion and lust can walk hand in hand, but lust goes beyond the deviant sexual desires to include covetousness of anything that can be possessed or pursued. Spirits of lust know no boundaries because they can cause us to covet anything that we feel will add to the pleasure or value of life. In fact, the things we lust after may be what we need for survival, but then we begin to see them as a means to our right to life, liberty, and the pursuit of happiness.

Lust can include material possessions, success, and fame and its byproduct is using jealousy. Unlike perversion, lust does not find inroads into the imagination but by way of fleshly attractions and appetites. A person must first see the possibilities or taste of the fruit before a spirit of lust can take hold of a desire. The process for this spirit to gain a foothold begins with the person partaking of the fruit (good or evil), and as the individual begins to think about the pleasure or fulfillment of it, he or she begins to focus on the idea of having more. Of course, this focus is idolatrous in nature and very self-serving in practice, but this idolatrous practice is what can give spirits of lust the foothold to play havoc.

The world has provided the fruit that entices people into the tentacles of this spirit. This fruit sets many people up to be open and driven by this spirit with such attractions found in money, prestige, pleasure, and any form of self-gratification and vanity.

Lust only finds temporary relief, but each time a person gives way to a particular lust, the spirit of lust enlarges his or her appetite in that area. As the appetite becomes greater, the spirit of lust accelerates into a driving, tormenting force in a person's life.

Mocking Spirit: A mocking spirit is the most sinister spirit I have come in contact with, especially in the lives of those who claim to be Christians.

Let me state, if a person claims to be a Christian, I am not going to argue with them because I see Satan's influence in his or her life. I take a person at face value and address him or her according to the person's claims. It matters little whether I agree or not. My goal is simple—bring the proper contrast to the individual so the person can clearly see where he or she is and, I hope, make the right decisions. It is important that we do not limit ourselves from properly confronting a situation based on our little doctrinal boxes. Obviously, a wolf in sheep's clothing is probably not saved, but initially we must always approach a person from his or her perspective and not from our limited, dogmatic understanding. It is not Scriptural to assure ourselves that a person who is influenced by Satan is not a Christian. We do not have the Scriptural backing to make such a judgment call up front.

Fruits in a person's life do not always determine if the individual is saved, but they do give you an idea where they might be spiritually and if they are oppressed in some way.

We have encountered mocking spirits in people who believe the Gospel. This spirit's influence seems to be on the rise thanks to the so-called laughing revival. This laughing revival has actually opened people up to mock or make fun of fundamental Christian conduct, values, and even the old hymns. It is very arrogant and condescending towards those who are opposed to the blatant disrespect it often displays towards the pure things of God.

This spirit also enters through unfulfilled expectations that have produced anger, unbelief, and rebellion. Countless people have opened themselves up to this spirit because in their mind God has failed to adhere to their expectations. This perception not only causes disillusionment but will produce desperation. This leanness of the soul will cause individuals to seek God in some type of spiritual manifestation or pseudo religious movements, which makes them susceptible to a mocking spirit. People who operate in unbelief also have this spirit. It expresses itself through skepticism but will openly mock true faith when it encounters it. This spirit actually taunts the one who has given way to it along with any legitimate servant of God who may cross its path.

A mocking spirit will cause people to see themselves as hypocrites because they are often surface in their Christianity and only have an appearance of righteousness. Since these people lack spiritual substance and character, nothing seems real. When they are presented with real Christianity, the mocking spirit raises its head with a vengeance because wherever spiritual character is lacking, pride will reign with a fervor. Often the mocking spirit will serve as a mask on their face that appears as a religious facade to the outside world but is a sinister means of mocking the person who wears it (and those who buy its hypocrisy). In fact, it openly mocks the things of God through snide remarks and demeaning statements.

Although small, it can be a difficult spirit to get rid of. The person has to face the fact that it gained an inroad into his or her life because he or she has, made Christianity nothing more than a surface appearance, believed a lie, compromised with sin, or judged God and found Him to be a failure. It is hard for a person who may see self as being pious and wise to admit he or she failed God or was foolish enough to judge the ultimate Judge of all souls.

Lying Spirits: Lying spirits are companions to every spirit or device of Satan. Satan is the father of lies and uses lies as a means to undermine a person's faith in God.[5]

Worldliness serves as a major entrance for lying spirits because a person who is subject to the world is under Satan's domain. Relationship

---
[5] John 8:44

with the world implies that a person has divided loyalties and is operating in idolatry, which is always founded on a lie. This is why people must become single in heart in their devotion to God to close down this avenue.

Lying spirits operate in what I call half-truths. They actually bring accusations against God, His saints and even the person they operate through, that seem reasonable, logical, or plausible. But there is always one important factor missing: That of God. When we compare Satan's lies with the character and promises of God, they are reduced to sinister, clever deceits.

The enigma is that people agree with Satan's evaluation of a matter rather than testing such accusations or conclusions according to the nature, word, and promises of God. When a person receives a lie, the lie begins to undermine the individual's faith in God, thereby ebbing away the person's confidence and authority.

By attacking a person's authority, Satan knows he can render a person powerless to effectively stand and fight against any other advancement.

In my years of dealing with the destruction caused by Satan's lies in a person's life, I have discovered ten major lies that serve as a springboard for hundreds of lies. In some cases, these lies become mindsets. Following is a summary of these ten lies.

1. I am unworthy.
2. I am a failure.
3. I am unlovable.
4. I will never get anywhere in life, so why try.
5. I have gone too far away from God and can't come back.
6. I have the right to do what I am doing.
7. I will never trust anyone again.
8. I am going to protect myself from ever being hurt again.
9. I am going to keep people at bay to avoid rejection (a form of control and fear).
10. I am going to call the shots in my own life because I can't trust anyone else to get it right.

Notice how each lie is given power by a determination of the will: I am, I have, or I will. These lies actually demand the person must become God in order to control or justify the condition of his or her world. As you can see, at the core of every wrong determination is a lie of Satan, which ultimately sets the person up to act as God.

When I encounter a lie in a person's life, I remind him or her that he or she must exchange it for the truth. Our Christian abilities and failures have nothing to do with our personal uprightness but rather with God's greatness. Granted, there will always be the constant reminder that each of us falls short of the glory of God, but this does not constitute a person's crime or their failure when it comes to the kingdom of God.

The spiritual crime that is being committed on a daily basis that makes each person susceptible to Satan is not believing (or having faith) that the work done by Christ on the cross reaches beyond all of humanity's hopeless plight to bring redemption and reconciliation to each of our lives. We stand upright, sanctified, and redeemed because we are in Christ and He is in us.[6] We receive this truth by faith, allowing us to receive and partake of it in confidence and joy.

I have realized that the cross of Jesus is about man's sinful plight. The perfect Son of God was beaten by man's jealousies, spit at by man's arrogance, mocked by his fear, crowned by his anger, and nailed to the cross by his hatred. Man's best was displayed on that cross, and it revealed why every man deserves to taste the wrath of God. But praise God, His best became an exchange for us as Jesus Christ became sin in our place.[7] Yes, the cross exposes man's best (his filthy rags), but Christianity in action displays God's best—the life of Jesus being worked in us in order to be manifested through us.

Every time Satan reminds me of my failures, I refuse to stop there. I take the lie by the hand and lead it to the cross and point to it, knowing that it clearly declares that my failures or sins were nailed to that cross with Jesus. But I do not stop at the cross; I go one step beyond the cross to the reality of Jesus. I claim the words of the Apostle Paul, *"I am crucified with Christ: nevertheless I live; yet not I, but Christ liveth in me:*

---

[6] 1 Corinthians 1:30; Colossians 1:27
[7] 2 Corinthians 5:21

and the life which I now live in the flesh I live by the faith of the Son of God, who loved me, and gave himself for me."

The cross is about me, but the Christian life is about Jesus becoming a reality. It is no longer my life but His life. It is not my abilities but His power and authority. He is worthy of all praise! He is lovely and victorious. He came from heaven to earth, went by way of the cross and rose from the grave, showing that He not only finished the course, but nothing could stop Him from fulfilling the plan of redemption. That, my friend, is getting somewhere!

Jesus went into the grave and the lower parts of the earth to preach to the captives, but He came back showing that His grace serves as boundaries to sin-laden people who have a sincere desire to once again come back to the land of the living.[8]

Are you an individual who feels you have the right to do your own thing to be happy? Jesus had the right to avoid the cross, but He didn't. As Christians we do have rights, but they have to do with having the power and liberty to do what is right. Jesus gave way to something of greater value—our eternal salvation. He gave way to another authority—His Father, and because of that He was given a name above all names.[9] The greatest right is the right to submit to that which is more honorable and greater than ourselves. This is the secret of spiritual success and godly character.

You may feel you can't trust anyone, but you need to trust Jesus because He truly cares for you. Perhaps you are trying to protect yourself? Jesus never protected Himself, and as a result you and I can now have eternal and abundant life, providing us with an important principle: What you try to hold and protect you will lose, but if you are willing to offer it up, you will find it.

Are you trying to keep people at bay? You must be lonely. Jesus knew what was in the heart of man, but He continued to touch, heal, rejoice, weep, and reach out to people. He knew that as He gave away self, His life took on a greater meaning. Our life does not belong to

---

[8] 1 Peter 3:9; Romans 5:20-21
[9] Philippians 2:5-11

ourselves but to God. He intended us to pour it out upon others in order to find its real meaning and purpose.

Are you trying to call the shots to get it right? I can tell you right now you are probably creating havoc in the lives of those around you. Jesus is God Incarnate, but He never did call the shots. He did what His Father told Him, and He got it right. You and I are not even close to being God, and the idea of trying to call the shots is absurd and can be traced back to the same old lie spoken in the Garden of Eden, *"Ye shall be as gods."*

It is time to do an exchange at the cross—our depraved, wicked life for the resurrected life of Jesus. It is time for our Christian life to be about Jesus and not about how good or important we would like to think we are in the scheme of things. It is time to replace the lies of Satan with the truth and the reality of Jesus Christ. After all, it is the truth of Jesus that makes a person free.

God has provided us with the means to overcome Satan. They are not complicated, but they require a person to get past any idea of self-worth.

Let us now examine the type of atmosphere that will put Satan on the run.

Overcoming Satan

James 4:7-10 gives us three necessary responses to overcome Satan. These responses correlate with Jesus' call to his disciples to deny self, pick up the cross, and follow Him. These responses are submitting to God, resisting Satan, and humbling self so God can lift us into identification and victory with, in, and through Jesus Christ.

It is important to realize that Satan entices the old man or natural spirit in each of us with the things of the world.[10] The world is made up of lust of the flesh, lust of the eyes, and pride of life.[11]

The reason the natural man is attracted to the things of the world is because he has personal agendas or inclinations that are bent on honoring and exalting self in every area of his or her life. Personal

---

[10] James 1:14-15
[11] 1 John 2:15-17

agendas are based on the flesh, while self is honored by heaping the things a person sees or covets upon itself. As self becomes the focus in this fashion, it will be exalted as a god that will demand everything that comes into its reach (or world) to obey its every whim and need.

Let me show you how the responses found in *James 4* and Jesus' command to His disciples take care of Satan's ability to entice man into his traps of destruction and death.

Natural Spirit	World	Responses	Discipleship
Personal Agenda	Lust of flesh	Submit to God	Deny Self
Honor Self	Lust of Eyes	Resist Satan	Pick up Cross
Exalt Self	Pride of Life	Humble Self	Follow Jesus

When you consider how our personal agendas lose their power when we submit to God by denying self, you can see how Satan is unable to entice us in the area of the flesh. If we resist Satan and pick up our cross, we will change our focus, fleeing worldly attractions, thereby changing what we value and pursue. By humbling ourselves, we can come under the authority of Jesus and follow Him into the abundant life away from all the enticements that would allure us into Satan's traps. As William Law stated, "Self is the whole evil of our fallen nature, but self-denial is our capacity for being saved; humility is our savior." [12]

It would be easy to escape temptations, avoid snares, and enjoy living waters and green pastures, but many fail to put *James 4:7-10* into practical application. This failure leads to utter defeat.

With this diagram in mind, let us advance into understanding Satan's traps. In the previous chapters I have shown how Satan reinforces walls, mindsets, and wrong patterns, but we must understand the devices he

---

[12] *God's Best Secret,* by Andrew Murray, pg. 272

uses to gain access into the different territories of man's soul. Some of these devices are also referred to as *avenues*.

As each of these devices or avenues are dealt with, take the time to examine yourself to see if any of them have given Satan any inroads into your life. These Satanic means can only grow and maintain their power in darkness and ignorance; therefore, allow the light of God's Spirit to shine in your life in order to expose any such areas. You will find that the light is able to quickly alleviate them of their rights and power in your life.

A. W. Tozer summarized the whole essence of a victorious Christian life when he said, "Always and always God must be first. The gospel in its scriptural context puts the glory of God first and the salvation of man second."[13]

In our examination of our life before our Lord, let us ensure God is first, last, and in between, making Satan an ineffective foe in our life.

---

[13] *Born After Midnight*, © 1989 by Christian Publications, page 23.

Chapter Thirteen

UNBELIEF AND IDOLATRY

Satan uses many devices against Christians. These devices can be traced back to the world's systems.

As stated in the last chapter, the world is made up of three enticing and seductive human attractions. *1 John 1:16* identifies these three culprits, *"For all that is in the world, the lust of the flesh, and the lust of the eyes, and the pride of life, is not of the father, but is of the world."*

The Apostle Paul tells us in *2 Corinthians 4:4* that Satan is the real god of this enticing, seductive world. For this reason, *James 4:4* tells us that if we are friends with the world, we are an enemy of God. Jesus makes it clear that it will be natural for the world to hate His followers because it hated Him.[1]

Satan uses the three elements of the world to lure us into his traps. The greatest trap of the world is that it is able to undermine true faith. In many cases, dependency on the world subtly replaces faith, which is trust, reliance, and dependency on God. You can see this worldly dependency in many Christians.

Jesus asked in *Luke 18:8, "Nevertheless when the Son of man cometh, shall he find faith on the earth?"* Notice He didn't ask if He would find churches, religious devotion, or deeds but if He would find real faith.

Jude 3 makes it very clear that we must contend for the faith that was first delivered to us. *Hebrews 11:6* states that it is *impossible* to please God without faith. *James 2* shows that real faith always ends in obedience. *Romans 14:23* summarizes active faith in the Christian realm, *"...for whatsoever is not of faith is sin."*

Faith walks hand in hand with other godly virtues. We are justified by faith, and it is counted as true righteousness in our lives. Our hearts

---

[1] John 15:18-19

are purified by faith, while our lives are sanctified because of it. Faith's basis and growth is found in the Word of God, and its motivation is found in the love of God. There is only one real faith; therefore, it creates real unity among true believers. It serves as our shield and helps us overcome the world. It is solely directed at and in Jesus Christ, and as a result we totally live by the faith of the Son of God.[2]

Our faith is what is tested and refined as gold in the midst of trials. In fact, God gives us the measure of faith to stand and endure to the end.[3] For example, the measure of faith is often determined by the revelation of Jesus that we receive or are entrusted with before or after each battle. This is why Jesus is the author and finisher of our faith.[4] *1 Peter 1:9* summarizes the fruit of real faith, *"Receiving the end of your faith, even the salvation of your souls."*[5]

What is true faith? It declares, "God said it; I choose to believe it." Faith comes down to knowing and believing God's Word about His character.[6] This basic concept of faith helps us to understand that when Satan undermines our faith, he is simply undermining our confidence in God's true character.

Satan undermines a person's faith in God by taking him or her into extremes in this area. The first extreme plays on the ignorance of a person's understanding of God's character. Even though the Bible is clear that people need to seek out God, few do, *"For he that cometh to God must believe that he is, and that he is a rewarder of them that diligently seek him."* [7]

Most people are left on their own to define God and the Christian walk. Their conclusions can demean and limit God, leaving individuals with a factual concept instead of a living and powerful entity. The problem is that when we need to believe that God is who He is, we lack

---

[2] Ro. 4:5, 9; 3:28; 10:17; Acts 15:9; 26:18; Galatians 5:6; 2:20; Ephesians 4:13; 1 John 5:4

[3] 1 Peter 1:5-8; Romans 12:3

[4] Hebrews 12:2

[5] For more information about faith see the author's book *In Search Of Real Faith*.

[6] Hebrews 11:6

[7] Ibid

real hope to cling to the immovable rock. We are like the man in *Mark 9:24, "Lord, I believe; help thou mine unbelief."*

Real faith is not a concept conjured up with intellectual dissection and observation but is a reality based on the character of the one true God. When God is defined without proper teaching and discipling, the faith that is acquired will simply lead a person back to self and not to God. Self chooses to trust in what it can touch, feel, understand, and see. This is why the Apostle Paul stated that *"we are to walk by faith and not by sight."*[8] Jesus made this clear when He told Thomas, *"Thomas, because thou hast seen me, thou has believed: blessed are they that have not seen, and yet have believed" (John 2:29).*

What Jesus was saying to Thomas in this verse is that what you may see will help you declare a truth, but faith will take you a step further by making it a reality that allows you to discover and experience greater depths or mysteries of God. Sadly, many Christians never get past the intellectual realm into the mysteries of God. Such Christians live on the fleshly or lower plane in their spiritual lives and have menial experiences with God.

Faith is a choice while its counterpart, unbelief, is the consequence. We either choose to believe what the Word declares or we walk in skepticism. The choice of faith takes place in the will, and if we choose to reject faith in God, we will automatically place faith in self. There is nothing that limits God or undermines real faith like exaltation or emphasis of self.

This becomes obvious in times of trials or testing. People whose religious journey leads them back to self will find they lack a secure root system, which causes them to be easily toppled because there is no foundation. Spiritual failure in such an individual will create introspection. Introspection means self becomes the ruler as all of the possibilities behind such failure are examined. Fear of rejection begins to raise its head, causing an unseen vice to grip the person's mind. As self begins to loom in the form of self-preservation, the one true God becomes shrouded in confusion. This confusion causes doubts as Satan seizes the opportunity to send darts of lies and accusations

---

[8] 2 Corinthians 5:7

against God's character. As the weeds of doubt take root among the rocky soil of self, offshoots of *unbelief* begin to unveil themselves.

Unbelief is a sin that wreaks the greatest havoc in a Christian's life. The religious facade of unbelief is superstition in regards to the unseen or self-righteous judgmentalism towards that which can be seen or observed. It grows in the shadows of the deceitfulness of sin, eventually producing a hard heart that will depart from the living God.[9] We can even catch glimpses of this hard heart among Jesus' disciples because they considered the obstacles instead of Jesus' greatness and provision.[10]

Many Christians are walking in unbelief, but few will face the harsh fact that it is present and causing inconsistency in their spiritual lives. This unwillingness to face unbelief comes down to reluctance of admitting that they have error in their hearts. This error is present and undermines faith because they did not know the ways of God. In fact, the major cause of unbelief is that Christians do not know God because they have failed to properly study the Word, *"to shew themselves approved unto God" (2 Timothy 2:15).*

The sin of unbelief not only limits God from being God but it also calls Him a liar. Although unbelief keeps God from intervening, its deception keeps a person from seeing that he or she is the real hindrance to spiritual maturity. Unbelief will turn around and mock God for not performing according to the person's unrealistic standards. It is ungrateful in nature and fails to recognize the many blessings of God. It is sinister in practice because it is self-righteous, angry, unforgiving, and accusing. In short, unbelief states that God is the biggest failure in the Bible and is blasphemous in attitude, for God's Word declares, *"The just shall live by faith."*

The second destructive extreme of faith in which Christians can operate finds its source in *idolatry*.

---

[9] Hebrews 3:8-13
[10] Mark 6:50-52

Idolatry

Idolatry is hard to pinpoint in our society. Unlike during Old Testament times and the Apostle Paul's day, idolatry is not a visible reality in this present age. The pagan people had idols of gold, wood, and stone and burned incense to the things of creation. Although people in many parts of the world still practice such idolatrous and pagan practices, the idols in America are culturally accepted and promoted. These idols are unseen, but they cause obsession, fear, and worship. They enslave people into paganism and cause them to hide in the shadows of unbelief, embrace superstition over truth, and chase after illusive rainbows.

Where are these idols located? Ezekiel identifies two major locations from which these unseen idols freely reign—the heart and mind.[11] It is important to realize these idols are as sinister and wicked as the gold, wood, and stone that the hands of man have erected. The difference is that self-serving desires and vain imaginations have erected the idols of the heart and mind.

Personal agendas and *fleshly* or *worldly inclinations* represent the main idols of the heart. The heart represents idolatry in secret places; therefore, it is easy to hide such idols behind religious cloaks and masks. This allows the individual to control his or her world and play the religious game without being called to accountability.

For the mind these idols are nothing more than *arrogant opinions of self* and *expectations*. The mind points to idolatry in high places and delusion.

The problem with these different idols is that people become accustomed to them because they have been a part of the landscape of their lives for years. People erect these idols in the beginning to serve their purposes. They usually give individuals some semblance of hope and direction and bring order into their lives. They arouse people's emotions and give them boundaries and a corner on what they consider to be reality, often making them elite or special to their way of thinking.

---

[11] Ezekiel 8:9-15; 14:4

Since they have been a part of their lives for years, individuals think nothing of them. In fact, they have become constant companions.

But what many fail to realize is that instead of being harmless desires, these idols subtly become gods, causing many unknowingly to bow down to them. These idols gain control as they become entrenched in people's lives and begin to determine their reality, priorities, pursuits, and judgments. They create an exclusive world that not only exists in the imagination but also feeds speculations and desires. In the end, people even adjust their Christianity to these idols, causing a destructive mixture of carnality and truth. Sadly, this mixture will define another god and defile the one true God's will and purpose for people's lives.

Let us consider how each of these idols work. Although we have already dealt with some of them, I feel it is important to understand them in the light of idolatry, which, once again, will reveal their wickedness.

Personal agendas are nothing more than personal desires and priorities. When you get down to the bottom of these desires, they are very self-serving and motivated by pride. They become competitive with God's best for the person and will cause divided loyalties. This mixture will prompt the person to justify unpredictable (ungodly) maneuvers, resulting in the loss of personal credibility and authority.

My encounter with personal agendas has made me realize I can't trust people who insist on holding on to them. In the end such people will offer up you or your relationship with them as a sacrifice in preference for their agendas. In fact, they will betray their high calling and unknowingly reject God's will in preference for these idols.

These agendas must be brought to the light, rooted out, and replaced with God's agendas. If they are not, individuals who bow down to them will be considered infidels as they walk a path of deception and defeat.

Wrong inclinations find their origin in vain imaginations, speculations, and lies. These inclinations represent the direction one will naturally walk in his or her life regardless of goals or spiritual desires. They will ultimately taint or defile the things of God, including a person's prayer life.

In fact, wrong inclinations will rule over God's will when a person is seeking it in prayer. Even though a person is seeking God in sincere prayer, the individual will lean towards that which serves his or her inclinations. Ultimately a person's inclinations will drown out God's will and he or she will end up adhering to them.

Inclinations represent individual incentives and find their power in the determinations that have been made by the person in his or her will. Since inclinations control the person, one must test or consider them in the light of the spirit that the individual is subjected to. This is why wrong inclinations can make a seemingly good person idolatrous and pagan in nature.

Wrong inclinations will cause a person to be double-minded or unstable in all of his or her ways.[12] In the end, these inclinations will close down a Christian who has not properly dealt with them, which produces slothfulness.

Arrogant opinions come in different disguises. People who hold to such cemented opinions see themselves as wise, logical, practical, and factual. This self-serving perception allows them to naturally serve as the judge and jury of everything that crosses their path.

These tenets justify wrong attitudes and actions and are cruel and unmerciful. They delude the person to his or her wicked disposition and to the Bible's warning not to think more highly of self than one ought to.[13] People who operate according to their tenets not only have high opinions of what they think they know, but they actually lord it over others to the point that they will eventually judge that which is godly as unacceptable or evil.

These arrogant opinions operate in two different ways. The first way finds its roots in conceit. Conceit deludes people into thinking that their conclusions actually constitute godly wisdom.

Wisdom involves three aspects: knowledge, application, and experience. These three aspects give birth to truth. Failure to properly apply these three aspects of wisdom will pervert truth rather than

---

[12] James 1:8
[13] Romans 12:3; Philippians 2:3

embrace it. This is why *Proverbs 26:12* states, *"Seest thou a man wise in his own conceit? There is more hope of a fool than for him."*

People who become wise in their own conceits accumulate knowledge but fail to apply it. Since their conclusion appears so wise, they believe they have reached the pinnacle or height of their knowledge or understanding, thus experiencing a form of mental or sensual escalation. As you can see, they fail to apply the knowledge, which simply means their understanding lacks the right spirit. Since the right spirit is absent, the individual will walk in a mental delusion that blinds him or her to how foolish he or she will appear to others.

This delusion can create an "iron clad" mind. This type of mind becomes god to the person as the mind determines truth regardless of the facts. This mind runs everything through it. What does not fit or confirm its present conclusions will cause great confusion or be considered stupid and be immediately rejected. Although the person may want to be teachable, his or her mind is a closed trap that will not let anything *in* that is contrary or *out* that serves this superior intellectual god. This is why the Word instructs such people not to be wise in their own conceits.[14] "Conceits" simply means that the individual does not really possess godly wisdom but the wisdom that is earthly, sensual, and devilish.[15]

The second aspect of opinions sitting on the throne comes from a person who is devoid of the grace of God. This person considers everything in light of personal righteousness.

This type of individual lives in denial about his or her spiritual depravity. This person clearly sees the wrongs of others because his or her focus appears to be sharp, allowing the individual to rightly judge others. It is true that these people's focus is sharp, but the reason for such sharpness is not based on their intelligence or insight but on arrogant pride that sees itself as superior and above committing acts of stupidity. In fact, this sharp focus comes from the board that blindsides them to their own wickedness.

---

[14] Romans 12:16
[15] James 3:13-15

This judgmental board mentioned in *Matthew 7:1-6* makes these self-righteous, whitewashed sepulchers focus on the discrepancies of others. They have a condescending attitude that follows their nose upward as their self-righteous speculations take them into the gutters and pigpens of their own tombs of selfishness and sin. Their so-called suspicions are nothing more than jealousies and prejudices that have been clothed behind a religious smoke screen. Their Christian concern is nothing more than a sinister tolerance that displays superiority or pity.

It is from the pigpens of their own prejudices, wickedness, and depravity that they harshly judge others of the very same unacceptable ways they stand guilty of following. In fact, the more they stand guilty of a sin or discrepancy, the more unmerciful and prejudicial they become in their judgment of it in others.

Jesus knew that unless a person is regenerated, he or she can only judge from the confines of his or her self-serving pigpen. This is why He said, *"For with what judgment ye judge, ye shall be judged: and with what measure ye mete, if shall be measured to you again" (Matthew 7:2).*

I have been around these types of people. Sadly, the emphasis of religion in many churches can encourage this self-righteous prejudice and idolatry. These self-appointed judges can't understand why people do not see it their way, but the truth is they often stand out in the crowd because they are miserable and hard. The spirit behind these people is self-loathing and full of hatred. These people not only try to destroy those who refuse to live up to or bow down to their high opinions of self, but they also wound Christians in the name of Christ while driving many away from the kingdom of heaven with their sharp whips of criticism and hatred.

Expectations find their origin in our rulers (concepts, standards, images, and ideas). Many Christians who live in disillusionment about Christianity have bowed down to these idols, expecting something to happen. But when these expectations fail to materialize, they find themselves questioning the character of God. After all, they just wanted to serve God; why is He not blessing their works? Questions arise like a Phoenix out of the recesses of their mind. "Is something wrong with me? Or maybe God doesn't love me; therefore, He doesn't really want me to serve Him." The doubts begin to take root.

The problem with expectations is that they are often based on grandiose fantasies or on self-serving ideas. Granted, they may seem noble or harmless, but in reality, they are very idolatrous and sinister.

Expectations are idolatrous because people automatically bow down to them, thinking they are honorable, logical, and right. They are sinister because people expect God to bow down to them as well, ignoring and defying His sovereignty, character, and will.

Unfulfilled expectations will cause a person to operate in despair and skepticism that often produces mockery.

As you study these idols you begin to realize idolatry is nothing more than the absence of true faith. *Hebrews 4:2* states, *"For unto us was the gospel preached, as well as unto them; but the word preached did not profit them, not being mixed with faith in them that heard it."*

Obviously, in the above Scripture, there is a lot of religion and activity but without real faith. This implies there is not only a mixed spirit, a divided heart, and a wrong foundation but also another faith.

As we can see, all of the idols of the heart and mind lack genuine faith. People have put their faith in their agendas, intellect, personal righteousness, and expectations. Although they have applied religion and good works and have tacked on Jesus, they find themselves being controlled by these idols. They eventually discover that they have ended up with a mixture that is carnal in nature and opposes God in attitude and action.

God condemns wrong mixtures. In *Deuteronomy 22:10-12* God speaks of three mixtures that are unacceptable. When we bring this into the spiritual realm, we can see what constitutes mixed spirits, wrong foundation, and a divided heart. These combinations will produce and exalt a pseudo faith or belief in another god.

Let's consider both the physical and spiritual implications of the text found in *Deuteronomy 22*.

1) *Sow vineyard with diverse seeds.* This combination represents *mixed teachings* in the Christian realm. It is not unusual to see

those in spiritual leadership combine with the Word of God erroneous teachings that are not only incompatible with truth but are carnal in nature. People who sow tares with the pure Word of God ultimately defile it. They often spiritualize the natural while naturalizing the spiritual. Good examples of a few of these erroneous combinations include such teachings as "Positive Confession, Word Faith," "Replacement Theology," and "Return to our Jewish Roots Movement." If you study these teachings, you will see that they all appeal to the lust of the eyes as people determine and pursue after the kingdom that best feeds their pride and satisfies their self-righteousness and, at the same time, serves their earthly purposes and agendas. In the end, these people exalt these false teachings, popular teachers, and the pseudo faith above the one true God. Such exaltation is idolatry. The Apostle Peter made reference to these people when he categorized them as being unlearned and unstable and who wrest the Scriptures unto their own destruction.[16]

2) *Yoking an ox and ass together.* This mixture represents *mixed service*. It implies a person is serving different masters. This combination states that the person's underlying motivation is self-serving and not Christ-centered. When there is more than one master, a person will be pulled in various directions because he or she has removed self from the yoke of Christ, giving way to the dictates of another master, mainly the "old man." When the "old man" is calling the shots, the pride of life or self has taken the throne and is now ruling. It is important to point out that if God is not reigning, the person is committing the sin of idolatry. The combination of God and self will eventually cause the person to become ineffective, plowing a crooked path of destruction. In the end, the person will actually destroy his or her spiritual life.

3) *Garments of diverse sorts.* This combination represents *mixed conduct,* which speaks of an inconsistent walk. An inconsistent walk means a person is trying to combine the Spirit of God with

---

[16] 2 Peter 3:16

the works of the flesh. When you try to mix the Holy Spirit with the works of the flesh, you end up with carnality.[17] Carnality in the Christian life verifies one fact: The individual has never gotten past the milk stage.[18] This mixture simply means you have kept flesh as your god. It will take authority away from your life in Christ and render your testimony as ineffective. An ineffective testimony leaves you unable to overcome Satan.[19]

Obviously, these wrong mixtures not only find their origins in the world (the lust of the flesh, the lust of the eyes, and the pride of life) but they also find their source in idolatry, which ends up producing the fruit of unbelief.

Hebrews 4:2 states that the Gospel could not profit those who did not have the faith to receive it. This shows us that without real faith the seeds of the glorious Gospel will fall to the wayside instead of taking root in a person's life.

The problem is that once the Gospel falls to the wayside, idolatry has no opposition. Spiritual darkness will invade every area of the person's life, producing the deception of sin, a hard heart, and finally unbelief.

Idolatry and unbelief walk together hand in hand. Any time you detect unbelief, idolatry is not far away. If idolatry is obvious, you will be able to see the fruit of unbelief operating in fear, rebellion, and disobedience. Both of these devices can serve as gigantic openings to Satan to work greater bondage and destruction.

You must ask yourself whether you are walking in faith in God or operating in idolatry and unbelief. Is the Gospel real to you because your faith is genuine, or do you have a mixture of idols and doubts that will produce spiritual ruin in the end?

---

[17] See Galatians 5:15-21
[18] 1 Corinthians 3:1-4
[19] Revelation 12:11

Chapter Fourteen

WITCHCRAFT, HERESY, AND REBELLION

Obviously, one of Satan's most popular avenues into people's lives is witchcraft. When most individuals think of witchcraft, they automatically think of the occult.

Satan does use devices such as magic, astrology, tarot cards, séances, fortune telling, palm reading, and the Ouija board game to open people up to his supernatural world. Many times people innocently participate with Satan's world because they are either flippant or scoffers of his existence. Others are looking for answers to their questions about the world beyond and will turn to the occult. Nevertheless, encounters with Satan and his demons, even in small ways, open a person up to the kingdom of darkness.

Witchcraft is a serious abomination to God because not only is it Satan's avenue to gain access into people's lives and God's territory, but it also offers a supernatural substitute for God's power. It defiles and perverts the things of God, dulls spiritual hearing, and causes a person to operate in total darkness and delusion. This is why anyone who operated within this realm in the days of Israel was put to death.[1]

Witchcraft is also associated with sins that are not considered supernatural in nature, but one must remember sin can serve as an open door to the supernatural.

In *Galatians 5:19-21* we see witchcraft being considered one of the works of the flesh. Witchcraft is very appealing to the flesh. It justifies lust, feeds the ego, and gives a person a sense of power and purpose. In fact, once a person becomes caught up with the power of witchcraft

---

[1] Exodus 22:18; Deuteronomy 18:10

it is hard for him or her to renounce it. It takes integrity and a sincere love for God not to be drawn back into its tentacles.

As in the days of Israel, witchcraft remains condemned. *Galatians 5:21c* states the consequences for those who operate according to the flesh, *"...that they which do such things shall not inherit the kingdom of God."*

Sadly, there is a growing movement toward witchcraft and the occult. People crave power over their circumstances and others. This attraction often exists because the church appears to be powerless, worldly, and foolish. This appeal to the occult usually starts out in the form of innocent curiosity, but eventually its subtle power envelops a person and leads him or her into a frightening world of nightmarish proportions.

People who subject themselves to the occult basically give Satan permission to come in and do his bidding in and through their lives. Victims who have been lured into the dark realm of Satan confess that they had to decide to take back the territory in order to be set free and live a victorious life. In order for a person to take the territory back in his or her life, he or she must submit to the lordship of Christ. This action puts the person under the authority and protection of Jesus Christ.

In modern Christianity, the lordship of Jesus is surrounded in controversy and is often downplayed. In fact, there is a popular unbiblical belief that those who claim Jesus must be Lord in a Christian's life are preaching another Gospel. This belief claims that God's grace is enough to ensure heaven; therefore, man has no responsibility to work that salvation out, in, and through his life.

People who proclaim this heretical gospel do great damage to others and show their ignorance concerning God's grace and the kingdom of darkness. The truth is that someone or something reigns in a person's life. If Jesus is not reigning, then Satan is because the flesh and the world are subject to him.

In deliverance, lordship becomes a major issue. People must choose to submit to the lordship of Jesus before they can embrace His truth and be set free from Satan's influences and oppression.

It is important to point out that salvation means deliverance, and my involvement in ministry has proved to me many times that Satan does not have to relinquish any claims in a person's life if he or she remains under his domain. After all, lordship determines who is really God in a person's life.

Satan is referred to as the prince (ruler) of the air or god of this world while Jesus is referred to as the King of kings and Lord of lords.[2] When we come under the lordship or ownership of Jesus, Satan must recognize that he no longer has any claims on our lives and must let go of the territory. The Apostle Paul made this comment in *1 Corinthians 12:3: "Wherefore I give you to understand, that no man speaking by the Spirit of God calleth Jesus accursed: and that no man can say that Jesus is the Lord but by the Holy Ghost."*

Once a person submits to Jesus as Lord, he or she must renounce all involvement with anything that is of the occult. This includes heretical beliefs and practices. This is a way of giving an eviction notice to Satan and his cohorts. If Jesus is Lord, Satan must comply.

Another source that is associated with witchcraft is drugs (which can include prescription drugs as well). The word "sorcery" in *Revelation 21:8* comes from a root word meaning drugs. Drugs are mind-altering substances that open a person up to Satan's realm because the person ceases to be in control of his or her faculties. This allows Satan free access.

Revelation 9:21 states, *"Neither repented they of their murders, nor of their **sorceries,** nor of their fornication nor of their thefts."* This unrepentant attitude about using drugs is evident in America. Recently on a TV news magazine a woman was interviewed about the mind-altering drug Ecstasy. Even though this drug has been proven to be dangerous, this lady had justified her use of it and why it should be legalized in the United States. Sadly, this unrepentant, stiff-necked attitude toward drugs is prevalent and can even be found in the church.

Another word for sorceries is poison. These drugs not only poison minds and bodies but relationships as well. They destroy lives and families, leaving innocent people bankrupt and holding the pieces of sorrow and destruction. After all, there are no boundaries or limitations to the havoc drugs work in the lives of people.

---

[2] Ephesians 2:2; 2 Corinthians 4:3-4; Revelation 19:16

Revelation 18:23 says, *"...for by thy **sorceries** were all nations deceived."* Drugs deceive their victims. They dull their senses and leave them vulnerable to any predator that decides to rob, kill, or destroy them.

Drugs are not the only means of altering the mind. The New Age employs various means to alter the consciousness, such as music, demon-inspired literature, meditation techniques, mesmerizing, hypnosis, astral projection, and trances that indoctrinate and change a person's worldview. These methods and practices are not only spiritual in nature but are designed to subtly open the mind to Satan's deception and power.

The New Age

Today the world is heading towards what many consider to be a "new age" or a dawning of a new society or world order. This new age is nothing more than old lies that have been repackaged with modern scientific or religious terms. In Scripture it is known as the mystery of iniquity and will be used to fulfill prophecy as it leads the world politically, economically, and spiritually into a one-world government and religion.[3]

This New Age philosophy has many tributaries that include secret societies, cults and mind science cults, the worship of mother earth, spiritualism, Hinduism, yoga, and Buddhism. It embraces all pagan practices, spiritualizes that which is natural, and deifies man. It believes there are many ways to godhood and shows tolerance to the different beliefs of others, except fundamental Christianity and Judaism. (Note: Islam doesn't fit into either category.)

Fundamental Christianity is the one great enemy of the New Age movement. The reason for this animosity is because the New Age believes in reincarnation instead of resurrection and denies the Fall and original sin. Fundamental Christianity teaches three truths that rip at the core of the New Age. These truths are: 1) There is only one true God; 2) there is only one way to salvation or heaven; and 3) there are eternal

---

[3] 2 Thessalonians 2:3-12

consequences for those who refuse to accept God's provision of salvation.

The problem today for blood-bought saints is that a form of the New Age has successfully made inroads into the church. The version of the New Age found in the church has many names (similar to branches on a tree), but the most popular name is the Manifested Sons of God.

Amazingly, this Christian counterfeit maintains the same basic beliefs as the New Age Movement, only it is clothed in popular Christian terms and platitudes. For example, it promotes a type of repentance and holiness, but these acts replace the work of Jesus on the cross and are designed to bring man to a place of immortality.

Oswald Chambers pointed out one should never confound eternal life with immortality. The reason for this is because eternal life has to do with the quality of life and not it duration. In fact, eternal life can only be found in the Person of Jesus Christ for He is the essence of everlasting life.[4]

This New Age heresy in the church seeks its credibility through "new revelations" and "signs and wonders," not the true Gospel. It does away with national Israel and replaces it with the church as "spiritual Israel," which often brings the church under the Law and encourages the keeping of the Sabbath and the Old Testament feasts for the purpose of righteousness. This belief emphasizes a new doctrine of apostles and prophets while cleverly discarding the foundation and cornerstone, Jesus Christ.

Like its worldly counterpart, this heretical belief mocks fundamental Christianity and sees it as its greatest enemy. Both groups believe that they will usher in peace and rule the world, eliminate those who oppose them, and unveil the real Jesus. They also believe that man will be deified while humanizing God. In fact, the Manifested Sons of God (MSOG) believe God became man so man could become God. The MSOG deny the blessed hope of every Christian, that Jesus is literally coming back in bodily form as the King of kings and Lord of lords to personally set up His future kingdom.

---

[4] *101 Days in the Gospels with Oswald Chambers*, © 1992 by James Adair and Harry Verploegh, pg. 82.

Following are three main beliefs from both of these New Age philosophies. Note how they are similar.

New Age	Manifested Sons of God
1. Birth of the Christ Consciousness	1. Born again (symbolized by the Feast of Passover)
2. Release from worldly desires and influences through Eastern meditation-detaching oneself. Typified by the baptism of Jesus at Jordan	2. Baptized by the Holy Spirit and led into the wilderness for a time of testing and preparation. (Symbolized by the Feast of Pentecost.)
3. Initiation given by the Lord of the world at which point one becomes divine.	3. Unveiled to the world as a Manifested Son of God. Sonship equal to Jesus Christ. (Symbolized by the Feast of Tabernacles.)

Like its earthly counterpart, MSOG's belief has many tributaries that reach throughout the Christian church. These tributaries can be identified by some of the other names this blatant heresy goes by, such as Overcomers, Restoration, Reconstructionism, Manchild Company, Kingdom Now, Kingdom Dominion, First Fruits, Kingdom Children, the Second Reformation, and the Prosperity Doctrine.

These movements often practice witchcraft to impose their will on others through such means as visualization. Those who are part of the Manifested Sons of God (usually called "apostles" and "prophets") even curse those who dare to oppose them. The ultimate goal for both of these movements is to rid the world of "narrow-minded" fundamentalists who refuse to submit to their cause and leadership. And they will do it all in the name of God.[5]

We know the end of both of these idolatrous, antichrist philosophies. God will not tolerate such blatant opposition. *Revelation 21:8* tells us, *"But the fearful, and unbelieving, and the abominable, and murderers,*

---

[5] John 15:18-21

and whoremongers, and sorcerers, and idolaters and all liars, shall have their part in the lake which burneth with fire and brimstone: which is the second death."

Rebellion

1 Samuel 15:23 states rebellion is another form of witchcraft, *"For rebellion is as the sin of witchcraft, and stubbornness is as iniquity. Because thou hast rejected the word of the LORD, he hath also rejected thee from being king."*

This statement was made to King Saul after he failed to obey God's instruction. Rebellion is associated with the sin of witchcraft in this Scripture.

Rebellion lies at the heart of all sin and witchcraft. It is ungrateful in attitude, is stiff-necked regarding submission, and displays anger and scoffing towards humility. It is man's way of deifying self while demoting God.

At the core of witchcraft is fierce independence from God and the need to control or reign over one's life. Man embraces rebellion because he does not want to submit to God. He wants to call his own shots or, in other words, be his own god. This is the same attitude Satan had before God judged his arrogance.

Isaiah 14:13-14 summarizes this rebellious attitude, *"For thou hast said in thine heart, I will ascend into heaven."* Man is forever saying in his heart that he will ascend, subdue all obstacles, and reign as supreme ruler of his world. He also silently believes that he will be exalted in the hearts of men and women whether in his home, church, or community. He strives to sit in places of power and prestige where he will be worshipped and honored. He arrogantly plans to ascend above all opposition and in the end be like the Most High.

Satan allows man to think he reigns as a god when in reality Satan is his true lord. Man may convince himself he is calling the shots, but Satan gives him free reign, for in time he will be able to require his soul rightfully.

There is only one God by nature. *Isaiah 45:22* declares: *"Look unto me, and be ye saved, all the ends of the earth, for I am God, and there is none else."* Rebellion and witchcraft simply reject the fact there is only one God. Notice how Samuel told Saul in *1 Samuel 15:23* that his disobedient action was an outright rejection of God and as a result God would reject him.

Rebellion may arrogantly lead man to believe in the end he will win, but the Word of God is clear--rebellion, erroneous beliefs, witchcraft, and all works of darkness will end in the lake of fire.

At this time it is important to help people discern between someone who is in rebellion and someone who is being oppressed by the enemy. Rebellion fluctuates emotionally. For example, a person in rebellion will emotionally go back or forth or escalate in frustration and anger. When a person is demonically oppressed, however, it is like hitting an immovable wall. They are unable to hear or receive in order to respond. If you hit a wall, you need to take authority over Satan. If you encounter rebellion, strive to gently bring instruction or rebuke to the individual.

There are times when you might encounter both rebellion and demonic oppression. Usually, people who are in this state have no intention of repenting. They have made up their minds to maintain their rights, and as a result, Satan is alive and present on the scene. The best you can do is use the sharp sword of truth in the hope that it might penetrate the rebellion and the oppression to bring a reality check to the individual.

It takes a lot of integrity on a person's part to subdue personal rebellion. It is a lifelong battle that only gets easier as a person submits to God and obeys His Word.

This submission first requires man to agree with God's evaluation of his spiritual condition, disposition, and actions. This form of submission involves the intellect and requires self-denial, which will produce brokenness, meekness, humility, and sobriety.

The second stage is for man to submit his will to God. This type of submission is a form of crucifixion because it requires mortifying self in order to allow the will of man to come into line with God's will. Once the will has been submitted, then the individual must take the initiative to follow Jesus as Lord. This involves commitment, which includes the emotions or senses coming under the control of the Spirit.

The problem with undisciplined emotions (or senses) is that they can subtly replace God's truth. In fact, the senses become the ultimate authority as to what is righteous or acceptable. This is why all emotions must come under the control of the Spirit of God to rightfully discern truth.

But before our emotions can come under the control of the Holy Spirit, we have to deny self and apply the cross. As we put self down and give way to God, we will be free to follow Jesus. It is as we follow Jesus that our emotions or senses begin to take on His likeness. This likeness is not a simple imitation of Jesus but an actual reflection of His mind and heart. It is the reality of Jesus manifesting itself in and through our lives.

This manifestation is like becoming an unveiled mirror or an unhindered light that reflects the awesome majesty of the Son of God. This reflection can't be ignored, denied, or subdued. It is the reflection that calls all men who reject God liars and brings conviction to those who hide in the darkness and shadows of sin.

This is why Jesus said: *"If any man will come after me, let him deny himself, and take up his cross, and follow me" (Matthew 16:24).* If a person fails to adhere to these three steps, he or she is in danger of not finishing the course.

Christianity is a race, but it is not enough to just start the race; a person must cross the finish line to receive the prize. Jesus is the only one who knows the course and can lead an individual to the finish line. This is why John gave this instruction in *1 John 2:6: "He that saith he abideth in him ought himself also to walk, even as he walked."*

The question one must ask is, does Satan have any right to my life through witchcraft, heresy, or rebellion? If you find the answer is yes, it is time to renounce all of Satan's claims and works, deny self, repent, apply the cross, and submit to the Lordship of Jesus Christ. After Satan flees, be sure to maintain your freedom in Christ by following and obeying Him. After all, life in Christ is a life of great joy, revival, and liberty.

Jesus said it best in *John 8:36, "If the Son therefore shall make you free, ye shall be free indeed."*

Chapter Fifteen

SELF-CENTEREDNESS

As I consider the days in which we live, I realize this book would have never been written except that the atmosphere of the church demands it. As never before, people, including Christians, are on an endless search for something or someone. And when you ask them what they are searching for, they sadly admit they are searching for identity and purpose.

This is an especially sad commentary on the Christian life. How can a life that promises fulfillment and substance leave its people searching and empty? It is almost as if Christianity is a failure because it appears to leave its people lost and prey to every wind of doctrine and error that comes along.

Does the problem lie with Christianity or those who lay claims to it? Are the people really empty? The answer is simple: The people are not empty, but rather they are full of empty things that have no merit. This state makes them unable to receive those things that would add substance and meaning.

In the previous chapters I have been discussing such subjects as unbelief, idolatry, and rebellion, but we must ask what lies at the core of these sinful actions. At the core of these destructive fruits is something called selfishness.

Selfishness is what consumes the fallen man but leaves him empty and miserable. It invades every area of his soul, perception, and ways. It chases after the world and is inclined to pursue every fleshly lust. The culture we live in appeals to it in every facet of life, but sadly so does much of the church.

Such concepts as self-esteem are being presented to Christians as a solution for the rebellion, fear, and destruction that is wreaking havoc in the home and among the body of believers. But selfism or the promotion of self at any point is nothing but self-realization.

Oswald Chambers made this statement about self-realization, "The more you realize yourself the less will you seek God." He goes on to explain that self-realization causes one to enthrone work rather than enthroning Jesus Christ in His work."[1]

The concept of self goes back to the humanistic religion that was designed to replace God with man. This religion is clothed in the philosophies of the world, which effectively promote all of the selfisms of the "me generation."

The idea of promoting a worldly, humanistic philosophy and religion in the church is bad enough, but sadly many are buying into this worldly concept that is not only creating the atmosphere for greater rebellion but is bringing destruction to the home as well.

Any teaching that promotes self is contrary to the Word of God, for Jesus clearly taught His followers to deny self. This denial is necessary because when self is exalted in any way, it simply means self is being deified and God will be put on the back shelf to consider, control, and blame when circumstances present themselves accordingly.

This deification of self is nothing more than another form of idolatry. All idolatry is inspired or enhanced by Satan's kingdom. This type of idolatry simply means self is reigning, implying the natural spirit (old man) is in operation and giving way to Satan's enticement and bidding.

Selfishness or self-centeredness is nothing more than unbridled introspection. Introspection causes darkness, perverted reality, and insanity. It is plagued by every type of sin, deluded by all forms of justification, and driven mad by insecurities and fear. Therefore, it is important to understand the traits of self-centeredness to ensure that we are not caught within the bondage of its world.

First of all, self-centeredness is motivated by pride. Oswald Chambers said this about pride: "Pride in its most estimable as well as its most debased form is self-deification; it is not yielding to temptation

---

[1] *My Utmost For His Highest*, June 10 and July 11 devotions.

without, but a distinct alteration of relationships within."² And at the core of pride are *personal rights.*

Being A Claim Jumper

I have agonized with the secret of Christians walking in victory. After years of struggling with this issue, I realize that most battles are fought and won or lost at the point of personal rights.

Rights often determine what constitutes love, acceptance, recognition, and happiness for individuals. And because of these rights, people believe that they deserve the best from life.

To deny self means to deny my right to self. But the problem is many Christians are claim jumpers at the expense of God's grace when it comes to rights in the kingdom of God. They actually claim rights that are not godly or scriptural while hiding behind God's grace. As a result, grace has become a cheap commodity that is treated as a doctrine and serves as a point of great spiritual discussion. It is greatly misunderstood, used, and abused in the midst of all the religious platitudes.

The reason few understand grace is because most fail to come to terms with the fact that they are in a fallen condition. People want to believe there is something good in them that allots them personal rights. Rights imply you deserve certain treatment or recognition because you have earned them.

These rights set people up to be offended. Offense is a significant snare of Satan because it looks justifiable but is often motivated by jealousies, anger, hatred, and unforgiveness. It often seeks vengeance, sows seeds of discord, and expresses itself in self-pity and an unteachable spirit. It serves as the judgmental board in the person's eye and will either come out on top as being right or become a victim, but it will always refuse to be accountable.

People who glory in their rights have a high opinion of self that causes them to be angry, especially at God when He fails to adhere to

---

² *Still Higher For His Highest*, July 22 devotion.

their conjured-up rights. This anger gives place to the devil as they begin to judge God and think Him to be cruel and unfair.

If people came to terms with the fact there is no real good thing in them, they would have to face the harsh reality that everyone born into Adam's race deserves hell. Therefore, if man deserves hell, what rights does he have to expect anything of value or substance from this life? **None**!

This is where the grace of God enters. Until people realize they are sinners who deserve ruin and destruction in this present life, they can't rightfully or humbly embrace His grace. Grace can only be applied when individuals recognize they deserve nothing except judgment and cling to His cross in need and desperation.

Personal rights are nothing more than man's free will to do his own thing according to his whims and desires. Whenever people reserve the right to determine the essence of the reality of their lives, they are insisting on reigning or sitting on the throne as God.

Submission to rights simply means you are submitting to the "old man," which subjects you to the game rules of the god of this world, Satan. In fact, anywhere a person holds on to or maintains these rights, rebellion and bondage will be found in that individual's life.

Holding on to rights is natural for each of us but ultimately erects another God and brings disillusionment and unbelief.

It must be pointed out that God gave us a free agency, allowing us the right to choose Him and the ability to submit to Him. Abusing such basic rights means people will eventually lose them.

Another characteristic of self-centeredness is *bigotry*. Selfishness constitutes a small world. In fact, where self reigns, a destructive and self-sufficient disposition exists that works within its own personal prejudices. There are four dispositions that can be seen among people. It is important to recognize each disposition because they not only determine what a person will accept in his or her world but how that individual will respond to truth.

The Beast Within

Jesus relates people's disposition to four different animals. These dispositions do not become distinguishable until Jesus' call to follow Him goes out to the people. This call will go out whenever truth is preached in power and authority.

The first people to respond are those who have the disposition of a *wolf*. Jesus made two references to this beast, in *Matthew 7:15* and *Luke 10:3*.

A wolf is a survivor or predator at heart; therefore, all actions are self-serving. This animal looks for helpless creatures or will patiently wear down healthy animals to tear, kill, and destroy.

Throughout my Christian years, I have encountered various people among God's saints who embody the viciousness of a wolf's selfish disposition. This sinister disposition knows no boundaries when it comes to personal survival. It is determined to live no matter how many lives it disrupts or ruins.

When the shepherd turns his or her back, people with this disposition begin to make aggressive advancements among the innocent. They look for helpless people to use, abuse, and devour for their own religious agendas. They are usually either working towards leadership or are in a leadership position. In fact, the most popular position for a wolf in sheep's clothing to hide his or her real intentions is the music department. I can't tell you how many wolves I have encountered that make a grandstand by leading worship. There is something about music and worship that becomes an excellent avenue on which to make inroads into innocent people's lives.[3]

The problem today is that many wolves no longer need to wear sheep's clothing to find free access to God's people. The church has become so worldly and fleshly that it seems to embrace anyone who can give enough money, fill a needed position, or entertain the crowd.

If there is a wolf among you, responsible leaders need to take the sword, the Word of God, to this predator. If the individual will not repent,

---

[3] This attraction could have something to do with Ezekiel 28:14-19.

these leaders need to protect the rest of God's people by warning them of this person and instructing them to flee from the individual's presence.

If you are part of a body where a wolf is in leadership, you must go to responsible leaders and state your concern. If the leadership fails to contend with the wolf, you need to personally flee from the "jaws" or influence of this person and find refuge elsewhere.

The next group that will become distinguished is the *swine*.[4] People with this disposition embody the slothfulness and complacency that is often found in selfishness. Their world of selfishness is very limited, perverted, and unrealistic. It can be best described as a cesspool or a pigpen.

This particular disposition of selfishness refuses to adjust to anything unless it serves its purpose. It will embrace everything, the good with the bad, and call it reality. The only time people of this group get excited is when you challenge their perverted, narrow reality with uncompromised truth.

When Jesus was dealing with people who clung to their cesspools of self, He basically told His followers to leave such people in their pigpens and follow Him. The problem the followers of Jesus have with those in the pigpens is that there is an enticement to get into these cesspools to try to save these drowning people from themselves.

Jesus assured His followers that the only thing that can happen in the pigpen is that the servant of God will become defiled and wounded, and the pure things of God he or she possesses will be trampled under with blatant disregard.

These small, narrow pigpens are full of every type of selfism known to man, for they represent the occupants' perceptions, which are arrogantly maintained and quick to display bigotry. The reason prejudices exist is because these swine test everything according to their self-centered pigpens.

The third group to be distinguished in the realm of selfishness is the *goats*. Goats are interesting animals to observe, and their similarities to a disposition in people reveal another side of selfishness.

---

[4] Matthew 7:6

People who have this disposition are able to fit in nicely among God's people, but they have one quality that sets them apart from those who follow Jesus: They mingle instead of follow. They may talk the talk but ultimately fail to walk the walk that sets God's people apart.

These people mingle in and out because they are easily sidetracked from the path. Like goats, these people may pursue anything that is desirable to the eyes and comfortable to their religious ears. Sadly, they end up remaining on the outside of the fringes of God's best, wandering around the camp of God but never becoming totally identified with Jesus.

The only time you realize that a person may fit in this category is when you challenge the individual to come all the way into the camp. That is when this person's selfish disposition raises up in the form of independence. This is made more obvious when the person opens his or her mouth with, *"Buuuuuut."* Eventually you realize that this person wants to determine what he or she receives and on what terms. In other words, this person does not want to pay the price to know God by coming under Jesus' lordship.

You also recognize that this person believes he or she can arrive at the same conclusion and destination without going the way of the cross and becoming totally identified with Jesus. This individual will always take the religious path of least resistance to get to some so-called religious pinnacle to avoid any inconvenience. In the end, such an individual will be separated from God's followers.[5]

As you compare these three dispositions, you will realize each disposition is protecting the essence of self in some way. For example, the aggressive wolf is bent on protecting the idea of its well-being while the swine becomes committed to protect its world. The goat becomes defiant as it guards its independence.

As you can see, the way a person responds to Jesus is determined by the depth of a person's selfishness. This is why the beast or the selfishness within a person's fallen nature must be killed: so that a new disposition can be resurrected within him or her.

---

[5] Matthew 25:33; Zechariah 10:3

The only disposition that is acceptable is not that of a self-sufficient beast but of a meek animal known as a sheep.[6]

Each of the first three animals displays survival instincts, self-sufficiency, intelligence, and personal strength. Their dispositions state that they do not need God; therefore, they can determine their lives on their own terms. Although they do not out rightly reject God, they will not allow Him to reign.

A sheep, on the other hand, is considered a stupid animal. It needs a shepherd to survive, for it is prey to every predator. As a result, it is subjected to every enemy and element, and without intervention it will be destroyed. This is why sheep know the voice of their shepherd--because they are totally dependent upon his leadership and protection.

What is your disposition? Are you like the wolf who watches out for number one or a pig that adjusts everything to his pigpen? Maybe you are a goat that is avoiding total identification with Jesus for a small pinnacle of independence and biased truth that has no power to change or save.

If your disposition is wrong, know that God is in the business of changing dispositions. Repent of your selfish disposition and deny or neglect its demands while killing its control and importance in your life on the cross. Do not be mistaken; there must be death to self to develop the disposition of a sheep and truly become subject to the Good Shepherd who gave His life for those who belong to Him.

Self-Expression

Selfishness hides behind many disguises and excuses. One of the disguises that selfishness stands behind is individuality. Individuality is nothing more than self-expression.

There is a distinction between individuality and personality. Individuality is an expression of the "old man" in us while personality is what God wants to regenerate and sanctify so that our life can serve as an expression of His Son. With these two aspects in mind, we can see

---

[6] John 10

where one represents rebellion and the other one represents our unseen potential to become the express image of Jesus.

It is not unusual to see young people clamoring for the right to express themselves without rules and responsibilities. I have even seen young people go to the extremes in dress supposedly to express themselves. This extreme is not an expression of self but of rebellion or hurt that often seeks attention or reaction. Sadly, most of these young rebels are lost and are trying to find themselves in their mode of dress. What a useless and disappointing search that must be for them.

We can see this same self-expression being promoted among many of the young people in Christianity who are trying to express themselves visibly through their dress. For example, I heard of a young man that was upset with his church because it would not allow him to minister due to his manner of dress. He declared if the church could not accept him as he was then he would forget about serving under its auspices. You could tell he was hurt and felt rejected because the leadership of his church would not accept him on his terms.

First of all, I can see the point of view of both this young man and his church. I believe the church has a tendency to be more caught up with presenting a false image rather than the person of Jesus Christ. But on the other hand, the young man's unwillingness to comply with his church's desires not only showed a great deal of immaturity on his part but also an unwillingness to submit over a matter that was very self-centered and not Christ-motivated. This unwillingness to submit is nothing more than rebellion and arrogance.

This arrogant attitude is expressing itself in various ways in Christendom. Many people want the right to serve God on their terms without any accountability for the way they present themselves. They become resentful and hurt when their church or organization refuses to let them represent it, or Christ, in a way that is unacceptable. After all, people must be drawn, not repelled, by what they see.

Apparently, this young man felt he needed to have the liberty to let his individuality hang out to be an effective minister. The real truth is that his individuality needed to be crucified so that through a meek attitude

Jesus could be expressed and lifted up and people would be attracted to Him alone.

This brings us to the main reason that ministers are ineffective--they are expressing themselves rather than serving as an expression of Jesus. This expression of the "old man" states that self has something of importance to offer outside of Jesus. A.B. Simpson stated, "A spirit of self-importance is fatal to all work for Christ. The biggest enemy of true spiritual power is spiritual self-consciousness."[7]

Because of self-importance and self-consciousness in ministry, many ministers have brought Jesus down from the glories of heaven and dressed him up in the latest clothes. Any time you demean the holy character of Christ, you end up presenting another Jesus that is often very worldly and can look like anyone ranging from a CEO to some heavily tattooed hard rocker.

This brings us to another subject, that of evangelism. There is a concept that we need to become identified with those we are evangelizing. I have watched people mark their bodies, color their hair, and wear the particular rags to become identified with their target.

I usually ask myself if this is really necessary. After all, I have effectively ministered to former drug addicts, and I have never taken drugs.

The Apostle Paul talked about becoming all things to all men, but he never mentioned becoming identified with people in their dress, peculiar worlds, or actions. I believe any good minister will always find common ground with people they are working with, but identification is another issue.

The Word of God is clear that there is only one Person we must become identified with, and His name is Jesus. I believe that what hurting people are looking for is love and compassion, not worldly identification. I know that I don't have to be like a person to show benevolence and genuine concern for his or her state. I also know that people are attracted to what is real and not put on. My goal as I express real love is that the person drawn towards it will be able to identify Jesus

---

[7] *Days Of Heaven On Earth,* July 29 devotion.

in me. This is the identification that should be distinct and obvious in every Christian's life.

People need to see the real, resurrected Jesus that went by way of the cross as a sacrificial Lamb but who now sits in glory on the right side of the Father.

As true ministers we need to remember that Jesus never expressed Himself. For example, He was the visible expression of the Father as He walked this earth, and while He was on the cross He was the visible expression of our sin.[8] He became sin for us, and if there is any doubt as to what our individuality looks like, just look at the cross of Christ. If you care to see the real revelation of your identity you will not want to maintain it, but rather you will want to leave it nailed on the cross.

This is why *Romans 12:1-2* instructs us to present our bodies as a living sacrifice so that our minds will be transformed, not according to the world, but according to the Spirit of the Living God. It is important to point out that individuality is tied into the world's identity, not our Lord's character. If a Christian is regenerated, individuality will never be an issue but a far-distant memory of vanity in action.

The problem with self-centeredness is that it leads to a total obsession with self. This obsession can erect destructive mindsets and cause endless pursuits that lead to emptiness and torment. As a result, the pursuit of selfishness results in endless cycles that become swallowed up by a vacuum of nothingness.

Are you being swallowed up in the vacuum of selfishness?

---

[8] John 14:9; 2 Corinthians 5:21

Chapter Sixteen
IN PURSUIT OF NIRVANA

When Adam disobeyed, the curse of struggle, toil, and death came upon all mankind and creation; therefore, the main pursuit of the fallen creation became survival. Although this struggle is natural, it often leads those with a living soul (people) into a state of emptiness, of hopelessness, and of being lost.

The concept of survival is humanistic in nature (that the fittest will survive) and pagan in practice (surviving regardless of who or what is sacrificed). Therefore, the pursuit of survival can justify compromise, unholy alliances, and sin. It can be hypocritical in action as it judges infractions in others but refuses to recognize or take accountability for personal actions.

This survival mode can be clearly observed in a disposition referred to as the street mentality. A street mentality can be seen in a person who has given way to perversion in his or her life. This perversion can be associated with ironclad determinations, rights, abuse, and immorality that will translate into an insatiable appetite to have attention or be adored as God.

We also see this mentality among people who have been heavily involved with drugs (including alcoholism), promiscuity, hard core pornography, and crime. This mindset can be very hard to deal with even in Christians because it refuses to operate in reality and personal accountability.

This mentality's consuming focus is to survive no matter what the person has to do. The goal to survive gives the individual rights to do whatever it takes regardless of how wicked and dishonest it is. After all, the person must survive; therefore, he or she has the right to con, flatter, steal, prostitute one self, or sacrifice others to live. This mentality is actually the combination of all three of the selfish dispositions put together into one mindset. For example, these people have survival actions of a wolf, a disposition of a swine, and the practices of a goat. In fact, this mentality represents selfishness at its height, and each of us would do well to understand that it is a blatant, visible expression of selfishness (rebellion) in operation. In fact, every evil fruit of selfishness can be observed in this type of individual.

The amazing thing about people with this mentality is that they have very high standards but they only apply them to the other guy. In fact, this mentality serves as the judgmental board in these people's eyes. They use this board to harshly judge others, but they fail to turn it on themselves because they must and will survive.

Another reason people with a street mentality fail to connect reality with personal actions is because they have seared some of their conscience in order to live with past and/or present wicked lifestyles. Even though they chalk their wicked actions up to a matter of survival, their iniquity remains a matter of justifiable sins for which they have failed to take full accountability for and repented of. Because their slates remain stained with the darkness of iniquity from this mindset (and not properly covered by the blood of Jesus through repentance), they remain indifferent and unrealistic to personal actions.

Since these people refuse to take responsibility for personal actions, character or integrity is never developed in them. When people are devoid of character, they fail to learn valuable lessons of life, thereby never really growing up or maturing emotionally, mentally, and spiritually.

Although these people can come across as self-sufficient and tough or hard on the outside, they are quite needy and insecure. They desire to have close relationships but show real gaps in their ability to interact with people on a healthy basis because they refuse to be vulnerable or submissive. In fact, they want to be gods in the world of others in order to protect self and ensure their personal survival.

Their need to be a god causes them to display perverted or unnatural attractions or expectations towards relationships. This unhealthy attraction can be seen in their relationships, but they refuse to give these expectations up to deal in reality. These expectations are a big part of the mindset because they make up an insatiable need that often demands to be satisfied at all costs. In the end they become unbearable burdens to others as they end up sucking the life out of those trying to help them and smothering close relationships with fear and insecurities. These expectations also serve as fantasies that they feel should be fulfilled because they have been victimized all their lives and now deserve the best that life has to offer.

They hide this fear, insecurity, and inability in relationships with cloaks, angles, games, and means of control and manipulation. They actually set themselves up for failure in any relationship because they only present images (surface), play games as a means to control emotions, con to get their way, and display self-pity, aggression, or anger whenever confronted or called to accountability.

These people make it hard for others to help them because they often believe that acts of kindness are not a matter of grace or sacrifice but something they rightfully deserve. Because of this need to survive, they will always take a mile rather than respect the inch that was allotted to them. Depending on how needy or desperate they are in their survival mode, they can go as far as trying to invade every area of your life. We have been around people with this mentality who laid claims to our home, life, activities, and mind.

It is always interesting to confront these people. Although they might admit that they did wrong, they will always add, "Buuuuuut." If you can get these individuals past their arguments, debates, and excuses to face their pathetic pigpens, you usually encounter tears of worldly remorse or self-pity.[1]

It is important to point out self-pity may confess spiritual devotion but falls short of taking personal accountability. In a sense, it can serve as a form of fake humility that admits wrong but has rights because the individual is simply a victim and not the instigator of the situation.

Oswald Chambers said this about self-pity, "No sin is worse than the sin of self-pity, because it obliterates God and puts self-interest upon the throne." He states that self-pity spits out murmurings as the people

---

[1] 2 Corinthians 7:10

become craving spiritual sponges that are devoid of anything that is lovely or generous.[2]

If you manage to get past these people's facades and "buts," you discover individuals who refuse to submit to any authority. Many of the games they devise are just their way of getting around authority without paying the consequences. Once you catch on to the game and call them to accountability, they resort to the victim syndrome or the pity party because they were trying to do what you asked even though it was on their terms.

As you can see, these people's rebellion is cleverly disguised. It is cunning (to survive) and slothful (to avoid doing right) as well as fearful, pathetic, and aggressive.

This rebellious mentality ultimately refuses to submit to anything without a fight even if it would best serve the person's purpose to do so. It will be in control; therefore, it will not give up its miserable, perverted, comfortable, little pigpens to embrace obedience, purity, and life.

Another fruit of this mentality is turmoil. In fact, these individuals love to create a crisis because it gives them the platform to come out on top in some way. For example, they either come out as the good guy who solves the problem with their actions or wisdom or the victim who has been misunderstood. After enough encounters with this mentality, not only do you begin to see a pattern in these people's crises, but you also realize the crisis is nothing more than their attempt to receive attention.

These people have no peace in their lives. They flutter around like some wounded bird that is too fearful to land because it would make them vulnerable. You can see this in their spiritual lives as well because they play the same games with God as they do in every relationship. The games eventually become obvious.

They may wear cloaks of righteousness, talk the talk and try to show super spirituality, but they have no real peace with God. They are very needy but will fight against God, making them poor and vulnerable in spirit. They need to be set free, but they fail to see the error of their ways. They want to land to experience healing but refuse to submit to true authority. They need to rest but will not take responsibility and

---

[2] *My Utmost for His Highest*, Oswald Chambers, May 16 devotional.

repent. They are weary of the essence of their lives but thrive on conflict. They desire to know peace but refuse to neglect their rights, exchange their expectations with reality, deem their fantasies as delusional, tear down the altars that represent their self-serving games, crucify their insipid self-pity, and out-rightly kill their selfishness or mentality. After all, the bottom line for these people is survival, not denial, crucifixion, and death![3] Consider the following chart.

Open Doors	Spirits	Outward Manifestations
Survival—I must survive	Slothful	Complacency—Self-Pity
Wrong Foundation—Self	Religious	Form of Righteousness
Perversion	Self-Righteous	Judgmental Board
Prefer fantasy over truth	Pride	No humility—Submission
Will not be vulnerable	Fear	Driven or paralyzed

The next question is, how can you help someone with this mentality? At best you can challenge them with the truth, but unless they are ready to face the wretchedness of their mentality, accept reality, and take responsibility for personal actions, they continue to play the game of survival no matter where they are.

I have watched these people defile and ruin everything in their lives and continue to play the same wretched game while blaming the destructive consequences on others and becoming angry with God.

This brings us to another subject that is greatly intertwined with this mentality and the idolatry of selfishness, and that is the right to be happy.

---

[3] For review purposes read chapter 10 to refresh yourself about what it takes to deal with the bottom line in a person's life.

In Pursuit of the Illusive God of Happiness

We have already considered personal agendas, but it is important to realize that they find their origin in selfishness. If you can get past the various stages of selfishness, you will discover that personal agendas are based on what an individual deems as happiness. Therefore, pursuit of personal agendas usually means the pursuit for personal happiness, and our culture and expectations often define this pursuit.

The Word of God talks about happiness, but the problem is that the church has become so worldly that many Christians have bought a cultural or worldly concept of happiness rather than a godly perspective.

This worldly perspective of happiness has caused many Christians to look to the world for their happiness. They believe that happiness can be found in relationships, pleasures, and material things. In fact, they equate holiness with material things, joy with worldly pleasures, importance with worldly relationships, purpose with worldly success, and contentment with sensual happiness.

In a sense, happiness in this text subtly becomes the god that replaces people's relationship with God, causing these individuals to become the visible expression of worldly vanity and foolishness. Since happiness is now god, they have a right to pursue this god regardless of the compromise or consequences that it entails.

I can't tell you how many Christians refuse to repent of sinful actions because in their mind the sin represented personal happiness. And as logic would have it, since God wants his children happy, He will certainly understand such actions.

This is a big problem with rights, fantasy, selfishness, and happiness: People actually end up erecting a god that fits their personal criteria. With this personal god, they can live in delusional bliss and ignorance. Of course, this god is not the one who will judge them in the end, but meanwhile they can enjoy their worldly pursuits and sin without feeling too guilty.

I remember one Christian who had been involved in fornication in order to pursue happiness. She had received a sexually transmitted disease in the process. Needless to say, this woman was quite upset and embarrassed. As she was trying to reason it away, I rebuked her and reminded her that it was the consequence of fornication.

The problem with the god of happiness is that this type of happiness is illusive and is often based on fantasy. Amazingly, people imagine happiness to be a utopia where everything revolves around them. For example, their spouse madly loves them, their children are well behaved, and their home is a beautiful sanctuary where there is blessed peace and happiness. If they manage to walk in this scenario at all, they quickly realize this type of happiness is fleeting and temporary and nothing more than a fairytale that leaves people disillusioned. This hard reality has caused tremendous anger and dissatisfaction in many Christians' lives.

This pursuit is passed down to each generation. As people pursue happiness in a worldly manner, the next generation becomes more "me oriented." Because of this unrealistic emphasis, young people are beginning to equate everything in the world as being here for their pleasure and enjoyment. They do not understand that all things require some kind of investment and sacrifice. As a result, I have watched each generation become more slothful in work habits, resentful of responsibility, and irresponsible with the things that have been entrusted to them.

Sadly, some Christian parents are instilling this philosophy in their children. Even though they may preach against association with the world, their personal relationship with the world often tells their children that everything of value and importance comes from the world. In fact, the parents' relationship with the world is basically training up the child in the ways of the world rather than the ways of God. This type of Christianity states, "As a Christian you can have the world too, as long as you remember to tack Jesus onto your life occasionally."

Words without proper examples become hypocritical to a young person who is already being attracted to the world by the other influences around him or her. Since the young person is inclined towards the world, he or she will naturally go the ways of the world. This evil association will give temporary happiness or pleasure to them but will leave them empty and miserable inside.

As I watch the worldly pursuit of Christians, I ask myself, "When are God's people going to agree with Him about such matters involving the world?"[4] As I ponder this question, I often wonder how many of our young people are being offered up to the god of happiness because of their parents' example.

Some Christians take the right to happiness in another direction. They act as if being good in most areas or doing good things allows people to break other rules that are not that important.

Let me state there is nothing good in us outside of Jesus Christ. We have no reality, identity, inheritance, godly personality, joy, peace, happiness, or life outside of the reality of Jesus.

The Bible is clear about where people's real happiness can be found, *"...yea, happy is that people, whose God is the LORD" (Psalm 144:15).*

When you study the Beatitudes in *Matthew 5:3-12*, which summarizes the essence of a happy life, you find out it is not about me, myself, and I but about having the right attitude towards the matters of life that produces the reality of Jesus.

When you consider the different aspects of selfishness, you can see why people end up empty, angry, and hopeless. For them to fulfill every desire and whim selfishness erects—whether it is recognition of individuality, getting others to bow down to a street mentality, or finding happiness in this world—they must become god.

The attempt to be god is plagued by tormenting insecurities. These insecurities exist because self is limited in its abilities to control or change circumstances. As this reality torments an individual who is caught up with the idolatry of selfishness, the more controlling and desperate a person becomes.

This brings us to another area of selfishness—that of fear.

---

[4] James 4:4

Rayola Kelley

The Fear Factor

Control issues produce tremendous fear. In fact, fear becomes a spirit that influences people, including Christians. This spirit plays on self-centeredness like a professional tap dancer does on a floor. It creates incredible havoc.

This spirit has been known to grip minds, causing bouts of confusion, depression, and even fanaticism. It has been known to sit on the chests of people and cause them to feel like they are having a heart attack or can't breathe.

A spirit of fear simply works from personal fears of powerlessness. It will either drive a person to destruction or paralyze the individual, preventing him or her from reaching out and up for help.

For example, I was contending with a woman who had been in great sin. She had to confront some of her past life in order to move on. I was trying to help her, but in the process a spirit of fear gripped her. Before I knew it, she was on the floor in a fetal position. She could not hear, perceive, or react. I realize this is an extreme example, but I have watched a spirit of fear literally shake people out of their shoes or put them in a state of limbo.

In another incident, a particular man was trying to sell an investment. As time went by he began to imagine that he would not be able to get rid of this albatross. He became anxious, and speculation started to run wild. Eventually, all he could envision was the worst scenario possible. One day he received an offer that was way below market value. Out of fear he impulsively accepted it. Later another offer was made that would have been sufficient. Because of fear, this man accepted the counterfeit that Satan sent in and was robbed in the process. Impulsiveness of this nature not only reacts out of fear, but it often puts God to a foolish test as well.[5]

Fear also has its disguises. One of its best disguises is fake nobility. For example, people who are fearful refuse to confront serious problems. They have reasons such as not wanting to hurt feelings or

---

[5] Matthew 4:7

cause undue stress in a situation. In reality, what they are saying is "I am afraid of the consequences; therefore, I will present myself as compassionate, kind, longsuffering, loving, and tolerant." This logic can give anyone a false sense of his or her nobility, but the bottom line is that the individual refuses to confront because he or she is watching out for number one. As you can also see, fear is also quite selfish.

2 Timothy 1:7 states, *"For God hath not given us the spirit of fear; but of power, and of love and of a sound mind."* This Scripture shows us the three areas a spirit of fear attacks in our spiritual lives.

First of all, it attacks our faith. Our faith in God has the power to move mountains, but fear produces doubt and unbelief towards the character of God.[6] It undermines faith by causing a person to take his or her eyes off of God and put them on the situation.

Crises are always going to be bigger and hopeless from fear's perspective. This perspective paralyzes a person mentally and spiritually. This is why *Hebrews 12:3* tells us the greatest type of fainting takes place in the mind: Once the mind has lost sight of Almighty God, it will be consumed by fear.

The second area this spirit attacks is God's love. A spirit of fear always causes its victims to doubt God's love and commitment to them. *1 John 4:18* says, *"There is no fear in love; but perfect love casteth out fear: because fear hath torment. He that feareth is not made perfect in love."*

People's limitations and insecurities cause them to have a fear of failure, rejection, incompetence, or loss of control. Since fear is motivated by pride, a person can't afford to be wrong, refuted, or considered inferior.

This brings us back to the rulers of pride (concepts, standards, images, or ideas). They ultimately condemn the one operating under this oppression because the person can't live up to his or her rulers. This condemnation produces hopelessness.

It is hard for people operating in fear to believe God wants to forgive, exalt, and restore them. They already feel the bitterness of personal failure, the sting of rejection, the condemnation of incompetence, and

---

[6] Matthew 17:20

doom because they have lost control. But *1 Peter 4:8* gives us this insight about God's unconditional love, *"And above all things have fervent charity among yourselves: for charity shall cover the multitude of sins."*

God's love covered sins with the blood of Jesus. As *1 John 1:9* says, *"If we confess our sins, he is faithful and just to forgive us our sins, and to cleanse us from all unrighteousness."*

In order to receive this forgiveness, a person must believe that God does love him or her in spite of his or her failures and that if there is any rejection going on, it is solely on the individual's part. When a person will not receive God's forgiveness, he or she is rejecting His perfect love. This is why *1 John 4:18* states that such a person has, *"not been made perfect in love."*

The final area that a spirit of fear will attack is the mind. A person who is being oppressed by a spirit of fear will have difficulty maintaining a stable mind.

According to *James 1:8,* *"A double minded man is unstable in all his ways."* When fear grips the mind, there is no stability or clarity in any area of the person's life. Eventually fear becomes the entity that defines a frightening, unrealistic reality for the individual.

Philippians 2:5 tells us to *"have the mind of Christ."* The mind that is plagued by fear is opposite of the mind of Christ. The mind of Christ is submissive, but the mind of fear is afraid of submission. The mind of Christ is humble, but the fearful mind is unteachable. The mind of Christ is sensitive while the mind of fear avoids involvement.

There are other forms of fear we must not ignore. The most popular one is worrying.

Worrying is often acceptable in our Christian life. We feel we have rights to worry because things are not going according to our preference.

Oswald Chambers calls worrying a form of slander against God's character. He goes on to say that such fussing always ends in sin and that we imagine that it is an indication of how really wise we are but in reality it shows how wicked we are because it springs from a determination to get our own way. He pointed out that our Lord never worried nor was He anxious because He was not out to promote His own ideas but to realize God's perfect will. [7]

A person worries about getting his or her way in a matter. After all, in a person's mind his or her ways represent the supreme scenario of happiness for his or her world. I must point out worrying is rarely in relationship with present reality but with the possible events of the future we have no control of. This makes worrying useless or a point of absolute vanity.

Worrying implies God is not concerned, nor aware of the needs and details of our life. This is why Jesus tells us to take no thought for our needs or for tomorrow because it shows unbelief. This wasteful exercise shows that the individual is not putting his or her trust in God or His word. *Romans 8:28* gives this promise, *"And we know that all things work together for good to them that love God, to them who are the called according to his purpose."*

Worrying turns into the cares of the world. A person begins to care more about the activities around him or her than about pursuing God.

Martha (the sister of Lazarus) showed through her example how these cares keep a person from enjoying the best God has for an individual.[8] Jesus said of the cares of the world that they actually choked out the Word of God. In other words, the cares of the world drown out the Word of God's authority and power in a person's life. [9]

Ultimately, any kind of fear can turn into worship of Satan. It is idolatrous in nature, and since Satan is after man's worship, this avenue greatly helps his cause and creates a greater bondage for the person who is being oppressed by it.

Revelation 21:8 tells us that the fearful will have their part in the lake that burns. The reason for this strict judgment of fear is because it is contrary to God's nature, His Word, and unfeigned love and faith. Fear is rebellious because it refuses to trust God. It is a constant companion of pride and the final product of all introspection or selfishness.

---

[7] *My Utmost for His Highest,* Oswald Chambers, April 20th and July 4th devotions.
[8] Luke 10:38-42
[9] Matthew 13:22

Jesus tells us we must deny self. As one understands self-centeredness, he or she can see why self-denial is not an option but a must if all of the selfisms along with pride and fear are to be stripped of all of their rights.

My co-laborer, Jeannette Haley, made this statement in regards to the liberty one finds once he or she gets past self, "One of the greatest blessings of getting past yourself is that you can be yourself."

As I encounter the various aspects and pursuits of selfishness, I have come to realize how absurd and heinous it is. It sets a person up with useless pursuits, entices him or her with unrealistic fantasies, and produces a disposition that enslaves and destroys and ultimately leads to emptiness and despair. Therefore, it is vital that we recognize it in our lives.

Does self still reign in your life? Let us consider Jesus. After all, He humbled Himself to become a servant to die for us. Therefore, can we not afford to deny self, for in so doing, God will exalt us into heavenly places with His Son, Jesus Christ? [10]

---

[10] Ephesians 2:6

Chapter Seventeen

THE SINS OF THE TONGUE

One of Satan's greatest weapons that he uses against man is the tongue. The sins of the tongue are not only many, but they can prove to be the most devastating.

The tongue robs innocent people of dignity, promises, hopes, and truth. It can kill reputations and credibility. It can destroy the work of God and cause the servants of God to be offered up on the altars of pettiness, wicked speculation, and self-righteous jealousies in the name of God.

No wonder the tongue is used by Satan in homes, churches, and the world. *James 3* talks about the power and destruction of the tongue.

> *Behold also the ships which though they be so great, and are driven of fierce winds, yet are they turned about with a very small helm, whithersoever the governor listeth. Even so the tongue is a little member, and boasted great things. Behold, how great a matter a little fire kindleth (James 3:4-5)!*

Although small, the tongue is the most powerful member of our body, and sadly it is the most uncontrollable. The tongue is usually uncontrollable because a person is not under the control of the Spirit. Since the person is not meek, he or she is not wise, especially when it comes to the tongue.

A bridled tongue is associated with a perfect man in the kingdom of God.[1] A disciplined tongue implies a person has come under the control of the Spirit by bringing all members of the body, including the tongue, under His direction.

The Apostle Paul talked about the necessity of bringing all the members of his body under control in *1 Corinthians 9:27*, "*But I keep*

---

[1] James 3:2

under my body, and bring it into subjection: lest that by any means, when I have preached to others, I myself should be a castaway."

I have no doubt Paul was talking about keeping his tongue under subjection as well. There is nothing that causes a person to lose credibility in his or her Christian life faster than an undisciplined tongue. *Proverbs 17:28* tells us even a fool who keeps his or her mouth shut appears wise.

This brings us to a harsh reality: The opposite of an undisciplined tongue is wisdom. A person who shows a lack of restraint with his or her tongue is considered unwise or a fool.

James 3:13-16 explains why an undisciplined tongue reveals a fool at heart,

> *Who is a wise man and endured with knowledge among you? Let him shew out of a good conversation his works with meekness of wisdom. But if ye have bitter envying and strife in your hearts, glory not, and lie not against the truth. This wisdom descendeth not from above, but is earthly, sensual, devilish. For where envying and strife is there is confusion and every evil work.*

Let me ask some questions. What does an undisciplined tongue cause among people? The answer is *strife.*

Why do people talk out of turn about someone else? The answer is often because there is *bitter envying* or *jealousy.*

Why do people lie about things? The answer is to *adjust the truth* to protect themselves from consequences.

James clearly tells us where there is envying and strife, there is confusion and every evil working. This is why the tongue is unruly, evil, and full of deadly poison. As *James 3:10* says, *"Out of the same mouth proceedeth blessing and cursing. My brethren, these things ought not so to be."*

The tongue has caused so much hurt and chaos in this world, not to mention poisoning countless relationships. And yet, few Christians will face the destruction of their tongues, confess the wickedness of this small member, and repent of the poison they have managed to spread.

I know personally the struggle to bring the tongue under control, and I also realize the tongue serves as a thermometer to a person's spiritual life. If the tongue proves to be constantly undisciplined or ungodly, there is something going on in the spiritual realm on a personal level that needs to be tended to.

It is important that as Christians we make sure that our tongues are not available to Satan. In order to do this, we must understand the sins of the tongue.

Cursing

Psalm 59:12 says, *"For the sin of their mouth and the words of their lips let them even be taken in their pride: and for cursing and lying which they speak."* Cursing can imply cussing, a destructive oath, or a verbal means to despise and bring someone into contempt.

Cursing can come in the form of verbal abuse or affliction, demeaning comments, perverted suggestions, or a form of vile disregard for a person's feelings and thoughts. Such cursing can cause a tremendous amount of damage. It can scar a person emotionally, cause bitterness, and wound a person's spirit.

Proverbs 15:13 says this about a broken spirit, *"A merry heart maketh a cheerful countenance: but by sorrow of the heart the spirit is broken."* I have watched spouses curse their mates. I have witnessed parents tear their children's spirits down with a vengeance. Some of these people actually called themselves Christians. What a terrible contradiction of truth, for cursing is one of Satan's powerful devices.

Spouses who curse their mates are basically cursing themselves.[2] And parents who would dare to curse their children are abusing the precious heritage that God entrusted to them. They might as well put a millstone around their necks and throw themselves into the deepest part of the ocean.[3]

---

[2] Ephesians 5:28-30
[3] Matthew 18:1-6

The Word of God is clear about the type of conversation that should come from the lips of a believer. *Ephesians 4:29-31* says,

> Let no corrupt communication proceed out of your mouth, but that which is good to the use of edifying, that it many minister grace unto the hearers. And grieve not the Holy Spirit of God, whereby ye are sealed unto the day of redemption. Let all bitterness, and wrath, and anger, and clamour and evil speaking, be put away from you, with all malice.

Obviously, our form of conversation can grieve the Spirit of God. He is holy and can only honor and embrace that which is holy. If He is to be part of our lives, we must control our wicked tongues and channel them as a means to edify and bless.

We must take note that evil conversation is classified with such things as bitterness, wrath, and anger. The reason is clear: Cursing comes from an angry, hateful heart. Such anger or hate is a form of murder. *1 John 2:9-11* confirms this,

> He that saith he is in the light, and hateth his brother, is in darkness even until now. He that loveth his brother abideth in the light, and there is none occasion of stumbling in him. But he that hateth his brother is in darkness, and walketh in darkness, and knoweth not wither he goeth, because that darkness hath blinded his eyes.

If our conversation with others can't be edifying then we must exercise our tongue by restraining it instead of giving it the power to flap and destroy others with the poisons of our own self-serving hearts. Sadly, many believe that they have a right to express themselves no matter how it may hurt others. This type of communication is self-centered and foolish. As *Proverbs 17:28* implies, it is better to appear wise than to open our mouth and let the whole world know just how ignorant, foolish, and hypocritical we are.

I must establish what edification means. Today people believe that if our words are used to warn, correct, and exhort that they are not edifying; therefore, they can be ignored and rejected. Edification is not flattery but uncompromised truth executed in love.

Truth is not always pleasant to fleshly ears, but it will always be embraced by a receptive heart. Therefore, those who desire the truth regardless of how it affects the ears will receive godly edification.

Words that are not edifying are vain or useless and will be judged as idle words. Jesus said this in *Matthew 12:36-37, "But I say unto you, that every idle word that men shall speak, they shall give account thereof in the day of judgment. For by thy words thou shalt be justified and by thy words thou shalt be condemned."*

What does your manner of conversation say about your heart? Will your words justify or condemn you in the end? Take heed!

Lying

Lying is a prevalent sin of the tongue. It is natural for people to lie as a means to protect self from uncomfortable situations or consequences of wrong actions. But no matter how we justify it, there is nothing noble about lying because it is a coward's way out of appearing moral, responsible, and godly.

John 8:44 tells us Satan is the father of lies. If a person is lying, he or she is imitating the father of lies, identifying himself or herself with his kingdom.

For a Christian to lie is a blatant mockery of God's character and truth. It shows the believer is not a lover of truth, which is spiritual suicide. *2 Thessalonians 2:10-12* warns us that, *"God is sending a delusion to those who do not love the truth that they might be damned."* As you can see, lying is no small matter in God's eyes.

The problem with lying in our society is that we categorize it. For example, little white lies, exaggeration, toying with words to create a false impression, and playing deceptive games to get our way are not considered deceptive or blatant lying. But the truth is that these so-called lesser forms of delusion have the intent of forming a false reality. In God's sight it does not matter how small, entertaining, diplomatic, or clever our verbiage may be. If it involves any form of delusion, it is a lie.

This is why Jesus said in *Matthew 5:37, "But let your communication be, Yea, yea, Nay, nay for whatsoever is more than these cometh of* evil." Jesus recognized man's tendency to stretch or manipulate the truth; therefore, He was encouraging men to keep integrity in the forefront by keeping answers or explanations honest, short, and to the point. He knew that by keeping their conversations on this simple level, people would avoid evil.

Man must avoid lying at all costs because the end of liars is the same end as the father of lies, Satan.

> *But the fearful, and unbelieving, and the abominable, and murderers and whoremongers, and sorcerers, and idolaters and all liars, shall have their part in the lake which burneth with fire and brimstone: which is the second death (Revelation 21:8, emphasis mine).*

The question is, are you falling into the trap of lying because you do not keep your answers and explanations short and to the point? Are you imitating the father of lies by trying to protect yourself and manipulate the truth, or are you becoming more like the truth, Jesus Christ? Your answer determines your eternal destination.

Gossip

The next most popular sin of the tongue after lying is gossip. Gossip can encompass many sins of the tongue. Its greatest offense is sowing seeds of discord among the brethren.

Proverbs 11:12-13 states, *"He that is void of wisdom despiseth his neighbour: but a man of understanding holdeth his peace. A talebearer revealeth secrets: but he that is of a faithful spirit concealeth the matter."* As we can see, those who gossip reveal secrets while those who have a faithful spirit will conceal a matter, knowing that such secrets can wound and cause discord among people.

Sowing seeds of discord is an abomination before God, a sin He hates.[4] Since gossip is a serious offense in the kingdom of God, it is important to understand the dynamics of it. The problem is that there are many misconceptions about gossip.

---

[4] Proverbs 6:16-19

For example, many people think that gossip is just spreading lies or rumors about people, but gossip takes in what many people do not consider offensive to God or to their brethren. Gossip is simply sharing people's business with others. For example, if I share with you the challenges in my life and you then turn around and tell other people about them, you have just committed the sin of gossip.

My co-laborer, Jeannette, made this statement, "Christians are in trouble because they can't mind their own business." Talebearers are nothing more than busybodies who put their noses in the private affairs of others and begin to share not only biased details but also personal opinions and speculations about the whole matter.

I am reminded of what Jesus said to Peter when he tried to make John's future ministry his business. Jesus said, *"If I will that he tarry till I come, what is that to thee? follow thou me" (John 21:22).*

People who get involved with other people's business rarely have time for God's business.[5] The problem is that busybodies justify their gossip by saying it is God's business. After all, they are just "concerned" about this person and feel led to share all of the details with their Christian brothers or sisters so they can pray about it. Needless to say, the justification for gossip is as lame as the activity itself.

Gossip is one of the greatest means of betraying someone's trust. People do not tell us their business so we can tell others. They tell us what is going on in secret because they trust us to be wise and discreet. They are not telling us about their private affairs so that we can turn around in our most pious form and spread it around in order to invoke others to pray, but rather they are telling us so we can pray privately in our own prayer closets.

The reason that we have few legitimate ministers in the church today is because they are talebearers, busybodies, and totally untrustworthy. Many lose valuable credibility as soon as they open their mouths with the latest news. Not only do they betray the trust of others, but they also start fires and keep them going with half-truths, misrepresentations, ignorance, exaggerations, speculations, false assumptions, and accusations. In fact, the one fruit that distinguishes busybodies is

---

[5] 2 Thessalonians 3:11; 1 Timothy 5:13

turmoil. These people love to start, spread, and perpetuate turmoil. As *Proverbs 26:20* so graciously reminds us, *"Where no wood is, there the fire goeth out: so where there is no talebearer, the strife ceaseth."* In the end, gossip becomes nothing more than a justified way of bearing false witness against real servants of God.

Many servants of God have been shredded to pieces by the pious, self-appointed, professional talebearer of Christendom. Sadly, many of these talebearers are in leadership positions and use their position as a means to spread their poisonous venom of jealousy, greed, lust, and hate by tearing down God's real servants with malicious gossip.[6]

If only Christians would put the fire out individually and expose it for the sin it is, less sin and casualties would occur among God's sheep. If they would pray more about what they hear and talk less, the church might begin to see souls saved, healed, and restored.

Gossip is one of the most sinister of sins, and until Christians recognize it as such, it will continue to be one of Satan's greatest means to rob, kill, and destroy the things of God. He will use it to defile the inner workings of homes and churches. He will rejoice as Christians justify its practices while it hypocritically breaks God's commandments and man's heart and confidence.

Are you a talebearer? Do you share people's private affairs with others in the name of Christian love and concern? You need to recognize that gossip is not the product of either of these Christian virtues but a dangerous playground for Satan. Repent quickly and ask the Lord to guard your tongue. Then show great discipline by refraining from opening your mouth. Ask the Lord to show you how to put out fires instead of starting or feeding them. The first obvious blessing from fleeing gossip is that you will be able to look God (as well as others in your life) in the face.

---

[6] Proverbs 25:23

Slander

Gossip can easily fall into the next major sin of the tongue, slander. This sin is the easiest way of getting away with murder without ever being brought to trial. It is a blatant form of jealousy and hatred because it has only one goal: To destroy the target. Most victims of slander have been condemned on the basis of biased prejudices, speculations, and self-righteous judgments. This sin should never be found among God's followers, but sadly it is easy to discover as a practice that brings neither shame nor conviction to those who are quick to use it.

Regardless of what is going on in a person's life, no one has the right to damage someone's life by destroying a person's reputation. Slander never comes from the point of truth but from hatred. It has been excused away as a warning or judgment upon someone who is considered guilty, but in reality, it is a form of personal vengeance. Such vengeance belongs to God, and in due time He will bring the proper judgment upon the real culprits.[7]

I must stipulate there is a difference between a watchman that is warning people about heresy and a person who is bent on executing judgment upon a person on the basis of scriptural or personal disagreement. The differences come down to spirit. A watchman exposes error that can send people to hell while the other type of individual tries to destroy a person because of personal vendettas and causes.

Slander is also right in line with Satan's character. His name, "devil," means slanderer, and he is busy slandering the character of God's servants through others.[8]

Therefore, slander does Satan's bidding and creates darkness and destruction, hindering God's work. This is why *Proverbs 10:18* tells us, *"He that hideth hatred with lying lips and he that uttereth a slander, is a fool."*

---

[7] Romans 12:19; Hebrews 10:30
[8] Job 1:7; Revelation 12:10-11

I wish I could say I am not guilty of committing sins with my tongue. I have cursed, lied, gossiped, and slandered. I have falsely accused my brethren and God. I have discredited myself and kept dangerous fires going among believers. I am certainly guilty of not disciplining my tongue, and only by God's grace have I begun to understand the damage this undisciplined member of the human race has caused in both my life and the lives of others.

Over the years God has chastised me for my tongue's destruction. He has graciously showed me the consequences of it. He has brought me to see that only He can help me tame this poisonous asp I carry around with me. He has used this vile member of my body to give me a glimpse of the wild, untamed beast of the old man in me that must be mortified. He has allowed it to show me that it can only be muzzled as I come under the power and leading of the Holy Spirit.

How about you? Have you taken the poisonous bite out of your tongue by bringing it under the control of the Spirit, or are you justifying the damage and victims it leaves behind? Have you repented of your tongue's sinful activities, or are you ignoring the fallout that it has left behind?

The Word of God is clear: If you don't bridle the tongue, spiritual maturity will remain far from you and your religion will be considered vain before God and those who especially know you by your tongue.

Chapter Eighteen

SOUL TIES

Soul ties are one of Satan's most powerful avenues to oppress and control people. These ties are greatly misunderstood and often shrouded in ignorance. Sadly, 85 percent of the people I have ministered to had soul ties that prevented them from moving forward in their life with God.

I must state there are two types of soul ties. Natural soul ties develop between people such as married couples. This type of soul tie simply means that the souls of two people have been knitted together in agreement.

God established this type of agreement especially for married couples. The knitting of two souls means that the parties involved are becoming like-minded in spirit, direction, purpose, and spiritual matters.

David and Jonathan had this type of soul tie.[1] It not only creates agreement but also a deep sense of loyalty and responsibility. It clearly establishes and maintains honor or respect among those who have this type of agreement.

The other type of soul tie is Satan's counterfeit. Instead of agreement, this dark, unnatural soul tie becomes a possessive form of control in the spiritual realm as seen in the case of Dinah and Shechem.[2] It serves as a bungee cord between people, keeping both individuals from moving outside of its influence, especially the person who is trying to move closer to God.

These unnatural soul ties create lust, fear, anger, hate, and rebellion. They actually prevent a person from seeing the destruction that is engulfing his or her soul. They create obsession and jealousy that

---

[1] 1 Samuel 20
[2] Genesis 34:3 & 8

causes those entangled with them to manipulate situations and events in order to be together. Even though these ties prove to be tormenting in nature, they make people feel like they belong and are special. They give an individual a sense of fleshly pleasure that provides a temporary euphoria.

Another factor that affects the relationships that have these soul ties is that one person is always more dominating in the relationship. The dominating one is the one who controls, toys with, or uses the other person for his or her purposes or agendas.

As you can see from the description of these ties, they pervert and create unnatural affections, attractions, and control.[3]

Over the years I have discovered that no relationship is exempt from these ties. If perversion, fear, or ungodly practices exist, Satan can weave a web that is unclean, unhealthy, and destructive. I have found these ties among parents and children, friends, and even married couples.

It is important as Christians to understand how these soul ties are attached and what to do about them.

There are different ways soul ties are attached. People who are fearful, needy, or insecure about a relationship can attach these unhealthy ties to unsuspecting friends or the people they date or greatly admire. For example, parents who fear constantly for their children's safety or fear being alone or unneeded can fasten a soul tie to their child.

I dealt with a mother who had affixed a soul tie to her son. She was afraid of losing him because he represented something that was decent and beautiful to her life. As the Lord began to deal with her about this issue, He showed her that her son was becoming frustrated by this unseen control that existed between them and that eventually she would lose him. The soul tie was broken and now she has a healthy relationship with him.

People who have been involved in pre-marital or perverted sexual relationships can have these unhealthy ties. That is why the Apostle Paul made this statement,

---

[3] Romans 1:26-27

> *What? Know ye not that he which is joined to an harlot is one body? For two, saith he, shall be one flesh. But he that is joined unto the Lord is one Spirit. Flee fornication. Every sin that a man doeth is without the body; but he that committeth fornication sinneth against his own body (1 Corinthians 6:16-18).*

I once ministered to a man who had been quite a Casanova in his day. He had committed fornication with almost every woman he dated. As the light came on concerning his past, he began to see that he had a soul tie with every one of these ladies. Not only did these soul ties play havoc with his spiritual growth, but they also caused some real emotional problems as well.

After he repented of fornication and the soul ties were broken, he felt an incredible burden lifting off of him.

As you can see, soul ties often drag the garbage of past lives into people's present relationships. I can't begin to tell you how many people I have met whose soul ties from the past have defiled their present lives and relationships.

Unnatural soul ties must be dealt with, but they must not be treated as a generic problem. For example, curses are often treated as generic. Many people think that all one has to do is come against them with one general prayer and they will be taken care of. In some cases a general prayer may work, but not in every situation.

We must understand the different devices of the enemy so that when we encounter them, we can properly deal with them. Unnatural soul ties are no exception.

Breaking Soul Ties

There are two types of unnatural soul ties, and each one must be dealt with accordingly. The difference between soul ties comes down to whether they have roots.

Some soul ties do not have roots into the soul area. These ties are often spiritually wrapped around an unsuspecting victim much like a rope tied around a person's torso. The victim did not participate in establishing the soul tie, but is prevented from moving away from the person who has attached it.

Since the attachment has no roots, the tie simply needs to be *cut* like a piece of ribbon. All a person has to do is humble self and ask Jesus to cut it, and He will quickly comply.

The next type of soul tie can be difficult to deal with because it does have roots that extend down into the will and emotions of a person. Some of these root systems are extensive, like tree trunks that are embedded in the earth. They run deep and can emotionally wrap a person up like a mummy. This simply means one person emotionally allowed another person into his or her world in an unhealthy manner.

In cases like these, I ask the Lord to reveal the roots so that a person can begin to understand how the soul tie has affected his or her life. Once the roots are exposed, the Lord is asked to pull out this soul tie.

I have actually witnessed people double over as they felt the roots coming lose and being pulled upward. Some have "heard" the roots being ripped out of their soul area. In one case, it took 15 minutes before all the roots had finally been loosened enough so the soul tie could come out.

I have also encountered a couple of cases in which each individual has attached a soul tie to the other party. In such cases, it is not unusual to find that one has to be cut while the other one must be pulled.

Obviously, once a place has been vacated by this evil influence, the person must ask the Lord to fill that area up with His Spirit.[4]

The results are incredible. People who have been set free from these satanic devices admitted that there was a radical difference in their lives.

Do you have an unnatural soul tie with someone? Are you tormented by some invisible source that keeps drawing you back to someone (or even something) in your past while keeping you from moving forward? Ask the Lord if there is such an avenue--He will be quick to show you and set you free from it.

---

[4] See Matthew 12:43-45

Chapter Nineteen

CURSES

Almost all bondage occurs because man opens some type of door to Satan, but Satan uses a few avenues to bring bondage upon unsuspecting people.

These avenues are either unknown or controversial because Christians in America have a hard time believing that Satan could have such authority.

I recall reading a book about an American missionary in Africa. A comment was made by one of the natives that reveals the attitude many American believers have about Satan. The native told the missionary that he was appreciative that the church in America understood and preached the Gospel but the one weakness that puzzled him was how many lived in denial about Satan's power.

What we in America want to keep as a mere fantasy, or control with theology, is a harsh reality in places like Africa. For years the attitude of most Christians in America was that Satan's activities happened elsewhere, in countries less educated.

Education does not exempt anyone from the activities of Satan, but it does often blind people towards it. Instead of facing the influence of darkness in our midst, we put names like coincidence, superstition, fate, or foolishness on some of Satan's works to explain them away.

It is hard for Christians to believe that they are not resistant to Satan's influences. Even though the Bible does not say it, many believe if a person comes to Jesus, Satan has no rights or authority in his or her life from that point on.

This concept sounds wonderful, but it is not realistic. The Bible tells believers that they are to be soldiers, which implies there is a battle raging. This brings us back to another issue: Since Jesus has the power to put Satan under our feet, why is he still raging?

Satan has his purpose in this world. It is to prepare and perfect saints. This perfection often comes out of fighting battles. God did not take away the enemy or his devices but provided the authority and armor to overcome him and his works.[1] And as soldiers of Jesus Christ, we are responsible to recognize the enemy and his tactics and push him back with the authority and weapons provided.

One of the avenues that can unfairly affect unsuspecting Christians is that of curses. Curses are a controversial subject in Christendom. Once again, we can see extremes in this subject. Many of those who hold a fundamental view of the Word of God raise much opposition to the idea that curses could be operating in a Christian life. After all, Christ became a curse for us, thereby wiping out this Old Testament avenue of Satan. They also have *Proverbs 26:2* to fall back on, which states, *"As the bird by wandering as the swallow by flying, so the curse causeless shall not come."* This logic may make perfect sense, but there is nothing in the Word of God that clearly states that Christians are immune from curses. The word "causeless" means there are (or can be) causes that allow a curse access. In fact, the Word tells us that Satan shoots well-aimed fiery darts and has cause to do so.[2]

According to *Strong's Exhaustive Concordance,* "curse" in *Proverbs 26:2* means a small, sharp source that somewhat moves. With this in mind, can we automatically dismiss that one of Satan's darts could be a curse? But the other side of this issue is God has also given us a shield of faith to prevent curses from making inroads.[3] Note, however, that the armor of God must be in place, especially faith, to ensure that such darts do not hit their mark.

This is why we are also told not to give place to Satan: It is easy to do so, allowing his darts to hit targets.[4]

---

[1] Job 1: 7-12 refer to Revelation 12:7-11; Luke 22:31-32; Ephesians 6:10-18
[2] Ephesians 6:16
[3] Ephesians 6:16
[4] Ephesians 4:27

The other camp believes there are curses, but the approach can be extreme or generic and all-encompassing. I have watched people develop ministries, doctrines, and causes out of curses. This type of approach often causes abuses on this subject, giving the opposition much-needed ammunition to reject the idea of curses altogether.

I must state that I do not claim to be an expert on this subject. Although I would love to agree with the concept that no curses exist in the lives of Christians, my experiences tell me there is something of a spiritual nature that grips the lives of people and their succeeding generations. I must concede that it may be lack for a better word that I use the term "curses" to describe such bondage. But there is something that is sinister and very much present in the lives of people that can't be ignored or brushed off because it does not fit within popular fundamental views.

In the years I have ministered I have encountered this bondage in the lives of Christians. In order for these people to be set free, this sinister entanglement was referred to as a curse and quickly broken by the truth that Jesus had become a curse for us.[5] Some of the results were phenomenal.

We ministered to a woman who had two sons who were plagued in their lives. One son seemed totally oblivious to the Gospel while the other one was autistic.

In ministering to her, we found what we referred to as a "generational curse" that came down through her husband and gripped both of her sons. We stood in the gap with her, but the real results came after we prayed with her husband months later. In a short time, the verdict was in. The son who was closed to the Gospel got saved and became an effective witness for Jesus in his school and on the streets of his hometown. The other one actually came out of his autistic state and began to function in a normal capacity.

We can chalk up such an event as coincidental, but in my years of ministry I have seen too many such "coincidences."

---

[5] Galatians 3:10-14

Why argue over a point that can be found in Scripture? If a person feels there is a curse in someone's life and seeks to break it, what will it hurt, especially if he or she is right?

Over the years I have discovered these debates are often a matter of ignorance, fear, and pride that is inspired by a wrong spirit. Since it is easy to sit behind our religious creeds and maintain our theological stands, we can always insist we are standing for truth; therefore, there is no room for error. One needs to keep in mind that doctrine is one test, but the real test for anything comes down to whether it will ultimately stand up in the real world.

On front-line ministry, all theology is tested. Over the years I have had to disregard much of the theology that is based on man's interpretation of the Bible along with popular religious platitudes. Even though these beliefs may line up with man's logic and reasoning in his interpretations of such matters, they will crumble and become ineffective when challenged with hard reality. It is hard for man to accept the fact that Satan does not play according to man's logic or theology.

Christians must get past comfort zones and recognize that they are in a battle for souls. We need to realize extremes in any area of theology are dangerous to the well-being of God's army. Satan's tactics can't be reasoned away by theological debates. Granted, in war everything is first fought on paper, but the real battle occurs in trenches, and to the soldiers on the battlefield it becomes a different war. According to hindsight, this is what happened in the Vietnam Conflict.

Our America troops were limited by various restrictions that came down to nothing more than lines on a map and unrealistic agreements behind closed doors. As a result, the soldiers lost a greater war, that of moral, purpose, vision, and worth. The Vietnam Conflict was a disaster that left a wound in America that still remains open.

This same type of disaster can be seen in the lives of Christians who are in a battle with an unseen force but are limited from winning it because it is not according to the accepted, written theology of man. This limitation simply arises out of the fact that Christians are being prevented from recognizing (or stepping into some of the enemy's territory) to take what rightfully belongs to God because of the theological lines that are concrete in theory but not practical in experience.

Because of theology, many experiences on the front lines are written off as just another misuse or abuse of the things of God, leaving many people to remain prey to the enemy. To avoid conflict with people who are considered to be of sound doctrine, do frontline soldiers comply with the rules set down on paper, or do they fight the real battle raging before them and risk court-martial? My answer is simple: I am responsible to the ultimate Commander, Jesus, and His desires and examples are consistent.[6] I must make the enemy retreat whenever I encounter him.

To be fair we must get this subject away from a theological point of view and down to possible reality. We must answer one simple question: "What constitutes a curse in this text?" After all, we know from Scripture that people can curse us; therefore, the debate over this issue could come down to personal definition and understanding of the word "curse."

Let me share with you my perception of what constitutes a curse. All curses that we have dealt with begin with a lie, claim, or perverted accusation that actually penetrates the soul and spirit of a person. This type of curse is what we call a *word curse.* Once this lie or claim takes root, Satan has the inroad he needs to set up circumstances that will make the curse a reality or a mindset.

For example, a curse we have encountered frequently is that a person is branded as a loser. Even though the person may be intelligent and capable, the individual finds that at every point he or she is faced with some type of failure. In fact, it appears as if the individual is always swimming upstream and never getting anywhere. Such a state defines a cursed life, which will eventually result in hopelessness.

Once the curse gains momentum it actually begins to determine what I call normalcy for the person. In other words, the environment of failure becomes the person's lot in life. Sadly, if the individual marries, it can also become the family's lot in life.

As people accept this "lot" in life, they will succumb to the environment that is now breeding the destructive fruits of a lie. This lie may affect each family member differently, but its tentacles are far-

---

[6] Acts 4:20; 5:29

reaching and destructive. It is in such an atmosphere that the curse is passed down to family members. When a curse goes down through succeeding generations, we call it a *generational curse*.

The Bible mentions that the sins of the father are passed down to succeeding generations.[7] As you can see, if a person accepts the lies and claims of the enemy, it will create the atmosphere that will breed this type of scenario.

Sadly, I have seen this breeding ground in families. I have dealt with family members that were the third or fourth generation victims of molestation in their family. Even though the sin was hidden under anger, hurt, and shame, it had become a sick, normal practice in the family.

I personally understand the tentacles of this type of breeding ground. My family was part of a perverted cult that laid claims on you as soon as you were baptized into its belief system. An elder of the church would lay his hands on your head and make claims over your life.

All my life I witnessed some kind of perversion occurring, not only in my life, but also in my family's life. I knew that this perversion, with all the guilt and shame, was often hidden behind a veil of religion and hypocrisy. Sadly, this perversion set each of my family members up for some type of failure and destruction as it became normalcy or a way of life.

The veil was taken off of my eyes years after I became a Christian and God revealed the nature of what had plagued me even in my Christian life. Since then, I have stepped outside of its destruction and witnessed the ongoing devastating effects on some members of my family. I have actually watched some of them sink deeper into the mire of this perverted pigpen.

As I thought about curses, I was reminded of Jabez.[8] The names of the people of the Old Testament were significant. They often revealed the atmosphere or circumstances that surrounded the birth of a child. Jabez's name gives us a sense that his birth or the atmosphere around his family was unpleasant enough to cause sorrow. His name (implies

---

[7] Numbers 14:18
[8] 1 Chronicles 4:9-10

sorrow or affliction) alone was a form of a curse that could have easily set him up for sorrow and affliction.

But Scripture gives us insight into Jabez's character. He was honorable and would not accept the lot put upon him. He went to God and asked Him to change his atmosphere, enlarge his boundaries, and to keep him from the evil that could so easily beset him.

Jabez's example is the key to ensuring that curses have no place in our lives. As Christians we do not have to accept the lot put upon us because of lies, hateful statements, family sins, erroneous religious affiliations, and the culture we live in. We can look to our Deliverer and know that He can change the face of our life, heritage, and future.

The problem is that people may hate what they see going on in their families but fail to look to the only Deliverer who can break the destructive patterns of sins, lies, and claims. If a person tries to break this pattern in his or her own strength, the individual usually succumbs even more to its tentacles.

Since hateful statements or words can have a tremendous effect on us, it is important to beware of "word curses" or claims and recognize them as a tactic of the enemy.

We also must be aware that curses are able to travel because there is a spirit attached to them. Again, we are not just contending with a tangible world but an unseen world. A former witch told me how she, along with her cohorts, would travel the neighborhood of their community at night and send word curses on homes.

We have heard from many sources that those in hard core witchcraft also send people into churches to curse honorable Christians. They boast of bringing down predominate Christian pastors and leaders as well as congregations. They also infiltrate and cause problems and division through lies and slander.

Cults are another source that Satan uses to put claims or curses on people and their succeeding generations. We dealt with an individual who came out of a cult in which the leader had put a death curse on her. She could not understand why she lost her unborn child or why destruction followed her until she realized her leader's curse had made an inroad into her life.

In another incident I heard of a man that called himself a prophet. He literally put curses on the members of his cult to bring fear and intimidation to keep them under control. In one situation he told a woman that one of her children would die if she did not line up to his teachings. Although she left the cult, she was plagued with fear that she would lose one of her children. Once the hateful claim was brought to the light, identified as being a lie from Satan, its power was immediately broken in her life.

Once again, you might be saying, "Don't give Satan so much power or credit." The point is that in the atmosphere of darkness he does have incredible power, but once the light of Jesus exposes his works, he is defeated. Keep in mind at all times that there is only one key of power in the demonic realm, and that is darkness.

Darkness represents ignorance, deception, and evil. Satan has the right to fully operate within each of these atmospheres.[9] God's authority, light, and truth quickly defeat Satan's power in a person's life.[10]

It is also important to realize that if a curse exists, other demonic influences can be present.

For example, there is a cult whose name means "god of the dead" in the Chinese language. Therefore, when you encounter someone who is a part of this cult, you will not only discover a curse or claim on the person's life but also a spirit of destruction or death.

These demonic influences may have a greater hold on the person than the actual curse. This is why a generic prayer to break a curse will not always be effective.

1 Corinthians 14:33 tells us that God is not the author of confusion but of peace or order. It is vital that a person who is wading through this satanic web seeks God as to the order in which the different demonic influences must be dealt with. For example, if there is both a curse and spirit in operation, only God knows which one is the stronghold. In some cases, the curse is the stronghold, and once it is broken the spirit has

---

[9] Note the state of darkness in Genesis 1:2; Isaiah 29:15; 30:1; John 3:19-21; 8:44; Ephesians 2:1-3; Ephesians 5:3-13
[10] 1 John 4:4

no rights and must let go of the territory. If a spirit has the greatest hold, then it must be confronted first before the curse will lose its power.

The key to overcome any device or curse is to immediately recognize it as an avenue of Satan, reject it as being from God, and renounce it in faith, always seeking God's perspective concerning it. No Christian has to accept a curse because Jesus became a curse to break the power of this satanic device. As blood-bought saints, we do not have to receive such aggressive advances from anyone, regardless of who they claim to be, in the kingdom of God.

In the Old Testament we see people falling into judgment under the curses of God because of disobedience. The judgment that often comes upon people is because they ultimately reap what they sow.[11] In fact, God will turn people over to the wicked consequences of their desires so that they will reap the bitter harvest and hopefully come to repentance.[12]

It is important to point out that it is man who curses not only others, but also himself. There are several ways in which people (this includes Christians) can curse their own lives and families.

Cursing Your Own House

One of the ways that you can bring consequences upon your life is by abusing the things of God. The Word is quite clear that if a person preaches another gospel, he or she will be cursed.[13] This particular curse causes grave concern for me because some of the church today has watered down the Gospel and made it powerless and ineffective.

The new gospel encourages nothing more than a mental ascension instead of a heart reality. It allows the ears to be tickled, pride to be lifted upon the throne, and the flesh to remain intact. There is no price of self-denial and no cross to bear. For this reason, some who are really on their way to hell may believe they are saved. Although the leader will stand accursed for those he or she has led astray, the poor souls who

---

[11] Leviticus 26:14-39; Galatians 6:7-8
[12] 2 Peter 3:9
[13] Galatians 1:7-9

bought the watered-down version of the Gospel will be doomed to a Christless eternity.[14]

Another area in which many stand cursed is in how they handle the Word of God. *Deuteronomy 4:2* and *Revelation 22:19* warn that no one should add to or take away from God's Word because in so doing, God will take the person's name out of His book of life. *2 Peter 3:16* talks about people who wrest Scriptures to their own destruction. Mishandling God's Word is intolerable because the true Word of God has one goal: To lead people to eternal life, which can only be found in Jesus Christ.[15] To misappropriate or incorrectly apply the Word of God simply means you will ultimately miss its real aim of salvation, resulting in judgment.

Another area in which abuse is not tolerated in the kingdom of God is communion. Many at the church of Corinth were being flippant about this sacred ordinance. The Apostle Paul spoke of the consequences that resulted from such flippancy, *"For he that eateth and drinketh unworthily, eateth and drinketh damnation to himself, not discerning the Lord's body. For this cause many are weak and sickly among you, and many sleep" (1 Corinthians 11:29-30).* In my observation I see this same flippant attitude about communion today, and when I do I have to question the quality of leadership and the type of teaching that such people have been exposed to.

1 Corinthians 3:16-17 gives us this warning about another area that is greatly abused, *"Know ye not that ye are the temple of God, and that the Spirit of God dwelleth in you? If any man defile the temple of God, him shall God destroy; for the temple of God is holy, which temple ye are."* It seems that many in the Christian realm do not see their bodies as holy temples and use them in pursuing after fleshly pleasures, the world, and unholy alliances. In fact, the body is greatly abused and misused for self-serving purposes rather than for the glory of God. This is also why the sin of fornication is considered a sin against a person's body or temple.[16]

---

[14] Galatians 1:9; James 3:1
[15] John 5:39
[16] 1 Corinthians 6:17-20

People can also bring themselves in contempt before God when they fail to keep vows.[17] Individuals who do not value their word are void of integrity and can't be trusted. This is contrary to the character of God, who keeps all of His promises.

I have heard Christians make vows that were disregarded or changed when convenient to do so. Some of these people will face grave consequences for their flippancy.

Proverbs 17:13 tells us of another area that can bring devastating consequences upon us, *"Whoso rewardeth evil for good, evil shall not depart from his house."* I have encountered people who call themselves Christians who, out of so-called Christian duty, return evil for good. Sadly, in ministry we encounter too many Christians who fit this mode of operation.

In one particular case my co-laborer and I ministered extensively to a couple who had five children. They became self-righteous over some issues and turned on us. I realized that they were cursing themselves and that the sorrowful consequences would most likely come through their children.

Another area that will bring a curse upon an individual's life is how a person responds to the poor, the widow, the stranger, and children. *Proverbs 22:16* tells us if riches are increased at the expense of the poor, the culprit will come to want. *Exodus 22:21-24* states if someone oppresses the stranger or afflicts widows and children and they cry out to God, He will kill the evildoer. And we have Jesus' famous words in *Matthew 18:6: "But whoso shall offend one of these little ones which believe in me, it were better for him that a millstone were hanged about his neck, and that he were drowned in the depth of the sea."*

Examine your life and see if you might be plagued by unseen curses. Do you find yourself subject to patterns that have plagued your family? Or maybe someone out of anger or hatred cursed you and it took root in your soul. Maybe you have cursed yourself because of a wrong disposition or actions.

---

[17] Deuteronomy 23:21; Ecclesiastes 5:4-6; Matthew 5:33-37

Rayola Kelley

Know that Jesus became a curse; therefore, this bondage can be easily broken as you repent or submit to the light, truth, and power of God, revealing and breaking the influence of any such wicked avenue.

Chapter Twenty

Self-Serving Prayer

One of the ways that Satan can effectively use Christians is in the area of prayer. *Romans 8:26* tells us that we do not know how we ought to pray. *James 4:3* states, *"Ye ask, and receive not, because ye ask amiss, that ye may consume it upon your lusts."* As you can see, prayer can be very self-centered and self-serving.

Prayer is an important part of the victorious life of a Christian, but few understand how to use this weapon properly. One of the reasons is that there are many improper teachings about prayer. For example, one teaching claims that God answers all prayers. His answer may be yes, no, or wait. This idea sounds good, but it is not Scriptural. In *Jeremiah 11:14* God gives Jeremiah this instruction, *"Therefore pray not thou for this people, neither lift up a cry or pray for them: for I will not hear them in the time that they cry unto me for their trouble."* [1]

1 John 5:14 tells us, *"And this is the confidence that we have in him, that, if we ask anything according to his will, he heareth us."*

The Scripture in *Jeremiah* shows us God will not answer those who are in sin, and *1 John* implies that God does not hear or adhere to prayers that are not according to His will. If He does not regard all prayers, He is not responding to them.

There are also those in Christendom who refute that prayer based on God's will catch His ear. These same people advocate that you must be aggressive and demanding with your prayers because that is a sign of active faith. Some have even criticized Jesus for praying according to the will of the Father, stating that it was a form of unbelief instead of the humble submission of obedience that it was.

---

[1] See also Isaiah 59:2; 64:7; Lamentations 3:44

James 4:3 indirectly explains why some prayers are not regarded. It is because a wrong spirit motivates the prayers, and as a result they are prayed amiss. Such prayers are self-serving in nature and are empty of spiritual significance as far as God's will and purpose; therefore, they never hit the mark or reach the throne of God.

This brings us to consider what happens to prayers that are asked amiss. Do these requests fall to the wayside, or do they serve as avenues for Satan to work his own type of havoc?

Keep in mind that a wrong spirit is behind self-serving prayers. This wrong spirit will serve as an avenue for Satan. *Ephesians 2:2* tells us this about Satan, *"Wherein in time past ye walked according to the course of this world, according to the prince of the power of the air, the spirit that now worketh in the children of disobedience"* (emphasis added).

Satan is the ruler of the air, which affords him the right to take possession of any self-serving prayers that are being carelessly sent and use them for his own form of oppression.

There are two types of self-serving prayers. In one form of self-serving prayer, me, myself, and I have certain desires that I feel confident God will fulfill because He loves me and wants me to be happy. These prayers are based on personal agendas and wrong inclinations. They are inspired by the idols of the heart and mind. The goal of these idols is to achieve personal happiness by heaping the things of the world on self.

The perverted logic escalates as the person believes that God wants him or her happy and prosperous and that, therefore, He will have no other choice but to meet the list of wants that are presented in prayer. Such an individual does not know the character of God and is misusing prayer to get his or her way.

You might ask how Satan could use these types of prayers to oppress. It is simple; these people sincerely believe they deserve to have all of their requests answered; therefore, it will be hard for them to accept God's silence in the situation. Since these people do not know God's will, confusion is caused when many of their prayers go unanswered.

Satan will use these unanswered prayers to bring accusation against God's character. Doubts, frustration, and anger replace hope as well as the misguided confidence these people have towards God. The end result can be a hard heart, unbelief, and skepticism. As you can see, Satan uses such prayers against the person, undermining any sincere faith that may be present.

This is why people must learn to pray according to God's heart. Even Jesus' disciples asked Jesus to teach them to pray. We see that Jesus taught a great deal about prayer through instruction and personal examples.

Although Jesus' disciples had a religious background, they realized that they were missing the mark and wanted to be effective. This is when Jesus gave them a model for effective prayer. We know this prayer as "The Lord's Prayer," but in reality, it should be called "The Disciple's Prayer."[2]

Let us consider the format and attitude that can gain God's attention in prayer and make a difference in our lives, homes, churches, communities, and world. I also believe this model prayer can show struggling believers why their prayer lives are powerless. This prayer is found in *Matthew 6:9-13*.

"Our Father which art in heaven, Hallowed be thy name!" The initial invocation shows us that our approach in prayer must not be one of arrogance or aggression but of humility and awe because our God is the ultimate authority and is infinite, full of mysteries and glorious wonders. It is not a prayer that demands that God listen but one that appeals to His commitment towards man, recognizes His character, and seeks to know His heart. In a sense, it is an appeal that automatically has the potential to lead one into the very presence of God in order to worship Him in spirit and truth.[3]

"Thy kingdom come." This part of the prayer should remind each of us that we are part of an unseen kingdom that can only be realized in

---

[2] Jesus' prayer can be found in John 17.
[3] John 4:23-24

the believer's heart because it has not yet come to full fruition on earth.[4] Such a revelation will put the correct goal in perspective.

The problem I see today is that many Christians are striving to build personal kingdoms on earth rather than establish the heavenly kingdom in the hearts of man. Christians' existence on earth is not about realizing self but about experiencing God's kingdom in a personal way and sharing it with others.

"Thy will be done in earth, as it is in heaven." Notice how the person's desire will be for God's will to be accomplished and not his or her will to be done. God's will is perfect and benefits all who adhere to it. It is not optional or meant to be considered as a smorgasbord where one picks and chooses according to personal whims. It is the only boundary that ensures that a person will steadfastly stick to the course set before him or her regardless of the obstacles.[5]

"Give us this day our daily bread." Notice that the request is not for mansions, big cars, or nice bank accounts, but rather it is simple—give me what I have need of.

This simple supplication reminds me of the prayer found in *Proverbs 30:7-9*,

> Two things have I required of thee; deny me them not before I die: Remove far from me vanity and lies: give me neither poverty nor riches; feed me with food convenient for me: Lest I be full, and deny thee, and say, Who is the LORD? Or lest I be poor, and steal, and take the name of my God in vain.

The wise writer of *Proverbs* realized that all the world could offer were lies, vanity, or lust that could cause him to forget his God, the real Provider. He recognized that being full of the world would cause him to become self-sufficient and ungrateful to God.

On the other hand, he did not want to be so poor that he would have to steal, bringing a reproach on God. This is why he asked God to feed him with food convenient for him.

---

[4] John 18:36
[5] 1 Corinthians 9:24; Hebrew 12:1; Matthew 7:13-14; 2 Timothy 4:7-8

"Convenient" in this text means what is necessary for that particular time or space.[6] This is why Jesus gave us this instruction in *Matthew 6:31, "Therefore take no thought saying, What shall we eat? Or, What shall we drink? Or, Wherewithal shall we be clothed?"* Notice there are only three things we are guaranteed—food, drink, and clothes.

I am sure most Christians will admit they have these three necessities, but they are not grateful because they are looking at what they don't have according to the lusts of the flesh and world.

The big mistake that Christians make is that they regard earth in the same light as heaven. They want their mansions, streets of gold, and a perfect paradise while on earth. In short, they want heaven here where they can abide in perfect bliss and avoid that which is unknown, that which must be accepted by faith. The problem with this scenario is that most Christians will never become homesick for their real spiritual home and inheritance.

When Jesus talked about preparing a place, He was not talking about a physical place on earth but a spiritual residence. I once heard that the place Jesus was preparing was a place in Him. *Ephesians 2:6* confirms this, *"And hath raised us up together, and made us sit together in heavenly places in Christ Jesus."*

The place of importance in heaven will not be mansions but the throne of God where the unhindered majesty of the Son of God will fill the temple. The beauty about heaven will not be the gold streets but the unobstructed light of the King of kings. The paradise of heaven will not be marked by its fruitful gardens but by the unbridled worship that exalts the real treasure and eternal inheritance of every believer, the Lord Jesus Christ.[7]

Obviously, in this world of vanity and lust many treat God as if He is nothing more than a Santa Claus or a sugar daddy. As a result, many fail to possess the real treasure that can only be unveiled in the light of God's glory and realized in the ages to come.[8]

---

[6] *Strong's Exhaustive Concordance*, #2706.
[7] Colossians 1:27; 2:3
[8] Ephesians 2:7

"And forgive us our debts, as we forgive our debtors." This leads us back to the cross of Jesus. We are reminded that we stand level with, not superior to, every individual who has come to Calvary seeking God's forgiveness. It was at the cross of supreme sacrifice that we began to realize God's mercy and grace provided a means of receiving forgiveness. Since God is so gracious to forgive, we must forgive.[9]

Unforgiveness gives way to the root of bitterness that produces a hard heart and unbelief. This sin of darkness makes us as the heathen that are motivated by conditional love and self-serving benevolence. Unforgiveness in our hearts makes us murderers, in attitude it makes us God, and in actions it causes us to resort to paganism and wickedness.[10]

Forgiveness requires getting past self in humility to create a right attitude. Godly forgiveness is the sign that one is dead to self, compelled by the love of God, and alive unto God for His purpose and will.

"And lead us not into temptation but deliver us from evil." This supplication shows us that God can direct our steps and keep us from falling prey to the flesh, the world, and Satan. He can give us a way through or out of temptation, but we have the responsibility to flee idolatry and lusts when we encounter them.[11] Sadly, instead of fleeing lust and idolatry, many toy with these sins, falling prey to their tentacles.

"For thine is the kingdom, and the power and the glory, forever. Amen." In this final statement we are reminded of what constitutes the kingdom that resides within man, the power that delivers, and the glory that consumes a person with the reality of God, the Person Jesus Christ.

The goal of our prayer life should never be to get our way but to know God's way. In fact, we should be motivated to know nothing but Jesus and Him crucified.[12] We must not be content in our prayer life until we have experienced Him in intimacy and worshipped Him in spirit and truth.

---

[9] Matthew 6:14-15
[10] Matthew 5:43-48; 1John 3:18
[11] 1 Corinthians 10:13-14; 2 Timothy 2:22
[12] 1 Corinthians 2:2

What are you pursuing after right now in your prayer life? Is it to know Jesus in a greater way?

The second type of self-serving prayer is best known as psychic prayer because it can disrupt an unsuspecting person's ability to function mentally with clarity.

Psychic prayer occurs when a person prays his or her will on someone else. Sadly, this is not an unusual practice in Christendom. Well-meaning Christians can easily fall into this trap. For example, a Christian may feel they know what another person should do and is convinced that they must diligently pray for the individual to "see the light." This strong, concentrated prayer is self-righteous in nature, limited to man's perverted evaluation, and not in line with God's will.

Since the prayer is not in line with God, it becomes a form of control or witchcraft for Satan to use for his own purpose. He uses this type of prayer to press against the mind of the person that it is being directed towards, causing oppression.

This oppression can express itself in different ways. It can make a person feel like there is a tight band around his or her head or that he or she is mentally walking through mud, making him or her tired and ineffective. Sometimes these prayers can cause a covering over a person or even turn into a curse or a claim on the person's life.

In extreme cases involving myself, psychic prayer has produced the sensation of an unseen rat nibbling on my ears. I know when I feel this sensation that there is some major concentrated prayer coming against me. The individual or individuals are doing everything in their power to get me to see it their way and bow to their will.

Because of my experience in this area, I eventually discern the fruits of psychic prayer. Once I recognize it as the culprit, I immediately go to God and ask Him to expose the source to me in order to determine my response.

For example, some people are innocent about the type of effect they are having on your spiritual life, but others are bona fide enemies that are bent on getting you to bow down to their sinister and evil whims. If the person is innocent, I come against the prayer itself to render it ineffective. If the individual is an enemy bent on hindering or destroying the work of God in my life, I send the psychic prayer back on the person to render the individual ineffective.

Psychic prayer that returns to the enemy will often create confusion, causing the person's focus to turn elsewhere.

This sinister type of prayer can easily be subdued. The results are quick and amazing as confusion quickly disperses and the victim's mind becomes clear.

It is important to recognize that we do not know how we ought to pray. This is why I pray according to God's will, regardless of how zealous I may feel about something. As soon as I subject all requests to God, I know without a doubt He will handle each prayer according to His purpose. If there is a prayer that is self-centered, I pray that it will be discarded instead of used against an innocent victim or myself.

Praying according to God's will is not only a safe bet, but it is also an act of real faith. By asking God to have His will in all matters, a person is showing confidence in His character and commitment to ensure the best for everyone involved.

How is your prayer life? Does a right spirit motivate you, or are you operating in a wrong spirit? Are you praying your will on God or you praying to find God's will? Are you skeptical about prayer, or do you see it as a privilege to commune with the One who provided free access for you to enter into the Most Holy Place of fellowship with Him?[13] The answers to these questions will determine how victorious you are as a Christian and how effective you will be in prayer.

---

[13] Hebrew 4:14-16

Chapter Twenty-one

WRONG LAYING ON OF HANDS

There is much to be said about the impartation of spirits. Spirits can be and are transferred through the laying on of hands. That is why it was a common practice for the apostles of the new church to lay their hands on someone who was to be baptized by the Holy Spirit or commissioned to be sent forth in the authority and power of the Spirit of God on a mission.[1]

The laying on of hands went back to Old Testament practices. Kings, prophets, and priests were commissioned by the laying on of hands. It was a form of consecration or being set apart to execute the service of the Lord or lead God's people.[2] Even the priest laid hands on the sacrifice that was about to be offered up as a form of consecration before the Lord.[3]

The practice of the laying on of hands in the New Testament involved the act of consecration, but it also included such areas as healing and gifts. In *Luke 13:13,* Jesus laid his hands on the woman who had a spirit of infirmity for 18 years and she was healed. In *Acts 28:8*, Paul laid his hands on a sick individual and prayed for him and he was healed.

In Paul's letter to Timothy, he instructed him: *"Neglect not the gift that is in thee, which was given thee by prophecy, with the laying on of the hands of the presbytery"* (emphasis added). Obviously, Timothy had received a gift of the Holy Spirit through the laying on of hands.

In Paul's second letter to Timothy he gives this reminder to him: *"Wherefore I put thee in remembrance that thou stir up the gift of God,*

---

[1] Acts 6:6
[2] Numbers 8:10-11
[3] Leviticus 1:4-9

which is in thee by the <u>putting</u> <u>on</u> <u>of</u> <u>my</u> <u>hands</u>" (emphasis added). Apparently, Paul is reminding Timothy of the gift that was imparted to him by the laying on of hands and instructed him to stir it up according to God's purpose.

This brings us to Satan's counterfeits. Through the laying on of hands, the kingdom of darkness transfers its spirit to others as well. A former witch confirmed that once a person decides what spirit he or she chooses to submit to, hands are laid on the person to impart that particular demonic spirit to him or her.

If you watch a New Age healing exercise, you will note that the healers place their hands on the heads of the recipients. These healers are serving as an avenue or conduit of the wrong spirit or transferring what they call "neutral energy."

One of my Christian friends ignorantly received healing by way of a metaphysical healer. Healers who are advanced in transferring their energy go into a concentration that is close to being in a trance state. They can actually send their energy by pointing fingers at the person; therefore, they do not always have to place their hands directly on the person to impart their pseudo power.

My friend learned her healing was not from the right spirit and renounced it. The spirit lifted and the pain came back, but she did not want to be involved with a wrong spirit, no matter what it offered her.

This is why the Apostle Paul offered this instruction in *1 Timothy 5:22: "Lay hands suddenly on no man, neither be partaker of other men's sins; keep thyself pure."* Paul clearly tells us that we must not lay hands on someone without first testing the spirit of the other person. Obviously, we could find ourselves being partakers of their sins, which opens us up to become defiled by a wrong spirit.

We have watched various people from immature, "wannabe" ministers to people with wrong spirits, such as religious spirits, running around the church and Christian meetings ready to lay hands on innocent victims. This is unscriptural, but many are pursuing after power and not truth. And according to the actions of many, truth is nothing more than a minor detail rather than a life-and-death issue.

Today impartation is the latest fad in Christendom. Many are running to meetings to get an impartation of something supernatural. It is true that they might be receiving something of a supernatural nature, but it is rarely from God.

Sadly, these people take this unholy impartation back to their churches. Leaders who are not discerning and who are ignorant about these matters are allowing their congregations to become subject to another spirit.

This new spirit that is coming into the church through counterfeit impartation is very religious but displays wicked fruits. It causes tremendous confusion and division among Christians. It makes a mockery out of true Christianity, often causing those in the Christian realm who are practicing it to appear foolish and ridiculous. Instead of people walking away with a greater faith and love for Jesus, they walk away with another spirit, mocking "old time" religion. Instead of showing meekness, people display great arrogance. Rather than preaching the real Gospel, they downplay it with the emphasis on the supernatural.

The Holy Spirit is not an entertainer, nor is He arrogant in how He presents Jesus Christ. He is gentle and usually comes upon a person when there is humility and sincerity. As Jesus said, He is like the wind and you never know how or from what direction He will come, for He is sovereign.[4] For this reason, I will avoid any situation where I might be exposed to any type of religious insanity.

Sadly, because people are ignorant about this subject, many well-meaning Christians have submitted themselves to the wrong laying on of hands. The results are devastating.

Over the years we have ministered to many people who had the wrong spirit imparted to them through these different avenues. A good example of this was a missionary from India who came to my co-laborer and me seeking help. He was very concerned because he had no interest in the Word of God and was fighting great depression. Upon questioning him about his lack of love for the Scriptures, we traced it back to a meeting in which the wife of a well-known religious leader laid hands on him and prayed for him. After he got up, he found himself

---
[4] John 3:5-8

laughing uncontrollably. Later he discovered he was being plagued by perversion and lust and realized she had imparted a perverted spirit on him. He managed to get rid of the perverted spirit but did not realize that he had inherited a mocking spirit.

This mocking spirit started to ridicule his Christianity and the Word of God. It not only succeeded in undermining his love for the Word but also caused his attitude towards it to grow cold, making him skeptical. We prayed against the wrong laying on of hands and he renounced it, setting him free to love the Word of God and move forward into effective ministry.

Over the years we have ministered to other people who jerked, twitched, and made grunting noises. We traced these unscriptural actions back to their involvement with popular movements that promised greater power and joy producing manifestations of uncontrollable laughter or making noises like an animal. These people came to us with major problems but refused to acknowledge that they had submitted themselves to a wrong spirit that needed to be renounced because they truly believed it was the Holy Spirit.

Obviously, these people did not know the character of the Holy Spirit and had accepted a sick, perverted counterfeit in His place. This counterfeit fed their flesh, appeased their pride, and made them feel spiritual and special. It saddened me that they preferred the counterfeit to the real Spirit of God. It also revealed to me why they had problems and were susceptible to receive the wrong spirit.

This brings me to another practice that is dangerous—that of holding hands. I have a problem when congregations in churches are told to stand and hold hands while they pray. Supposedly, holding hands represents unity or agreement, but if you are holding the hand of a person who has a contrary spirit, it will not mean unity but rather personal bondage.

It is a known fact that witches visit churches to curse Christians that serve as a threat against the kingdom of darkness. The idea of holding the hand of someone who is a stranger or contrary in spirit is unacceptable to me, and I will either bow out or leave.

I have been innocently put in positions where I held someone's hand during prayer, and once I actually felt a spirit crawling up my arm. The sensation I had was almost as if acid was slowly engulfing my arm. It took major warfare for me to get rid of it, which instilled in my mind the seriousness of this avenue.

Recently, I found myself in the midst of a bona fide New Age meeting. The leader declared that those who refused to see the value of his New Age teachings were from the Dark Ages. As he required us to hold hands, he subtly begin to use visualization and astrology to open us up to the energy that would bring us healing. As I stood in the circle, I prayed against any wrong spirit and closed my mind to his demonic persuasion. I know he could sense I was not impressed and did not agree with him. I'm also sure he was not surprised when I left the meeting in its early stages.

Over the years I have realized that God protects those who are innocent, but He allows fools to fall into the trap. The difference between the innocent and the fool is the heart. Innocent people walk into something without realizing they have stepped into a hornets' nest and are often being protected by God. On the contrary, the fool knows what he is walking into but believes he can handle it and thereby falls into the trap.

As you can see, the laying on of hands is a serious matter. Do not be foolish or ignorant about this subject. You must not let just anyone lay hands on you. You need to know the spirit of that person and know that he or she possesses the right Spirit. On the other hand, you must not lay hands on someone until you know you have the freedom to do so.

Maybe right now you are struggling in your relationship with God. If so, ask Him if you have had the wrong laying on of hands. If so, seek out someone who will know how to stand in the gap. Make sure that you renounce it as not being from God and decide that you want no part of it.

The last few chapters covered the major avenues Satan uses to entangle people into oppression. Now it is time to understand the means Jesus uses to set a person free.

Chapter Twenty-two

THE GREAT PHYSICIAN

The Word of God points to Jesus as the Great Physician.[5] This shows us that Jesus is the only one who can heal us or set us free in all spiritual matters. But we need to understand what it means for Jesus to be our personal physician.

When we think of a physician, we think of a person who is able to take care of what ails us. When we think of Christ as the Great Physician, we think of someone who takes care of our sins and its consequences.

It is true that Jesus took care of the consequences of our sins, but He did that as the Lamb of God, not as the Great Physician. Oswald Chambers made this observation: "Deliverance from sin is not deliverance from conscious sin only, it is deliverance from sin in God's sight, and He can see down into a region I know nothing about."[6] Jesus must confront this unseen region as the Great Physician to bring about real healing or deliverance from sin.

The death of Christ took care of our blatant sins and redeemed us. This redemption is complete. As Oswald Chambers said, "Jesus Christ is not working out the redemption, it is complete; we are working it out, and beginning to realize it by obedience." [7] As the Physician and High Priest, Jesus must deal with our sin nature. The core of people's problems does not rest with sinful actions but with who they are. Everyone is a sinner by nature, prone to sin or rebel against God. Jesus came as the Great Physician to deal with man's fallen, miserable nature. Consider what He said in *Matthew 9:11-13,*

---

[5] Matthew 9:12-13; Luke 4:18-19; 5:17
[6] *Studies In The Sermon On The Mount,* Oswald Chambers, © 1995, Oswald Chambers Publications Association Limited; pg. 24
[7] *101 Days in the Epistles With Oswald Chamber,* pg. 280

> *And when the Pharisees saw it, they said unto his disciples, Why eateth your master with publicans and sinners? But when Jesus heard that, he said unto them, They that be whole need not a physician, but they that are sick. But go ye and learn what that meaneth, I will have mercy, and not sacrifice: for I am not come to call the righteous, but sinners to repentance.*

Man is a sinner, but note Jesus didn't say, "I have come only to take care of man's sins." He came to call man unto Himself so He could take care of what really plagues him.

This brings us to another principle. A person must seek a physician out before he or she can be helped. This only happens when a person recognizes that he or she has a problem that requires expertise intervention beyond personal abilities.

Therefore, we must note that the real issue in *Matthew 9:11-13* is not about sins but wholeness. In other words, man's problems encompass more than wrong actions. It is an inward problem that entails a wrong disposition or attitude that must be dealt with.

When people consider their spiritual condition in light of their sins and not their disposition, they fail to recognize the extent or seriousness of their problem and come to terms with God's grace. The reason for this is that people can change their actions and cease from outward sin but they can't change their disposition of sin. When we treat the sin but not the cause, we are still headed for failure and destruction. A good comparison would be trying to treat cancer as if it were the cold or flu.

People treat their sin nature with such remedies as religion, good works, pious sacrifices, etc. But the Word of God is quite clear that these attempts are futile. For example, to treat the sinful disposition with religion simply makes a person a white sepulcher that houses dead men's bones.[8]

To attempt to make the sin nature whole with pious sacrifices is to ignore the heart of the problem. After all, Jesus said, *"I will have mercy, and not sacrifice."*[9] The Apostle Paul made this comparison, *"And*

---

[8] Matthew 23:27
[9] Matthew 9:13

though I bestow all my goods to feed the poor, and though I give my body to be burned, and have not charity, it profiteth nothing" (1 Corinthians 13:3).

As you can see, sins are an outward manifestation of the inward disposition. Christ visibly took care of the sins on the cross, but now He must work behind the scenes to take care of the real problem of man.

Jesus takes care of the disposition of man by changing the environment within which man is functioning. The length of the process is determined by the attitude and response of the person.

The first thing the Great Physician must do to address man's sinful nature or his spiritual environment is to transform the mind or will area. Environment determines how one perceives God, and perception influences how one responds to or interacts with God. Destructive environments prevent God from showing Himself while the right atmosphere allows God to be God.

The type of environment comes down to knowledge, possession, expectations, emphasis, and confidence. To have a right environment, a person must *know* Jesus. As individuals know the real Jesus, they begin to find their position in Him.

Position defines who the individual is in the kingdom of God more than any other means. This position or identity is never found by looking in or looking around but by looking up towards the King of kings and Lord of lords.

As an individual finds his or her place in Christ, *values* begin to change. Much of what people seek today is to possess material things rather than eternal treasures. A wrong pursuit will set people up for disillusionment and disappointment.

It is important to realize that the worth of a person's life is not based on how much treasure he or she possesses but on *what types of treasure possess the person's heart.*[10]

For example, I have encountered people who are possessed by material things that bring emptiness to their lives. This is why all Christians must pursue the treasure of heaven to ensure that Jesus (and not earthly, temporal things) owns and possesses them.

---

[10] Matthew 6:21

The type of *expectations* we operate within determines what we value. Expectations cause a person to live in some type of expectancy and encourage some form of delusion. When an expectation does not come to fruition, doubts and unbelief flood the soul.

Many Christians have expectations concerning God that are not based on His character but on grandiose dreams. Granted, Christians should live in expectancy—not with the intent of seeing their will and dreams realized, but to encounter the reality of Jesus. In fact, Christians should be motivated by one constant expectation—the reality that Jesus is coming back.

Maintaining this blessed expectation in the right spirit influences a person's daily walk. As he or she prepares, watches, and prays for this glorious day, he or she will walk in sobriety and obedience.[11]

Once a person gains the right expectation, he or she will develop a right emphasis. *Emphasis* comes down to motivations and inclinations and will determine a person's priorities or agendas.

Most people's priorities are self-serving and not Christ-centered. Such people are caught up with what God will do for them rather than what He wants to do in and through them. This selfishness causes them to miss God's blessings while it overlooks the supernatural that is expressed in practical ways, and passes by God's intervention because it appears too insignificant.

After a person's emphasis is realigned to God's heart and purpose, he or she will begin to put *confidence* in the Person of God. This confidence produces the environment that allows God to be God. It will transfigure the will of man, giving him the power to stand in confidence of the true God no matter what is going on.

The will lies at the core of the sinful nature. To take care of this problem by creating the right environment, Jesus is calling man to get beyond the futile attempts to cover up, ignore, or justify his spiritual condition. He wants man to recognize his spiritual depravity, own up to his inability to change his disposition, and give up his attempts to try to make this spiritual condition right. He wants him to repent.

---

[11] Matthew 24:32-51; Mark 13:34-37; Luke 21:29-36

Matthew 4:17 tells us, *"From that time Jesus began to preach, and to say, 'Repent: for the kingdom of heaven is at hand.'"* Jesus calls man to himself by way of repentance.

Repentance is a complete change or about-face from present lifestyles. This act is the prerequisite to a person's disposition being changed by the Great Physician.

The problem is that many people think repentance is a matter of abstaining or ceasing from doing wrong things, but this act goes further. It involves a person changing his or her mind, direction, inclinations, and lifestyles.

This repentance can be seen in the Apostle Paul's life when he encountered Jesus on the road to Damascus in *Acts 9*. Study his repentance because it shows that repentance is not only a complete reformation but also a revolutionary change of the soul.

This complete turnabout will cause a person to respond to Christ's second call: *"If any man will come after me, let him deny himself and take up his cross, and follow me" (Matthew 16:24).*

The disposition that the Great Physician must confront is ruled by the "old man." The flesh must lose its influence and power over a person. This can only occur if a person adheres to Jesus' command in *Matthew 16:24.*

Self-denial takes all authority away from the "old man" while the application of the cross subdues all of his claims or rights. This will bring the natural spirit under control and begin to close any gaps or avenues by which Satan could gain access into a person's life.

Repentance also entails humility, submission, and a change of lordship. When man walks according to his own ways, he is serving as his own lord and in reality submitting to the authority of Satan. In repentance, man ceases to walk according to his ways and turns around to begin to walk in the ways of God. The change in direction brings the individual under the lordship of Jesus.

Lordship lies at the core of all deliverance. For example, if Jesus is not Lord, then something else will serve in that capacity.

This became clear in a situation where my co-laborer, Jeannette, and I ministered to a woman who was demon possessed. She had officially married Satan and practiced what she considered to be "good" witchcraft. (There is no such thing as goodness in any form of witchcraft.)

She came to us because her many demons were tormenting her. She said she wanted deliverance from them. During a period of 24 hours spread out over four different days, we cast out many demons. It took us five hours to get down to the person and another two hours before she could admit she started to distinguish what we really looked like. This may seem strange to most, but people who are possessed or greatly oppressed see through a dark tunnel that is narrow and perverted.

At the end of 24 hours, we could tell she was not being set free. It finally dawned on us she wanted relief from the torment of her demons and not deliverance from the power they gave her. She not only liked the power, but they also greatly entertained her when they were not tormenting her.

In my last encounter with her I told her we could cast out demons but unless she was willing to submit to the lordship of Jesus she would never be delivered from Satan and his claims on her life. She made a decision to walk away from the Lord Jesus Christ.

I was humbled as I thought about the narrow, perverted vision of those on the broad road leading to destruction. Many people avoid the narrow path that leads to heaven because it is too constricting. But after dealing with extreme cases of oppression or possession I have come to realize a person will encounter some form of hardness or narrowness in his or her life no matter which path the individual follows.[12]

The type of hardness a person encounters comes down to how the individual will respond to Jesus. I have chosen the narrow path that actually frees me of bondage rather than the broad path of self that narrows a person's perception in such a way that he or she experiences greater bondage, failing to recognize impending destruction and eventually missing heaven.

Since everyone chooses a narrow avenue, what kind of narrowness is guiding your steps?

---

[12] Matthew 7:13-14

Finally, deliverance or bondage comes down to rights and territories. Rights determine authority and territory determines rule. To ensure a person is not under Satan's domain, he or she must bring all of his or her rights under the lordship of Jesus and ask Him to rule his or her life.

As Lord, Jesus is responsible to provide for a person's needs, protect him or her from enemies, and ensure each of His followers spiritual well-being. In essence, He must come to mean everything to the individual by becoming a person's all in all.

Have you just looked to Jesus to take care of your outward sins and their consequences, or have you looked to Him to deal with your inward disposition as well? Is He Lord of your life or is He a passing consideration, a concept tacked on to your religious life, a good guy who is wimpish, unrealistic, and a pushover? Be honest with yourself.

Let *Isaiah 53:5* give you a reality check as to how far Jesus must reach into a person's life to bring wholeness, *"But he was wounded for our transgressions, he was bruised for our iniquities: the chastisement of our peace was upon him; and with his stripes we are healed."*

Chapter Twenty-three

THE GLORIOUS LIGHT

Jesus made this statement as the Great Physician in *Luke 4:18-19, The Spirit of the Lord is upon me, because he hath anointed me, to preach the gospel to the poor: he hath sent me to heal the brokenhearted, to preach deliverance to the captives, and recovering of sight to the blind, to set at liberty them that are bruised. To preach the acceptable year of the Lord.*

As the Great Physician Jesus came to deliver man. So many times we think we need to be delivered from Satan and the world, but in reality we need to be delivered from ourselves.

Notice how Jesus is not dealing with the outward bondage that enslaves man but the inward oppression that cripples him. For example, people are spiritually bankrupt or poor. Poverty in any area causes great oppression and will end in destruction. *Proverbs 10:15* brings this out, *"The rich man's wealth is his strong city: the destruction of the poor is their poverty."* But spiritual poverty makes a person a candidate for deliverance and restoration if he or she is willing to face it.

Jesus came to heal the brokenhearted. Most bondage originates with a broken heart. Broken hearts set people up to make determinations and erect walls of protection. This type of heart usually means various unresolved issues have not been dealt with. These issues will cause a struggle in the individual as he or she pursues after peace or wholeness.

Christ came to preach deliverance to the captives. People are captive at the point of their wills. They become subject to the determinations of their wills instead of the Spirit of God. He came with the sword of truth to break all such ropes and chains off of individuals.

Jesus came to recover sight to the blind. In other words, He came to restore the emotional level so that man could begin to perceive the character and things of God in the right way.

Finally, Jesus sets at liberty those are bruised. Sin is what spiritually bruises man. This terminal disease of man not only bruises the individual but also damages relationships. It is unfair as it causes innocent people to taste the bitterness of oppression and destruction due to the sins of others.

He came to preach the *acceptable* year of the Lord. What does it mean to preach the acceptable year? It means He came to present the reality of salvation, or deliverance, to all who will hear and receive.

Many people live in hopelessness because they feel that spiritual healing or deliverance is for others or for the future but not for them or the present. *2 Corinthians 6:2* states, *"For he saith, I have heard thee in a time <u>accepted</u>, and in the day of salvation have I succoured thee: behold, now is the <u>accepted</u> time; behold, now is the day of salvation"* (emphasis added). The question is, how can I embrace Jesus' deliverance? It begins by embracing Jesus as the glorious light.

Jesus was anointed to penetrate every area of bondage. *Isaiah 10:27* says, *"And it shall come to pass in that day, that his burden shall be taken away from off thy shoulder, and his yoke from off thy neck, and the yoke shall be destroyed because of the anointing."*

The Holy Spirit had to anoint the Man, Christ Jesus, to break these various yokes off of people. In fact, the Son of God exchanged an easy yoke with man's harsh, unbearable yoke.[1] We know this anointing took place at the River Jordan when Jesus submitted to water baptism.[2] This anointing served as a prelude to His life of ministry.

This breaking of the yoke started when Jesus, as the light, began to penetrate the darkness of man's mind. *Matthew 4:16* states, *"The people which sat in darkness saw a great light, and to them which sat in the region and shadow of death light is sprung up."*

---

[1] Matthew 11:28-30
[2] Matthew 3

Before man can be healed and set free the light must first penetrate his frame of reference. This wonderful light came in the form of the glorious Gospel. *2 Corinthians 4:3,4,* and *6* say,

> *But if our gospel be hid, it is hid to them that are lost: In whom the god of this world hath blinded the minds of them which believe not, lest the light of the glorious gospel of Christ, who is the image of God should shine unto them....For God, who commanded the light to shine out of darkness hath shined in our hearts, to give the light of the knowledge of the glory of God in the face of Jesus Christ.*

We are told that if the Gospel is hidden it is concealed to those who are lost (those who do not desire the only true God and His truth). The reason is simple,

> *Men loved darkness rather than light, because their deeds were evil. For everyone that doeth evil hateth the light, neither cometh to the light lest his deeds be reproved. But he that doeth truth cometh to the light, that his deeds may be made manifest, that they are wrought in God (John 3:19b-21).*

We also know from *2 Corinthians 4:4* that Satan has been able to blind minds because of unbelief. In other words, these lost people chose not to believe the witness about Jesus that has been given by the Bible.

The Gospel is about the Person of Jesus. The problem is that the Gospel has been summarized into a sinner's prayer or a doctrine. This has rendered this supernatural message powerless.

The Gospel is not just a message about Jesus' death on the cross, but rather it is about the Person of Jesus, who He is, and who He must be in the life of man. He is the Son of God, God Incarnate, the Messiah, Living Word, Savior of the world, and the true light of the Gospel. Presenting a watered-down gospel or another gospel is incapable of saving a person's soul because there is no light in it to penetrate the darkness of man's heart and mind. It is the light that exposes the terrible condition of fallen man and his need for salvation. Because of who Jesus is, the Gospel has become the most powerful message the world has ever known and is able to save the worst of sinners.

This message turned the upside-down world right–side up. Its light shined into man's great darkness to bring hope, truth, and sanity.

This Gospel is the power of God unto salvation or deliverance.[3] Not only does it save, but it also changes lives. The problem is that many people only see the Gospel as a means of salvation. But one can only reason that if the Gospel has the power to save, it has the power to change lives as well.

I have learned that the greatest evidence of salvation is a changed life. This new life manifests itself as the image of Christ shining forth.

The Gospel is not only about Jesus, but He makes it a reality. *2 Corinthians 8:9* tells us how Jesus accomplished this impossible task, *"For ye know the grace of our Lord Jesus Christ, that, though he was rich, yet for your sakes he became poor, that ye through his poverty might be rich."*

At this point we are reminded that Jesus came to preach the Gospel to the poor. In order to preach to the poor, He had to become poor. And for poverty-stricken man to be made spiritually rich, he must recognize his spiritual pauperism before God. As Jesus said, *"Blessed are the poor in spirit: for theirs is the kingdom of heaven"* (Matthew 5:3).

Before a person is able to recognize his or her spiritual destitution, the glorious light must penetrate man's wretchedness to expose the works of darkness.

It is only in the light of truth that all works of darkness can be revealed, confronted, and dealt with by the Great Physician. But how can we ensure that the searchlight of God will not only penetrate the intense darkness of our souls but also continue to shine? *Matthew 7:7* answers the question, *"Ask, and it shall be given you; seek, and ye shall find; knock, and it shall be opened unto you: For every one that asketh receiveth; and he that seeketh findeth; and to him that knocketh it shall be opened."*

Jesus is the way, the truth, and the life.[4] In order to understand Him as the way, we must *ask* Him to change our perception. Once our

---

[3] Romans 1:16
[4] John 14:6

perception is changed, we can begin to embrace and understand the ways of God.

Jesus is the truth, and we must *seek* to know Him. It is only as Jesus is revealed to us by His Spirit that we will begin to interpret everything according to Him. It is only when we get past self to see Jesus that we can know liberty.

The life that Jesus constitutes is eternal life. If Christ is in us, *eternal life* is present. But we are also in Christ, and this relationship points to the *abundant life.*

The abundant life can only be defined within an intimate and sweet fellowship with God. It is in the secret place with God that people can experience this satisfying life as He becomes their consuming reality. Consider the following diagram:

The Way	Ask to understand Him	Correct Perception
The Truth	Seek to know Him	Correct Interpretation
The Life	Knock—to perceive Him	Correct Definition

Many people ask God for things, but they fail to ask Him to meet them as the glorious light that will expose the things that are destructive to their lives and reveal His character and ways. They seek, but it is often to satisfy self-serving purposes. They knock on the doors of fleshly blessings, and the result is anger. Such people are walking in darkness. They only desire relief from torments and emptiness while avoiding deliverance from bondage brought on by fleshly, temporary pleasures and pursuits.

Jesus did not come to relieve or pacify us. He came to deliver us from the bondage of darkness and destruction. He can only accomplish this as the Great Life that is the light of the world, which must be able to shine unhindered in people's dark minds. This light can only come forth as individuals give way to Him in faith and obedience.[5]

---

[5] John 1:1-7

Another reason the glorious light fails to penetrate the dark souls of man is that man fails to listen. Most people do not expect God to answer them, which is a form of unbelief. It is hard for people today to believe Jesus came to heal and restore each and every individual. But the Great Physician has not changed nor has His mission; therefore, healing did not cease when Jesus ascended to sit on the right hand of God. In a way, this spiritual healing has escalated because the work of the Holy Spirit is available today for this present generation and can be experienced within seconds by those who open up their hearts.

Jesus is the Great "I AM," the ever-abiding reality and presence of God. But to be receptive of His power, anointing, and presence we must believe it as truth with the sincerity of a trusting child who has confidence in the heart of the Father. As the child reaches up towards God in trusting faith, the loving Father automatically reaches down to touch the receptive soul with the glorious reality of Jesus.

This is when the healing and restoration of the Great Physician becomes a reality. As His healing light shines in a person's heart, the glory of God will express itself in the face of Jesus as He is unveiled not only to the person but also to the world.

And oh, what a face Jesus has! It is not only precious, full of grace and truth, but it is the very image of God.

As we behold His face, His very reflection will manifest in us. 2 Corinthians 3:13, 14, 16 and 18 talk about this glorious transformation,

> And not as Moses, which put a veil over his face, that the children of Israel could not steadfastly look to the end of that which is abolished: But look to the end that which their minds were blinded: for until this day remaineth the same veil untaken away in the reading of the Old Testament; which veil is done away in Christ....Nevertheless when it shall turn to the Lord, the veil shall be taken away....But we all, with open face beholding as in a glass the glory of the Lord, are changed into the same image from glory to glory, even as by the Spirit of the Lord.

Is the image of Christ being reflected in your life? If not, the glorious light of Jesus has not penetrated every area of your life and bondage and works of darkness are preventing liberty and growth.

If this is true, you need to get serious about asking God to turn the light on in those areas. Make sure you are ready to humble self, stop, listen for His voice, and repent of any dark works that are revealed.

By child-like faith, accept the reality that Jesus has come to take care of the spiritual poverty that will bring you to ruin if ignored. He took care of the poverty by breaking through the darkness with truth and by cleansing receptive hearts with His Living Waters.

By sincerely asking for His light to search every area of your life, you are asking for something that touches God's heart. You are not only asking Him to go deeper, but you are asking for more of His influence and presence in your life. For where light is, there will be truth or reality and the incredible presence of God will be opened unto you.

As *Luke 11:13* says, *"If ye then, being evil, know how to give good gifts unto your children: how much more shall your heavenly Father give the Holy Spirit to them that ask him?"*

Chapter Twenty-four

WHOLE HEARTED

As the saying goes, "At the heart of man's problem is the heart of man." If man has trouble with the quality of his spiritual life, it is because his heart is not functioning properly. Jesus confirmed this truth,

> *Do not ye yet understand that whatsoever entereth in at the mouth goeth into the belly, and is cast out into the draught? But those things which proceed out of the mouth come forth from the heart; and they defile the man. For out of the heart proceed evil thoughts, murders, adulteries, fornications, thefts, false witness, blasphemies (Matthew 15:17-19).*

Proverbs 4:23 summarizes this whole matter with these words, *"Keep thy heart with all diligence; for out of it are the issues of life."*

The heart is the breeding ground for all that is vain, wicked, and ungodly. As *Jeremiah 17:9* states, *"The heart is deceitful above all things, and desperately wicked: who can know it?"*

There is no way a man can know the depth of his heart's wickedness because the heart is deceitful even about itself. It hides behind pious acts, fleshly empathy, unbridled emotions (zeal), and fake nobility.

This reminds me of what King David said in *Psalm 139: 23-24*, *"Search me, O God, and know my heart: try me, and know my thoughts: And see if there be any wicked way in me, and lead me in the way everlasting."*

David understood the fickleness of his own heart. He had realized that the unguarded inclinations of his heart were silently against God and His righteousness. He knew it was untrustworthy and self-serving. He also knew that only God could cleanse and change it, and that is why he cried out, *"Create in me a clean heart, O' God; and renew a right spirit within me" (Psalm 51:10).*

Battle For the Soul

When you study the heart in the Bible, you can see that God is after the heart of man. We are to seek and love God with all of our hearts.[1] We are to do the will of God from the heart to ensure there is no hindrance or division in our obedience, loyalty, and devotion to Him.[2] The problem with many is that they mistake good intentions towards God as seeking and loving Him with all of their heart. This mistake gives a false security about the person's real heart condition and falls short of true commitment.

Consider this promise,

A new heart also will I give you, and a new spirit will I put within you: and I will take away the stony heart out of your flesh, and I will give you an heart of flesh. And I will put my spirit within you, and cause you to walk in my statutes, and ye shall keep my judgments and do them (Ezekiel 36:26-27).

God recognized that to change the terrain of man's life, He had to change his heart. Jesus continues this theme in *Luke 4:18b*, "*...he hath sent me to heal the brokenhearted.*"

Everyone experiences the bitter sting of a broken heart, which robs us of innocence. Broken hearts occur when people experience abuse, rejection, loss, betrayal, hopelessness, broken dreams, disillusions, or feel misunderstood. Sadly, broken hearts cause people to make determinations that set them up for life instead of letting God have His way.

The truth of the matter is that the heart must be broken before God can change a person's disposition. This was made evident on the cross when Jesus' heart was broken.

Ruth Specter Lascelle gave a vivid description of Jesus' broken heart in her book, *A Dwelling Place for God*. She pointed out that *Psalm 22:14* declared that His heart was melted, which meant it was "liquefied." This heart condition implies that it was not only broken but was ruptured. She points out that In John 19:34 the original text is "...there gushed out blood and water." (She compares it with Psalm 105:41; water gushed forth from the Rock!) Water points to lymph fluid that is formed within

---

[1] Jeremiah 29:13; Mark 12:30
[2] Ephesians 6:5-6

the walls of the pericardium (a sac which surrounds the heart). Since the heart was ruptured, the blood also enters this sac, causing the heart to become enlarged. This state implies that an intense suffering had taken place. This blood and water GUSHED forth when the Roman soldier pierced the side of Jesus and entered the pericardial space.

Mrs. Lascelle pointed out that blood does not GUSH from one who is dead. For this type of effect to take place, the heart must be beating. But Scripture clearly states that Christ was dead when the Roman pierced His side. Mrs. Lascelle made this observation: "Crucifixion would not BY ITSELF have killed Him in so short of a time. The only explanation is that Christ had died of a broken heart (according to the prophecy in *Ps. 22:14*)." She goes on to point out that when the soldier pierced Jesus side from below, he penetrated the outside wall of the pericardium. Once the pericardium was pierced, the force of gravity caused the blood and water that had greatly extended the sac, to GUSH out of the opening made by the spear."[3]

If Jesus' heart was broken, then it is made to reason His followers' hearts will be broken in the process. The question is, why must the heart be broken?

In *Matthew 13,* Jesus talks about four heart conditions in the parable of the sower and the seed. The soil symbolizes the heart conditions while the seed represents the glorious Gospel. As we will see from the parable, the heart determines the type of impact the Gospel will have on a person's life.

The first three heart conditions in the parable imply serious heart problems.

The first heart is a *hard heart*. Because the heart is hard, the Gospel is prevented from penetrating it. In fact, the enemy is able to steal the seeds of the Gospel so that they will never take root in the heart and produce godly fruit.

It is not unusual to encounter this heart condition among people, even those who call themselves Christians. A hard heart simply represents a heart that is hard towards God's truth and reign. Pharaoh, in Moses' time, had a hard heart. He was challenged with God's truths

---

[3] *A Dwelling Place for God*, pg. 168. Also see Psalm 69:20

and warnings, but instead of responding in obedience he mocked or justified his disobedience. Each time he refused to heed to God's truths, his heart became harder.

I believe this is why God took credit for hardening Pharaoh's heart.[4] He knew that it was His truth that would cause this man's heart not only to turn against Him, but against Israel as well.

I have watched certain Christians who, when challenged to obey simple truths of God such as charity, gentleness, or forgiveness, end up justifying ungodly responses and attitudes. Each time they gave way to ungodly justification instead of God's truth, their hearts became harder.

Hebrews 3 tells us a hard heart is the product of unbelief, which walks hand in hand with pride. It produces people who may be very religious crusaders of righteousness but lack the fruit of the Spirit. People who do not obey God's truths do not believe Him because they do not personally know and love Him.

Needless to say, watching people harden their hearts towards God is frightening. Considering the fruit of such hearts and the possible future prospects is dreadful, for Pharaoh was greatly judged in ways that brought him to his knees in utter despair and sorrow.

This brings us to the healing of a hard heart. Before Jesus can heal such a heart, it must be totally broken.

The intense suffering caused by the sin of man broke Jesus' heart on the cross, and likewise the intense consequences of personal sins are sometimes the only hammer that can break a hard heart. As the hard heart is broken, the seed of the Gospel can make its way into the person's soul. As the light of the Gospel begins to reveal the person's sinful condition, the heart will become even more broken or tender, allowing the seed to take root to produce salvation.

As we see, hard hearts are indifferent to the truth and God's reign until broken--it is only in brokenness that a person can become identified with Jesus.

Identification is everything in the kingdom of God, and when people become identified with Jesus' broken heart over sin, they can begin to identify with those who have broken lives as well.

---

[4] Exodus 11:10

This is why Jesus came to identify Himself to each of us. He allowed Himself to be fashioned in the form of a man and be tempted in the same ways. He became sin so we could be made the righteousness of God.[5] *Isaiah 53:5* also humbly reminds us of how identified He became: *"But he was wounded for our transgressions."* His example shows us we must become identified with Him if we are to understand His righteousness and purpose for our lives.

Granted, not all hard hearts broken by harsh consequences will see the light. Some people become harder by the crushing instead of recognizing that they are rightfully paying the consequences for their evil actions. They will continue to justify sinful actions and blame others for their circumstances, permitting Satan to steal what seeds of the Gospel remain. These people will eventually become haters of God and will blatantly scoff and rebel against Him.

Once the seed of the Gospel begins to take root, the Holy Spirit will use it to bring greater brokenness so that greater works can take place. After all, it is not enough for the Holy Spirit to convict man of sin; He must reprove him of righteousness and judgment as well.[6]

Convicting of sin may show a person how far from the mark of God's glory he or she is, but reproving people of righteousness gives them an idea of what needs to take place to fulfill their purpose (or potential). And reproving people of judgment shows them that separation from evilness unto God is required in order to avoid judgment.

The second heart is a stony heart. A stony heart represents a self-serving heart that is receptive to the seed of the Gospel but will not allow the Gospel to take root. This type of heart is very deceptive because these people may have an appearance of righteousness, but they lack the goods that set them apart. This means that Christianity at best will be surface, emotional, and religious but never a life-changing reality. The person's love, worship, and service will remain conditional, fleshly, and powerless.

The reason the seed of the Gospel can never take root in this type of person's heart is because the seeds have to develop roots around

---

[5] Philippians 2:8; Hebrews 4:15; 2 Corinthians 5:21
[6] John 16:6-11

the many embedded rocks of self with all of its rights and expectations. These seeds of the Gospel must replace self, but if self remains intact, they become stifled because they are limited and cut off by worldly priorities, quenched by personal agendas, and drowned out by selfish pursuits.

Obviously, people who have self-serving hearts are also established on the foundation of shifting sand.[7] When the storms come into their lives, they will cave in to the pressure, which often causes them to become offended with God because He didn't perform according to their rights and expectations.

The only remedy for the self-serving heart is that it must be plowed up or broken down by the truth of God. *Jeremiah 4:3-4* commands,

For thus saith the LORD to the men of Judah and Jerusalem, Break up your fallow ground, and sow not among thorns. Circumcise yourselves to the LORD, and take away the foreskins of your heart, ye men of Judah and inhabitants of Jerusalem lest my fury come forth like fire, and burn that none can quench it, because of the evil of your doings.

Fallow ground is land that is full of debris such as hard clods or rocks that will prevent the seed from properly growing. To plow up the ground forces all of the debris to be brought to the surface. These hard clods must then be broken down or separated just as self must be crucified and separated from the Christian life so that the seeds of the Gospel can take root and bring forth life.

This plowing and separation should remind us that the body of Jesus was plowed or ripped up by the whips of self-serving man. He was separated from all compassion and kindness as He made His way to the cross. His wounds were made deep so that the Gospel could come forth. This is why *Isaiah 53:5* tells us: *"...with his stripes we are healed."*

With this in mind, how could we not allow our hearts to be plowed up so that they can embrace the depth and width of God's love and salvation? Is it any wonder that the warning of swift and extreme judgment was given by Jeremiah to those who would not submit to such work?

---

[7] Matthew 7:24-28

Rayola Kelley

This separation was also made evident when God told the men of Judah to circumcise the foreskins of their hearts. Foreskin of the heart symbolizes all the unclean residue of self or the old man. This type of separation allows for an exchange to take place. This is why God stated in *Ezekiel 36:26*, "A <u>new</u> <u>heart</u> also I will give you, and a new spirit will I put within you: and I will take away the <u>stony</u> <u>heart</u> out of your flesh, and I will give you an heart of flesh" (emphasis added).

Notice how our Great Physician will have to do radical spiritual surgery by exchanging our "old" heart with a "newness of His life. He will do this by replacing our old life with a new life (making us a new creation). He will replace our natural spirit with His Spirit and the self-serving intents of the stony heart with the inclination to respond to Him in unhindered love and adoration.

The third heart is a worldly heart, implying that it is a divided heart. Such a heart is divided between devotion to God and associations with the world.

Hosea 10:2 says this about a divided heart, *"Their heart is divided: now shall they be found faulty: he shall break down their altars, he shall spoil their images."*

A divided heart means an idolatrous heart that is trying to fit Christianity into its fleshly world. The world is nothing but a big idol that falsely promises to fulfill all of our needs and appetites.

Jesus is very clear about the negative results of a divided heart in *Matthew 6:24*, *"No man can serve two masters: for either he will hate the one, and love the other; or else he will hold to the one, and despise the other. Ye cannot serve God and mammon."*

The problem with a divided heart is that the person is apt to allow the influence of the world to win and totally choke out his or her life with God.[8] As the world chokes out the things of God, a spiritual wilderness and leanness in the person's life will result.

As the endless appetites and attractions of the world drown out the voice and life of God, they will eventually become swords that will pierce and finally break the person's heart as emptiness and leanness invade the individual's soul.

---

[8] Matthew 13:22

I have seen this type of broken heart. The problem with this kind of broken heart is that people usually try to put their own hearts back together instead of going to the Great Physician. Their hearts remain cracked shells as their lives remain miserable, inconsistent, and ineffective.

Jesus is the only one who can heal hearts. As *Isaiah 53:5* states, *"...he was bruised for our iniquities."* He is the One who heals us from the harsh realities of the world and the consequences of all of its enticements and attractions.

The final heart is the *whole heart.* This is a heart that has been submitted to the Great Physician. It is a heart that has experienced the reality of Jesus' death on the cross by realizing that, *"...the chastisement of our peace was upon him" (Isaiah 53:5).*

This heart is solely inclined towards God and receptive to His leadership and truths. It is a heart that has dimension because it is open to the Living Waters of His Spirit. It is rich with His wisdom and abounding in revelations of His character. Most of all it is a complete heart for it is seeking, trusting, and pure towards God. This type of heart will wholly follow the Lord.

We can see this type of heart in a man named Caleb. Caleb was one of the 12 spies who went into the Promised Land, but he was the one along with Joshua that encouraged the people to go into the land for God would fight the battle. Forty years after wandering in the wilderness he remained strong, vigorous, and eager to enter the land. Instead of choosing an easy opponent, he set his sights on the mountains and the Anakims who had great, fenced cities.[9]

Because Caleb was not divided in his devotion, he had a strong heart that knew no fear. This courage was the product of faith. His faith was securely placed on and in His God; therefore, he could not be moved as a young man or an old man. His spirit was strong, his mind quick, and his body ready for battle. He was an overcomer in every sense of the word.

I am aware that much of the church lacks this total devotion. During ministry for the Lord my heart has been broken mainly by people's sins

---

[9] Deuteronomy 1:36; Joshua 14:10-14

and their rejection of the Great Physician. Every Christian's heart should be broken by the condition of our nation, the church, and the home, but many hearts are angry because people in countries that are blessed with abundance are so spoiled and unrealistic. The idea of a broken heart is unattractive and causes many to try to save their life rather than lose it.

My greatest fear as His servant and daughter is that my heart can't be moved or broken by sin or the heavy hand of discipline. If my heart fails to break, it serves as proof that something is wrong with my heart condition, something that is possibly causing separation from my God. In fact, I rejoice when my heart is broken over that which is displeasing to my Precious Lord and Savior. A broken heart is a blessing in many ways and nothing to be feared or avoided because I know the Physician who will make it whole in a matter of seconds. His name is Jesus.

Like Jesus, I am aware that one must be cautious with how available he or she makes his or her heart to others.[10] But each servant of God must keep his or her heart open or vulnerable to God's work regardless of how much it might be used, broken, and discarded by others.

What about your heart? Is it hard, stony, worldly, or open? Is it broken or whole? Are you protecting it, or have you entrusted it to Jesus for His care?

Let me suggest that you do as King David did and give God permission to search your heart in order to allow present sin to break it, Jesus to put it back together, and God to use it as a means to express His love and compassion to others.

---

[10] See John 2:24

Chapter Twenty-five

THE KEY TO FREEDOM

Jesus said, *"He hath sent me...to preach deliverance to the captives" (Luke 4:18)*. Notice that preaching, not some miracle or great act, sets the captive free.

Few understand that preaching is such a powerful key because they do not understand the *spirit* behind the Gospel message that can set people free. The spirit behind this simple but incredible message is supernatural in nature and stands at the heart of salvation.

Although only one key can set the captive free, the lock itself is like a combination lock. You must know the combination before you can unlock the doors of captivity in a person's life.

The first part of the combination begins with the right message. If this message is not presented correctly, it will lack the power to reach through the entangled bars of men's hearts and minds to unlock the door.

The message that Christ brought started with this initial call: *"Repent: for the kingdom of heaven is at hand" (Matthew 4:17)*.

Today repentance is misunderstood, making the presentation of it weak or lacking the right spirit. For example, repentance in some circles has no substance to it because it never requires any change in attitudes and lifestyles. It is nothing more than a mental ascension that falls short of God's purpose. This makes for a weak repentance at best that will fail to set the captive free.

The other extreme found in preaching about this subject is a form of repentance that actually lacks Jesus. It is not enough to call for repentance; you must direct and guide the person in the right way. Therefore, godly repentance will always lead a person back to the only source of hope for his or her life, Jesus Christ.

Repentance minus Jesus encourages a worldly sorrow that leads to greater bondage and destruction.[1] It calls for conformation instead of transformation. This is when a person puts on a religious cloak to hide a heart that has not yet been cleansed or regenerated.

The next part of the message is known as the Gospel. Both Jesus and John the Baptist prepared the way for the Gospel by first calling for repentance. This call was a prelude for man to consider the plight of His spiritual condition. His plight would be more so revealed in the Gospel.

According to the Apostle Paul in *1 Corinthians 15:1-4,* there are three main parts of the Gospel. The first part of the message is that *"Christ died for sins according to the scriptures."*

This brings us to the very source that actually enslaves man. *Romans 6:20* tells us we *"were the servants of sin."* All men are born into servitude to sin. Sin mars man's potential, robs him of purity, and results in spiritual death. Jesus provided the combination that would set man free from sin's destructive tentacles. Repentance calls man to turn or run from that which enslaves him in order to embrace the solution.

Jesus' initial preaching called man to turn from sin in order to embrace the freedom He offered. It is important at this point to understand how the bondage of sin works.

As stated in previous chapters, bondage actually takes place in the will area because of ungodly determinations and mindsets that are based on the lies of Satan. For review purposes note the illustration on the following page,

---

[1] 2 Corinthians 7:10

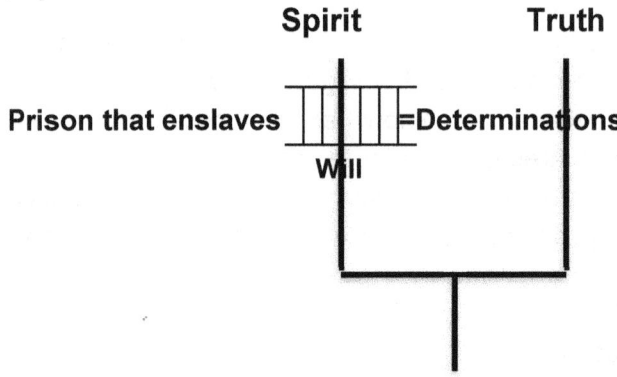

These lies can only take root and grow in darkness. They encourage the one enslaved to them to succumb to works of darkness, all the while deluding the individual as to the consequences.

John Owens made this observation about sin, "The basis for the efficacy of deceit is its effect upon the mind. For sin deceives the mind." Owens explains that when sin attempts to enter into the soul by other means such as affections, the mind checks and controls it. But once deceit influences the mind, the chance of sinning multiplies.[2]

James 1:14-15 tells us the progression of sin, *"But every man is tempted, when he is drawn away of his own lust, and enticed. Then when lust hath conceived, it bringeth forth sin: and sin when it is finished, bringeth forth death."* This verse in James tells us the majority of temptation comes from personal lust and not Satan. It is as people give way to the temptation that they open themselves up to Satan's oppression.

John Owens adds this insight about temptation, deceit, and sin: "Temptation sometimes arises gradually. Little by little it insinuates the poison until it gradually prevails." As this poison is cast into a false frame of reasoning, Owens explains that the soul turns against the grace of the gospel, causing the will to become spiritually debauched.[3]

---

[2] *Sin And Temptation*, pg. 36.
[3] Ibid, pg. 68

This brings us to the very nature of the Gospel. It is truth and, therefore, is able to set man free. This is why truth is the main key to all spiritual bondage. We find this truth in the very preaching or words of Jesus.

John 6:63 states, *"...the words that I speak unto you, they are spirit, and they are life."* Jesus' words bring both hope and healing to a sin-laden soul.

This brings us to another important fact: Truth is a choice of life. There are four aspects of truth that must be applied to all beliefs and practices.

First, a person must know the truth in order to properly discern between darkness and light. This means a person must willfully make the Word of God the final authority in his or her life.

It is not unusual for people to claim that they believe that God's Word is the ultimate authority but never treat it as such. In other words, it is authority in concept but not in practice. It can be debated and ignored if the circumstances warrant such a response.

It is easy to debate, dissect, quote, and use the Word of God for personal, self-centered purposes, but in this capacity it never becomes the living word of God that brings healing, deliverance, and life. In fact, few tremble before God's Word, which results in disobedience.[4]

This brings us to the second aspect: Godly truth will not lead a person to some great doctrine or philosophy but to a greater revelation of the Person of Jesus Christ. It is Jesus who sets a person free. As *John 8:36* states, *"If the son therefore shall make you free, ye shall be free indeed."*

The third aspect of truth is that there must be a willful exchange of the lies with the Word of God to accept it as the only standard. People who have given way to a lie must now choose to renounce the lie and believe the truth.

Once a person receives a lie as truth, it gives access to Satan to pervert or put into question the credibility of the Word of God. Once Satan gains this territory, the truth will be compromised and incapable of setting a person free.

---

[4] Ezra 9:4-5

Battle For the Soul

    This is why an exchange must be done. It requires faith on the part of a person. He or she must choose to believe that God's Word is truth and that it exposes, judges, and discerns all lies. If anything contradicts His Word in the individual's life, no matter how logical it may sound, it must be considered a lie of Satan and immediately rejected.

    We see a similar exchange occurring on the cross of Jesus. He came as man to take our place on the old rugged cross. This meant He became sin so we could be made into the righteousness of God.[5]

    It was on the cross that Jesus was bruised for our iniquities. A bruise is purple in color, and the color of purple is the combination of red and blue. The red signifies blood and blue represents heavenly, and when these two colors are combined to produce purple, the result is the color for royalty. These three colors point to the person, ministry, and work of Jesus Christ. Because of who He is and what He did we are not only healed by His stripes but we are made royal kings and priests of God.[6]

    The final aspect of truth is that it has no life or power without the Holy Spirit. The Holy Ghost is the One who makes truth more than facts or theology by making it living as He unveils Jesus in a personal way. Each revelation of Jesus that is revealed, makes truth alive and powerful, setting the captive free from all sin and its web of darkness and delusion.

    The next part of the Gospel message, after it reveals man's sinful condition, reveals that Jesus died for men's sins. *Romans 5:8* tells us, *"But God commendeth his love toward us, in that, while we were yet sinners Christ died for us."*

    Because of Jesus' death everyone can find forgiveness. *Psalm 103:12* gives us this promise, *"As far as the east is from the west, so far hath he removed our transgressions from us."* There must be forgiveness or pardon for sin before judgment can be sufficed.

    But this forgiveness is not given unless there is repentance. Oswald Chambers points out that when we say we are sorry, Jesus has pledged that we will be forgiven, but he emphasizes that a person must turn to God to obtain forgiveness. He goes on to say: *"...but the forgiveness is*

---

[5] 2 Corinthians 5:21
[6] Revelation 1:6

not operative unless we turn, because our turning is the proof that we know we need forgiveness."[7]

The next part of the Gospel is that Jesus was buried. Every repentant person can be sure that his or her sins were taken to the grave and no longer have any power or rights in his or her life. In fact, the grave silences the consequences of sin, *"Death is swallowed up in victory. O death, where is thy sting? O grave, where is thy victory?" (1 Corinthians 15:54b-55)*

The final part of the message that brings ultimate life is *"that he rose again the third day according to the scriptures."* Jesus' initial call shows people what their response must be to embrace the words of life. They must turn from darkness and death to embrace life and light.

Jesus is not a dead Savior but a living Lord. So many people bank that there is life after death but yet they live as if Jesus' resurrection is another myth or as if He is just a creed or concept. Jesus is sitting on the right hand of the Father.[8] He is alive and reigning, and one day He will come back to judge every person's words and deeds. His main judgment will be determined by what people have done with Him.[9]

In order to live for eternity, man must embrace life by believing every bit of the Gospel. He first must recognize his sinful condition and his need for intervention from God. He must then believe in his heart that Jesus died on the cross as a substitute for him to quench the judgment of sin. From this point, he can trace Jesus to the grave, where his sins were taken not only to silence their accusations but also to terminate the consequences of death. But the final part of the message is about victory, that Christ rose, for if He had not, *"...then is our preaching vain and your faith is also vain" (1 Corinthians 15:14).*

Our faith is not based on a dead martyr but on a living Intercessor. He not only died to redeem us, but He lives to ensure salvation. [10]

Because Jesus lives, all those who cling to Him live as well. Since Jesus lives, we can have assurance that His words will bring total liberty

---

[7] *101 Days in the Gospels with Oswald Chambers,* pg. 114
[8] Hebrews 8:1
[9] John 3:15-20
[10] Hebrews 7:25

and restoration to our souls so we may be able to embrace this incredible life. Since Jesus lives, we can overcome because we have a High Priest and all the tools to victoriously finish the course.[11] And what are the tools? The answer is found in the last book of the Bible.

Overcoming

At the core of the Gospel is the reality of Jesus Christ. Because of Jesus we have the promise of deliverance and restoration. Deliverance points to being set free from bondage while restoration points to a new life, an overcoming life.

When we think of Jesus Christ, the Gospel, and the Holy Spirit, we can see how Christians have the tools to overcome. In fact, this is brought out in *Revelation 12:11, "And they overcame him (Satan) by the blood of the Lamb, and by the word of their testimony; and they loved not their lives unto death"* (parenthesis added).

This Scripture relates to overcoming Satan in the time of tribulation, but the principle holds true for today. Although I have already covered some of these subjects, it is important to know how these three tools help us overcome the greatest onslaught of attack.

The first tool in *Revelation 12:11* is the blood of the Lamb. This tool points to Jesus and His redemptive work on the cross. 1 *Corinthians 6:20* and *7:23* tell us that we have been bought with a price. This price was the blood of Jesus being shed on the cross for our sins and points to the Gospel.[12] You might say His blood served as the principal payment while His sufferings served as the interest payment. Nevertheless, He paid the full price to redeem us.

Because Jesus served as the ultimate sacrifice and paid the complete price, we now have rights to embrace a new, complete life. These rights include the following benefits:

Forgiveness. *1 John 1:7* tells us that the blood of Jesus cleanses us from all sins. In *1 John 1:9* we find this statement, *"If we confess our*

---

[11] Hebrews 7:24-26
[12] Hebrews 9-10

sins, he is faithful and just to forgive us our sins and to cleanse us from all unrighteousness."

There is no salvation without the forgiveness of sin. It is forgiveness that allows people to taste mercy and experience grace. This pardon is not only an act of God that ensures salvation but is necessary for deliverance from bondage as well.

Most bondage occurs because people are unforgiving. All unforgiveness begins with anger and unbelief that produces bitterness and hatred. The root of bitterness defiles a person because it is unforgiving in nature and insists that it has a right to operate regardless of how contrary it is to the character of God.[13]

Covenant. The blood of Jesus established a new covenant. The Old Testament Covenant of the Law, *"made nothing perfect, but the bringing in of a better hope did; by the which we draw nigh to God" (Hebrews 7:19).*

The new covenant involves a new heart and spirit. It allows those who are part of it to boldly draw near to God bringing forth reconciliation.[14] *Colossians 1:20* confirms this hope, *"And, having made peace through the blood of his cross, by him to reconcile all things unto himself; by him, I say whether they be things in earth or things in heaven."*

2 Corinthians 5:19 says, *"To wit, that God was in Christ, reconciling the world unto himself, not imputing their trespasses unto them; and hath committed unto us the word of reconciliation."* As you can see, the blood not only cleanses us from sin and reconciles us to God, but it also places us positionally into an intimate relationship with God.

Children of God. This New Testament Covenant allows us to enter the throne of grace boldly because it designates us as children of God. *John 1:12* states, *"But as many as received him, to them gave he power to become the sons of God, even to them that believe on his name."*

As children of God, we have been guaranteed a heavenly inheritance.[15] Because we have a Heavenly Father we know we *"...have*

---

[13] Hebrews 12:15
[14] Ezekiel 36:26; Hebrews 8:10; 10:19-22
[15] Ephesians 1:11-14

not received the <u>spirit of bondage</u> again to fear; but (we) have received the Spirit of adoption, whereby we cry, Abba Father" (Romans 8:15, emphasis added).

What a great privilege Christians have because of the blood of Jesus. We have been bought with a price; therefore, we belong to Him and not Satan or the world. We have forgiveness of sin, thereby experiencing the mercy and grace of God. We have entered into a new covenant that ensures reconciliation with God and brings us into an intimate relationship of that of a father to a child.

It is important to remember a covenant is a two-sided agreement. God is true to His part of it, but Christians must be responsible to keep their end of the agreement.

In order to keep our end of the agreement, we must become bondservants to Jesus, for He owns us. We must forgive to receive forgiveness. We must honor the covenant by walking in the light, and we must become children in heart and attitude to experience a pure, intimate relationship with the Father.

Today many within Christianity are divorcing themselves from the blood of the Lamb as they compromise with other beliefs that ignore, downplay, or reject the blood of Jesus. There is no hope for such people because a bloodless religion that rejects the sacrifice of Jesus becomes a Christless belief that will ultimately cause advocates of this foolishness to taste the torment and fires of hell.[16]

The second tool is the word of our testimony. *1 Peter 3:15* instructs us to be, *"ready always to give an answer to every man that asketh you a reason of the hope that is in you with meekness and fear."*

What is the Christian's hope? When I ask Christians to give me their testimony, they usually tell me about their pastor, denomination, church activities, or doctrine. This religious rhetoric does not constitute a testimony that will stand in tribulation or overcome Satan. In fact, Satan will mock such empty rhetoric. He is not impressed with name dropping of leaders, denominations, or "sacred" doctrine. He only has to recognize the authority of Christ in our lives and respect the Word of God when it is spoken in spirit and truth.

---

[16] See the warning in Hebrews 10:26-31

This is why *Colossians 1:27* states that the only hope of a Christian, *"...is Christ in you, the hope of glory."*

Powerful testimonies consist of the revelation of Jesus. Such testimonies proclaim the reality of Jesus. They often include the Gospel message in a personal way. These proclamations grow as the Person and life of Jesus develops in the individual.

A testimony that is based on Jesus and finds life from Jesus is unwavering. I have seen this many times in my own life. For example, it is easy to debate doctrine as one does with religious issues, cults, and atheists, but such discussions are dead ends. But when a person shares his or her personal testimony of the risen Jesus Christ, it invalidates people's arguments. Why? Because a personal testimony implies one has experienced Jesus on a personal level.

Personal experience takes the subject of Jesus out of a mental or philosophical realm and puts Him in a personal reality that can't be debated or reasoned away. It states that Jesus is alive and that the individual has personally touched, tasted, seen, smelled, and heard Him.[17]

People who never experience Jesus do not have the immovable foundation to stand upon. This was made real to me after I heard the story of a man who was asked to write his testimony. He wrote down a date on his paper. When asked about the date, he explained that on that date he accepted Christ and up to that date and after that date nothing of significance had happened to him. Two weeks later the man committed suicide.

The salvation of Christ is a pivot point in man's spiritual life and not a stopping place. His reality should not only change lives but also change an individual's priorities, direction, and substance.

For the man who committed suicide, Jesus was a date and not a reality. He was a mental ascension and not a Person. This type of scenario is the reason that Christians fail to be victorious in their walk.

The substance or value of a Christian's life is determined by what he or she does with Jesus. The Son of God must become a person's all in

---

[17] 1 John 1:1

all to ensure a testimony that will silence Satan even in the midst of great loss.

The third means to overcome is death. *Revelation 12:11c* states, *"and they loved not their lives unto the death."* In essence, these people are already dead. They have denied self, picked up their cross, and learned to die daily to the self-life so they could follow Jesus into a greater life.

This principle was clearly brought out to me early in my Christian life. I heard a comment about Russian Christians that unveiled the power of death in overcoming. Russian authorities who persecuted Christians made this comment about them: "How can you threaten or kill someone who is already dead?"

There is such freedom in the death of the self-life. It truly allows people to live unto Christ.

The Apostle Paul made this clear in *Romans 6*. Positionally, every believer is dead in Christ, but that death has to be worked in, through, and out of our lives by the Holy Spirit.

This work can only occur when an individual knows he or she is dead; therefore, he or she refuses to respond to the self-life. Once the individual knows the status, he or she can count all things of the fleshly, self-centered life as dung.[18] Since the person counts the self-life and all of its affections as insignificant and dead, the individual can embrace the new life of Christ by submitting to the work of the Holy Spirit. At this point a person can count his or her new life as alive unto God for His purpose and glory.

Satan can't intimidate or threaten a person who knows his or her life is hidden in Christ and that he or she is dead. In fact, the enemy has no power to sway such an individual, which allows the person to live for and unto God.

The question is, can you stand and overcome the enemies of your soul? How much of your life expresses Jesus? How much of the quality of your life actually remains intact will be determined by how much bondage exists in your soul area? Are you still in captivity because you have not allowed Jesus' words to set you free from the reign of sin? Do

---

[18] Philippians 3:5-8

you understand what it means for Jesus to be bruised for your iniquities, or is it some foreign concept that has no real, life-changing meaning? Do you have a testimony of Him, or have you failed to come to terms with the Lamb of God?

Remember that Jesus' words bring life and healing, but they must be received by faith and obeyed in spirit and truth in order to set you free from the bondage of sin, self, and Satan.

Chapter Twenty-six

SIGHT AT LAST

Isaiah 53:2 tells us, *"For he shall grow up before him as a tender plant, and as a root out of a dry ground: he hath no form nor comeliness; and when we shall see him there is no beauty that we should desire him."*

One of the problems men have is that they can't see Jesus for who He is. They see no beauty or significance in Him that they would desire. For example, many see Him as an historical fact that is nothing more than a dead issue instead of a living reality. When some consider Him, they see Him as a dreaded enemy who poses a threat to their lifestyles instead of the One who provided a way for man to be reconciled to God. Others see the Son of God as having no significance because He is nothing more than a myth or a good man, prophet, or religious leader. These "eye problems" show many are blinded to His existence or true identity; therefore, they have no desire to see Him in all of His glory.

This inability to see the real Jesus also hinders one from knowing the real God. It is at this point that the greatest bondage occurs for man. Because man fails to know the true God of the Bible, he is plagued with a false foundation, faulty beliefs, tormenting insecurities, and unrelenting unbelief. He finds himself believing the lies and accusations of Satan and giving way to taunting, anger, depression, and disillusionment.

In *Luke 4:18* Jesus tells us there is a sight problem that He came to deal with. A. W. Tozer put it this way, "To FIND THE WAY we need more than light; we need sight....Light alone is not sufficient." Tozer points out that light is a figure which the Word of God and religious teachers interchange with the word, knowledge. He summarizes this concept in this statement: "As long as men do not know, they are said to be in darkness. The coming knowledge is like the rising of the sun."[1]

Jesus is the light of the world, but He is also the knowledge we must seek. He declared that He would bring this sight or knowledge to man by revealing Himself to him.

You might be saying right now, "I know of Jesus." Let me remind you that the Israelites knew of Jesus. Several of their Old Testament Scriptures made reference to Jesus' coming, but when He came, they refused to see Him. *John 1:9-11* tells us this about Jesus, *"That was the true Light, which lighteth every man that cometh into the world. He was in the world, and the world was made by him, and the world knew him not. He came unto his own and his own received him not."*

The reason Israel refused to see Jesus is that He did not live up to many of their preconceived notions. They expected to see a victorious king, not a suffering servant who would die on a cross. Because He failed to fit their criteria, they rejected and crucified Him.

Is this true for today? Are those who claim to know Jesus rejecting Him in their hearts just as the Jews did? Sadly, the answer is yes. Just as in the days of Jesus, some who claim to know Him in religious circles are rejecting Him.

Why is it that some individuals who claim to have the ability to recognize Jesus fail to do so? They have the same problem the Jews had. They are blinded to the real Jesus because they have already erected another Jesus in their minds.

Man defines Jesus in two ways. He either defines Him according to his own standards and ideas or according to the Word of God. Most people define Jesus according to their own concepts. These concepts limit the real Jesus Christ in a person's life, resulting in bondage.

The religious Jews had their concepts, and likewise the religious people of today have theirs. These concepts are not based on spirit and truth but on man's vain speculations and conclusions.

1 Corinthians 2:14 states, *"But the natural man receiveth not the things of the Spirit of God: for they are foolishness unto him: neither can he know them because they are spiritually discerned.*

---

[1] *Born After Midnight,* A. W. Tozer, pg. 60

Man can't discern the things of God with his own mind. In fact, he will pervert the things of God. Eventually, he will end up with another Jesus who is not the Jesus of the Bible. The problem will escalate as a person continues to build on his or her false Jesus and adjust all beliefs to this erected idol.[2]

Conflict occurs when the real Jesus is presented. The real Christ will not only challenge the false Christ, but He will collide with him just as Jesus did with the religious notions of His day.

The struggle that is incurred can be great and will often end with the religious people crucifying the real Jesus to hold on to their false gods. Here again we see the sad commentary of mankind even in the religious realm.

Many religious pilgrims seek for knowledge, but few seek to know the real Jesus. This is why we read this warning in 2 *Timothy 3:7, "Ever learning, and never able to come to the knowledge of the truth."*

Obviously, man wants to gain truth according to his own means. Recently, I had a discussion with a man whose philosophy was to debate the Word to get at truth. When I showed him the Scripture that tells us such debates are unprofitable, he justified his worldly pursuit and handling of the truth by saying that debate is popular among man; therefore, it is an accepted avenue to discover truth.[3]

The purpose of debate is not to seek truth but to show others how artful one is in debating. This unfruitful dialogue can't change minds that are already persuaded but it appeals to those who are wavering and it struts worldly intelligence. Such debates among the religious are nothing more than a form of unbelief and serve as a sick substitute for faith and submission to truth. As long as people are discussing or debating spiritual matters, they can believe that they are actually searching for truth when in reality they are trying to find ways around believing the truth that is challenging their concepts or comfort zones. And like all of man's ways, most debating is perverted and leads back to prideful conclusions and destruction.

---

[2] 1 Corinthians 3:11
[3] Titus 3:9

For example, debates have escalated into cults and what we now refer to as higher criticism. And how does this higher criticism view the Word of God? As nothing more than a myth. There you have it; man's means of seeking truth leads to arguing away the validity of the Bible or changing it to suit himself.

This destruction of the validity of the Bible is Satan's tactic. He knows if he can close down the spiritual perception of people concerning the real God, He will be successful in binding them up with limited concepts, muzzling them by stifling standards, enslaving them to unrealistic images, or caging them by harsh ideas or belief systems.

This is why the Word of God is not to be debated but believed and obeyed. Faith comes from hearing (not debating) and hearing from the Word of God, not man's opinions.[4]

Man can only perceive the Word when he simply chooses to believe it. Childlike faith allows the Spirit of God to make the truths of God's Word revelation. This revelation means Jesus is being unveiled as a reality to the spirit of the person.

Jesus came to heal this perverted reality by giving people the ability to see Him. This type of healing requires Jesus to heal the emotional area of a person's soul. Keep in mind that this is the area where man interprets what is going on in his environment. If this area is closed down by Satan's tactics, sins, or compromises, the person will be unable to perceive spiritual truths that would set him or her free.

Emotional healing can only begin when pride's rulers are crossed out and the will is under the influence of the Holy Spirit.[5] Once the emotional area is healed, Jesus will enlarge this limited area so that the person is capable of embracing greater revelations of Him.

This emotional area represents the four ways people sense or perceive God. Note the following illustration.

---

[4] Romans 10:17
[5] For review on man's rulers see chapter seven of this book.

Battle For the Soul

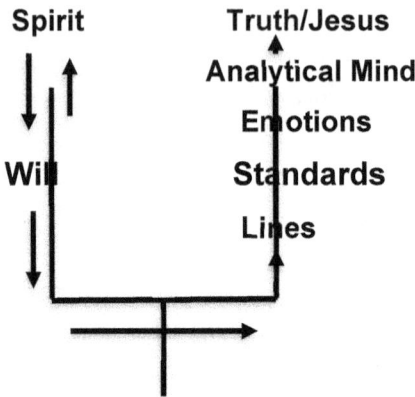

We must understand the four ways that man perceives or senses the things of God. But it is important to realize that all four of these avenues must be under the control of the Spirit of God and not pride's rulers. If these four types of interpretations are not under the right spirit, they will pervert truth while constructing a false Jesus, causing the person to reject the real Jesus.

People who operate with analytical minds will sense the reality of God. The Holy Spirit actually reveals the *ways* of God to these individuals. As they understand His ways, they will understand His nature and how He works. This is why *Proverbs 3:5-7* tells people who interpret according to this approach, *"Trust in the LORD with all thine heart; and lean not unto thine own understanding. In all thy ways acknowledge him, and he shall direct thy paths. Be not wise in thine own eyes: fear the LORD and depart from evil."*

A person who analyzes everything must choose to love Jesus with all of his or her mind. This individual must also understand that unless his or her thought process is under the power of the Holy Spirit, it will be perverted and untrustworthy.[6]

The next group of people is comprised of those who interpret Jesus according to how they *feel* or their *emotional state* instead of the Word of God. For example, if this type of person does not feel God loves him or her he or she will struggle with doubt and insecurities. These insecurities will lead to depression.

---

[6] 2 Corinthians 10:5

I have watched emotional people allow their emotions to take them on a roller coaster ride. They can become moody and unpredictable as their emotions swing like a pendulum. Because of their need to feel on top of their emotions and circumstances, they can easily operate in unreality, which can turn into insanity.

Such an individual needs not only to bring his or her emotions under control of the Holy Spirit, but the person must also choose to believe the Word of God over his or her feelings or conclusions. Instead of letting feelings consume him or her, he or she must strive to give way to God's truth so that the reality of Jesus can begin to serve as the only measure of reality. This form of submission requires the individual to choose to love God with all of his or her heart.

As this type of person strives to see the real Jesus, the Holy Spirit will enlarge the individual's emotions to embrace and know the Great I Am and His ever-abiding presence and glory. Once the individual embraces God in the right way, he or she will be able to worship Him in spirit and truth.

Those who operate with standards in the emotional area must clearly see the Jesus of the Bible. This is necessary to ensure that their standards do not line up to false images but line up to the attitude, heart, and actions of the real Jesus.

All false images must come down so that the Holy Spirit can line up their standards to the only spiritual cornerstone, Jesus Christ.

Standards that are established by false images are hard and tyrannical in nature. Standards that are under the Spirit's control are flexible and capable of being adjusted and shaped according to the Person of the Son of God.

A person who perceives Jesus according to standards must love God with all of his or her soul. This means the person submits his or her will to God, brings all thoughts into captivity, and abandons all standards that cannot be shaped or changed according to the purpose and will of God.

It is only as this person sees Jesus in humility, servitude, and glory that he or she can possess the correct Jesus and worship Him in spirit and truth.

Finally, the people who operate between ideas and lines must mortify their concrete ideas so that the Holy Spirit can adjust their lines to allow Jesus to be who He is.

People who function between these two harsh boundaries have no real dimension in their perception; therefore, Jesus is often flat, unfeeling, and harsh in their conclusions and presentation.

The Holy Spirit has to make Jesus a living Being that can't be cornered or put into neat packages of doctrine, philosophies, or expectations.

People who have a tendency to cage Jesus up with strong ideologies must choose to love Jesus with all their strength. In other words, they must bring the strength they invest into their ideas under the power of the Holy Spirit.

Strength under the Holy Spirit is flexible and can be channeled in the right way. Once such an individual's strength is channeled, his or her lines can be adjusted to the real Person of Jesus Christ, adding depth and clear vision so he or she can decisively see Jesus and accept Him on His terms.

Jesus' purpose for healing a person's spiritual sight is to help the individual truly see Him. Many of the great men of God who were spiritually successful had a heavenly vision of God. For example, Enoch walked with God and was translated. His walk implied he did personally experience God, and as a result he was translated into eternal glory.[7]

Abraham was considered a friend of God.[8] Obviously, Abraham had a close relationship with God very few could understand. Because of this relationship Abraham had to perceive God in an up close and intimate way.

Moses spoke to face to face with God and asked Him to show Him more of His glory. Joshua stood in the presence of the Lord, captain of the Lord's hosts, and ended up leading Israel into the Promised Land. Isaiah saw God in His glory and totally abandoned himself to His work.[9]

---

[7] Genesis 5:24
[8] James 2:23
[9] Exodus 33:18; Joshua 5:13-15; Isaiah 6

The Apostle Paul was taken up to the third heaven. He was a man that had been transformed by his encounter with Jesus on the road to Damascus but was in a way translated when he witnessed heavenly things that were beyond description.[10] He was able to make this declaration, *"...for I know whom I have believed, and am persuaded that he is able to keep that which I have committed unto him against that day"* (2 Timothy 1:12).

Jesus came to heal man's emotional area so he could rightly perceive Him. This will not only change how man interprets his environment, but he will also begin to see beyond his material world to see the essence of real life—the Person of Jesus Christ.

Once healed by the Great Physician, man's mind will be able to rightly see the ways of God in the midst of perversion. His feelings will be fine-tuned to Jesus and not to self, enabling him to embrace truth. Man will be able to perceive the Person of Jesus in the midst of unrealistic standards and false presentations that loom in front of him. Finally, he will be able to get beyond ideas that would pigeonhole Jesus in order to see the real Person of Jesus and become adjusted to His greatness.

What man must see about Jesus is His glory as God. It is not enough to perceive Jesus as Man, but one must see Him as God in the flesh.

Jesus came to take the blinders off of man's eyes and put healing salve in them. It is only as people gain their spiritual sight that they will be healed. Once their eyes are open, they will see Jesus—not only in His love, grace, and truth, but also in His glory.

Have you seen the glory of the Only Begotten Son? If not, you need to humble yourself before God and find out how you can receive your spiritual sight. If you have received your sight but you are having eye trouble, find out if personal sin or compromise has hindered your sight.

We all need to see Jesus, and as Job declared in the midst of great struggle, *"I have heard of thee by the hearing of the ear but now mine eye seeth thee"* (Job 42:5).

---

[10] Acts 9: 2 Corinthians 12:1-9

Chapter Twenty-seven

A LARGE PLACE

As the Great Physician, Jesus is able to set at liberty those who are bruised. In reality, nobody can get through this world without being bruised because the type of bruising Jesus is talking about in *Luke 4:18* is caused by sin.

We see this in Jesus' own life. He was greatly bruised by man's sinful deeds as He traveled to Calvary. He knew the pain of both physical and spiritual bruising caused by man's brutality and hatred.

It is important at this time to point out that bruising is caused by some outside source. The spiritual bruising Jesus is talking about is no exemption. The bruising that enslaves us is often caused by the wicked actions of others that we encounter along the way. This was made evident by what happened in the Garden of Eden.

Adam's action of disobedience bruised the whole human race. Everywhere man turns he is plagued by the harsh reality of the ongoing blows of sin. It breaks hearts, maims lives, and blinds men. It enslaves men to unseen forces, handicaps them from embracing the fullness of life, and keeps them from moving forward.

Like what happened to Jesus on His way to Calvary, the bruising comes from the outside upon that which is innocent. It is neither your fault nor mine that Adam sinned; therefore, why should we be constantly bruised and experience the bitter taste of death and separation from God?

It is for this reason that Jesus came. God is a righteous and just God. He would not allow Adam's actions to send all men to hell, so He sent the second Adam, Jesus, to take all the necessary bruising and enable man to be healed and restored.

The problem is that man refuses to accept God's provision or remedy and as a result condemns himself.

People justify sin by saying it does not hurt anybody else. How wrong this deceptive and self-centered logic is. Sin affects the people around us. It robs, kills, and destroys.[1] If you don't believe me, consider how much money, time, and energy is spent to compensate for man's many abuses from theft, drugs, fraud, and other crimes. Look at how the sins of spouses and parents emotionally affect mates and children. Space doesn't allow this author to fully cover this subject here, but it is evident that the sins of others always cost those who are innocent.

Since man is in a fallen nature and prone to be selfish and sinful, spiritual bruising abounds all around us. Therefore, none of us can protect ourselves from experiencing these spiritual contusions.

Jesus was saying that He came to set at liberty those who have been bruised by the sin that operates in the world. But man avoids Him as the antidote, using his bruising as an excuse for present sins and insisting on remaining a victim because of past wounds. As a result, man fails to enjoy the quality of life that has been made available to him.

Life, without the proper application of the antidote, makes man a casualty of life and sin. The bruising that occurs eventually becomes a serious matter as it begins to form into spiritual complications that eventually rob people of life.

The question is, why won't man accept the antidote and experience an abundant and satisfying life? The answer is simple: Man does not want to change comfortable habits or lifestyles no matter how godless and vain they are.

My co-laborer in the Gospel, Jeannette, went through a physical crisis in which her life hung in the balance. Physical death knocked at her door, and she consciously had to choose to live to keep death's tentacles from taking her down into the grave. She had to change every area of her lifestyle from what she ate down to how she washed her clothes. She later admitted that she could see why people would give up because it was so hard and drastic to change ingrained lifestyles—especially when you are already struggling for your physical life.

This is true for the spiritual realm as well. Many people want spiritual well-being. God has graciously made it available, but they refuse to give

---

[1] John 10:10

up the destructive lifestyles that beset them.[2] They don't want to go through the process of change because there is a price tag that comes with it.

This price tag usually includes such things as taking responsibility, self-denial, discipline, and submission to the work of the Holy Spirit. This shows us that man's spiritual condition rests solely at his door and not with God. He already has done His part, and now every individual must correctly respond to His solution.

But the price tag is not attractive, easy, or comfortable. This is why people talk about overcoming with great zeal but never seem to have the power to carry it out, making their talk cheap and deceptive.

This talk is a form of game playing without the actions or results. In the kingdom of God, Jesus is looking for those who will respond to His words without talking or debating about what He says. He wants to see action in the form of obedience.

Obviously, man is at a grave place. This place, where sin reigns, is dark, small, and empty. It is a place that can only cause distress and sorrow. It is where war rages in the recesses of man's mind and where loneliness and isolation subdue hope and resolution. It is a place of utter despair.

One has to wonder how hopeless or lonely a person will have to become before he or she looks up, calls out, and reaches up towards heaven, where the solution awaits. Sadly, most people have to hit bottom before they will cry out for help. A desperate cry means the person is now ready to receive the antidote.

Psalms 118:5 states, *"I called upon the LORD in distress: the LORD answered me, and set me in a large place."* What is the significance of a large place? It means a person is no longer in bondage, isolated from life, light, hope, and truth. This person now has the freedom to seek out God and find Him.

This search is all about maturing in a relationship with God. It is about growing in the knowledge of Jesus Christ. It is about an active, satisfying life in which an individual can now discover new territories in

---

[2] Hebrews 12:1

the endless character of God and obtain unsearchable riches that can only be found in Jesus Christ.

Many people believe that salvation is the key that sets people free. I have discovered that people must be set free by truth before they can embrace the salvation that is truly found and secured in a relationship with God. King David verified this in *2 Samuel 22:20, "He brought me forth also into a large place: he <u>delivered</u> <u>me</u>, because he delighted in me"* (emphasis added). This is why truth is a prelude to salvation instead of salvation serving as a door to truth.

The problem is that people put the cart before the horse. They offer salvation as the solution first rather than lift up the truth. Christ must be lifted up so that people have a reality check about sin, a comparison about righteousness, and a vision of judgment.

As the Holy Spirit brings forth this comparison, the eyes of the individual will begin to see the truth that will set him or her free enough to be able to make a proper determination. This is when the Holy Spirit can set him or her in a large place to begin to explore the possibilities of our Great God.

This freedom allows the individual to submit his or her will under the direction of the Holy Spirit so that He can bring down all false concepts, standards, images, and ideas of Jesus Christ. At this time the Spirit of God will be able to enlarge a person's frame of reference to embrace the deep treasures of God.

The Apostle Paul said this in *2 Corinthians 3:17, "Now the Lord is that Spirit: and where the Spirit of the Lord is, there is liberty."*

This book is about deliverance, but deliverance often means liberty. This liberty is not only based on overcoming Satan, but also on being overcome by the Spirit of God. Liberty is not about doing what you want to do, but about having the authority and power to do right. It is not only about overcoming the enemy, but rather it is also about having such an intimate relationship with God that the enemy can't find any avenue in which to take hold of or take root into your life.

Spiritual freedom is not just about giving, but about the ability to receive from God. It is not about having great knowledge about God but about having the ability to reach great heights and depths in Him. This liberty is not about happiness but holiness. It is not based on comfort and convenience but on self-denial and the cross, which leads to overcoming victory.

This liberty is not determined by the lack of prison chains but by the type of chains. For example, Paul knew the chains of sin and the chains of man. He declared that the chains of sin caused the greatest bondage in his life, and he rejoiced when locked in the chains of man because he had spiritual liberty in Christ.

Spiritual liberty carries chains as well. Paul was a bondservant to Jesus, and his chains were not physical but spiritual. These chains were made up of love that was shed abroad in his heart, grace that abounded in the midst of sin, hope that stood above persecution, and supernatural devotion and faithfulness that preserved him in the midst of fiery trials.

The Apostle Paul knew that his liberty did not hinge on greatness, power, or authority but on his relationship with God through Jesus Christ. Jesus even made reference to this in *Luke 10:20, "Notwithstanding in this rejoice not, that the spirits are subject unto you; but rather rejoice, because your names are written in heaven."*

The fact that our names are written in heaven means we have access to enter into an intimate relationship with God. We have the right to discover what it means to be His children, experience His love, know His grace, and realize that He is all in all, bringing satisfaction to the soul.[3]

This brings us to the final conclusion to this whole matter: that none of us has to be a victim of sin, self, and Satan. Jesus came as the Great Physician, and if we become a casualty of these spiritual culprits of our souls, the responsibility will solely rest on us.

Jesus encountered every known wound to medical science when He was going through His ordeal to bring us spiritual healing. According to Ruth Specter Lascelle's research, there are only five such wounds. They are bruising, laceration, penetration, perforation, and incision.[4]

As you can see, Jesus was wounded in every way in order to bring complete healing to each of us. *Isaiah 53:4-5* makes reference to Jesus'

---

[3] Ephesians 1:20-23; Colossians 3:11
[4] *A Dwelling Place For God,* pg. 117.

wounds to show us that we can be made whole: 1) stricken, smitten of God, 2) wounded for our transgressions, 3) bruised for our iniquities, 4) chastisement of our peace was upon him, and 5) with his stripes we are healed.

Jesus' invitation to each of us is simply to come to Him. His cry reaches down through centuries of sin, destruction, and death, but man still avoids coming. Oswald Chambers said that in every degree in which a person is not real, he or she will dispute, quibble, or do anything rather than come the last lap of unutterable foolishness, "Just as I am."[5]

If man would only come without any reservations, abandoning all to experience a fulfilling life, he would be satisfied. Jesus can meet us at all of our needs. Are you in need of trustworthy companionship? His invitation is, *"Come with me..." (Song of Solomon 4:8).*

Are you tired of running around the same mountain and encountering the same obstacles? Try stopping and face Him. Put forth this invitation to Him, *"Come my beloved, let us go forth..." (Song of Solomon 7:11)*. He is also waiting for your invitation.

Are you tired of carrying the world on your shoulders? His proposal to you is *"Come unto me, all ye that labour and are heavy laden..." (Matthew 11:28-30).*

Maybe you are hungry for something that has meaning, is sustaining, and is nourishing. His proposition to you is, *"I am the bread of life: he that cometh to me shall never hunger..." (John 6:35).*

Are you thirsty? His arms are open, and His cry has not changed for all these years, *"If any man thirst, let him come unto me, and drink" (John 7:37).*

Jesus stands at the door of a person's life and knocks.[6] He so desires to come in and fellowship with us for He possesses the power to heal the heart, the anointing to set the captive free, the life salve to open eyes, and the Living Waters to heal our bruises. But we must let Him into the inner core of our lives to receive the healing that will make us whole and complete.

---

[5] *101 Days in the Epistles with Oswald Chambers,* pg. 339.
[6] Revelation 3:20

Battle For the Soul

The Apostle Paul summarizes this glorious healing that comes out of an intimate fellowship with God through Jesus with these words, *"But we all, with open face beholding as in a glass the glory of the Lord, are changed into the same image from glory to glory, even as by the Spirit of the Lord" (2 Corinthians 3:18).*

The invitation has gone out to all, and Jesus is waiting at the door to meet with you and heal whatever spiritually ails you. Do not wait any longer. Go to the door of your life and accept His longing and loving invitation to you: *"Rise up, my love, my fair one, and come away* (with Me)"[7] (emphasis added).

---

[7] Son of Solomon 2:10 & 13

Bibliography

Strong's Exhaustive Concordance of the Bible.

Webster's New Collegiate Dictionary, G. & C. Merrian M. Co © 1976.

Studies in the Sermon of the Mount, Oswald Chambers, © 1995 by Oswald Chambers Publications Associations Ltd.

My Utmost for His Highest, Oswald Chambers, © 1963 by Oswald Chambers Publications Associations Ltd.

Biblical Psychology, Oswald Chambers, © 1995 by Oswald Chambers publications Ass. Ltd.

Sin and Temptation, John Owens, © James M. Houston.

Jesus Among Other Gods, Ravi Zacharias, © 1984 by International Bible Society.

The Normal Christian Life, Watchman Nee, © 1972 by Angus I. Kinnear.

Born After Midnight, A.W. Tozer, © 1989 by Christian Publicatiions.

101 Days In the Epistles with Oswald Chambers, Adair & Verploegh, © 1994 by Victor Books.

101 Days In The Gospels With Oswald Chambers, © 1992 by Adair & Verploegh

A Dwelling Place for God, Ruth Specter Lascelle, © 1990 by Hyman Israel Specter.

Other books by Rayola Kelley:

Hidden Manna
Stories of the Heart
Transforming Love & Beyond
The Great Debate
Post to Post: (1) Establishing the Way
Post to Post: (2) Walking in the Way

Volume One: Establishing Our Life in Christ
My Words are Spirit and Life
The Anatomy of Sin
The Principles of the Abundant Life
The Place of Covenant
Unmasking the Cult Mentality

Volume Two: Putting on the Life of Christ
He Actually Thought it Not Robbery
Revelation of the Cross
In Search of Real Faith
Think on These Things
Follow the Pattern

Volume Three: Developing a Godly Environment
Godly Discipline
Prayer and Worship
Don't Touch That Dial
Face of Thankfulness
ABC's of Christianity

Volume Four: Issues of the Heart
Hidden Manna (Revised)
Bring Down the Sacred Cows
The Manual for the Single Christian Life
Parents are People Too

Volume Five: Challenging the Christian Life
The Issues of Life
Presentation of the Gospel
For the Purpose of Edification
Whatever Happened to the Church?
Women's Place in the Kingdom of God

Volume Six: Developing Our Christian Life
The Many Faces of Christianity
Possessing Our Souls
Experiencing the Christian Life
The Power of Our Testimonies
The Victorious Journey

Volume Seven: Discovering True Ministry
From Prisons and Dots to Christianity
So You Want to be in Ministry?

Devotions:
Devotions of the Heart: Book One and Two
Daily Food for the Soul: OT and NT

Gentle Shepherd Ministries Devotion Series:
Being a Child of God
Disciplining the Strength of our Youth
Coming to Full Age

Nugget Books:
Nuggets From Heaven
More Nuggets From Heaven
Heavenly Gems
More Heavenly Gems
Heavenly Treasures

Gentle Shepherd Ministries Series:
The Christian Life Series:
What Matter Is This?
The Challenge of It
The Reality of It

The Leadership Series:
Overcoming
A Matter of Authority and Power
The Dynamics of True Leadership

www.ingramcontent.com/pod-product-compliance
Lightning Source LLC
Chambersburg PA
CBHW071653090426
42738CB00009B/1513